D0928729

Comic Drama

THE EUROPEAN HERITAGE

Edited by

W. D. HOWARTH

METHUEN & CO LTD

First published in 1978
by Methuen & Co Ltd
11 New Fetter Lane, London EC4P 4EE
© *1978 Methuen & Co Ltd*
Phototypeset in VIP Palatino by
Western Printing Services Ltd, Bristol
Printed in Great Britain at the
University Press, Cambridge

ISBN 0 416 85080 4 *(hardback)*
ISBN 0 416 85090 1 *(paperback)*

TO

THE MEMORY

OF

NEVILLE DENNY

COLLEAGUE AND FRIEND,

THIS BOOK

IS DEDICATED

Contents

Editor's foreword

WHEN I was invited to edit a volume on the subject of comedy in Europe, I welcomed the opportunity this presented for a collaborative undertaking on the part of colleagues living and working together, who might be able to meet from time to time in order to talk about comedy, and thus plan the shape and content of the book. I was fortunate in being able to recruit a team of specialists within the University of Bristol, though the project suffered a grievous setback at an early stage through the tragic death of Neville Denny, Senior Lecturer in Drama. Neville's blend of enthusiasm, judicious common sense and expert knowledge of his subject had already made their mark in our discussions, and we are all only too conscious of how much this book lost through his untimely death.

The introduction in particular owes a great deal to the exchange of views, and the pooling of specialist knowledge, that took place at our initial meetings; though as the actual author of the Introduction I must bear the responsibility for any residual shortcomings. As regards the other chapters, no attempt was made to impose a uniform method or style, and contributors were free to develop their own individual critical approach. Although the conveying of factual information was not our primary object, we have tried to ensure that each chapter presents a clear and coherent narrative as well as a personal point of view. Above all, it is our hope that the book may reflect something of the intellectual stimulus that we all experienced in meeting together to talk about a subject which, in spite of its central importance in our teaching and research activities, has always proved singularly resistant to critical analysis.

WDH
Bristol, 1977

Introduction:
theoretical considerations

W. D. HOWARTH

DESPITE the substantial body of writing devoted to theoretical discussion of the nature of comic drama, it cannot be said that this
provides a very satisfactory basis for the study of the genre. Scholars
still argue over the etymological derivation of the word 'comedy';
there is no general agreement on the boundaries prescribed for this
kind of drama, or the aesthetic purpose which animates it; and we
possess no challenging formulation of the essence of comedy, such as
the *Poetics* provide for tragedy, with sufficient authority to make it the
necessary starting point for any theoretical inquiry. It would be
absurd even to try to produce a comprehensive definition, let alone a
far-reaching theory of comedy, where so many better minds have
failed; so that what the present essay attempts is no more than a
'minimal definition', a sort of 'highest common factor'.[1] That is to say,
it offers a series of preliminary considerations, based, it is hoped, not
on *a priori* notions but on observed evidence, taking into account
important theoretical writings as well as the dramatic works themselves, and also noting significant exceptions to those distinctive
features which can be identified as characteristic of general practice.

It will often be easier to adopt a negative approach, to point out
what comedy does *not* do, than to assert positively a characteristic
content, style or flavour. For instance, one of the clearest distinguishing features of comedy seems to be its lack of that metaphysical
dimension which is of prime importance when we come to define
tragedy. The tragic hero wrestles with his destiny; and even when he
does not in the end lose his life, his predicament must bring home to
the audience, by means of threatened catastrophe, the implications of
this fateful struggle. This would be out of place in comedy: here, fate

---

[1] This approach owes a debt to R. C. Knight's example in his article 'A
Minimal Definition of Seventeenth-Century Tragedy', *French Studies*, X
(1956), pp. 297–308.

is replaced by a more trivial, or a more impersonal, chance; and if the comic character is permitted to indulge in philosophical reflections (such as are put into the mouth of Jaques or Figaro), these are reflections made as it were on the audience's behalf, as comments on what life has in store for us all, and are very different from the tragic hero's apostrophe to a malign fate that has singled him out for destruction. Northrop Frye says of this relationship between the audience and the events of comedy:

> The word 'plaudite' at the end of a Roman comedy, the invitation to the audience to form part of the comic society, would seem rather out of place at the end of a tragedy. The resolution of comedy comes, so to speak, from the audience's side of the stage; in a tragedy it comes from some mysterious world on the opposite side[2]

– and more generally, one might suggest that this worldly quality is one of the most fundamental attributes of comic drama. Shakespeare's comedy, it is true, does introduce the supernatural, but never in such a way as to disturb the reassuring world-view we associate with the genre: Caliban poses no real threat to the omniscient genius of Prospero. One example of a comic subject entirely dependent on the supernatural is the legend of Amphitryon, which has inspired so many dramatists from Plautus to the present day. But two things are noticeable about this story of men mocked and deceived by the gods (with a dénouement by *deus ex machina* in flat contradiction to Frye's dictum): first, that Plautus seems to have been so uneasy about the intrusion of the gods into comedy that he coined the label 'tragicomedy' to fit his play; and, second, that if Giraudoux's *Amphitryon 38* is easier to accept as comedy than the other well-known versions, from Plautus down to Kleist, this is largely because the omniscience and omnipotence of the gods are compromised, so that not only Mercury but also Jupiter behaves in a remarkably human way (and the same is surely true of Shakespeare's Puck and Titania). In other words, comedy might well claim as its motto Terence's 'humani nihil a me alienum puto' ('I count nothing that is human indifferent to me') – with the implied corollary that all non-human, or supernatural, material must normally be excluded unless it can be 'domesticated' and accommodated to a purely human scale of values.[3]

   If comedy is a form of drama whose subject matter is limited to the

---

[2] N. Frye, *Anatomy of Criticism* (Princeton, NJ, 1957), p. 164.
[3] A. Cook (*The Dark Voyage and the Golden Mean: A Philosophy of Comedy*) borrows Dryden's terms 'probable' and 'wonderful' and applies them respectively to comedy and to tragedy.

affairs of this world, a further step towards our minimal definition would be to say that its protagonists are – unlike the heroes of tragedy – nearly all of 'middling fortune': representative men and women, engaged in ordinary pursuits. Comedy, said Cicero in a phrase that was to be much quoted and glossed by medieval commentators, is 'an imitation of life, a mirror of custom, and an image of truth'. Donatus, writing about 350 AD, speaks of its subject matter as being 'civic and private concerns'. The characters of comedy lack the elevation, or superior dignity, which entitles those of tragedy to our admiration – that essential component of Aristotle's tragic catharsis, alongside pity and fear; and though neoclassical theorists frequently sought further to restrict the social relevance of comedy by excluding the popular and the vulgar – Corneille's definition of 1660, 'a portrayal of the manners and conversation of men and women of good breeding', is one of the most clear-cut of such attempts – nevertheless in practice comic drama has always been fairly tolerant on the score of social rank, and embraces not only the clodhopping peasants of popular farce but also the princes and courtiers of heroic comedy. The essential thing is that, when comedy does introduce characters of exalted status, it should still present their 'civic and private concerns': courtship, marriage and adultery, the acquisition of money and social status, we take to be the common interests of all men, whereas treason, murder and revenge are part of a ruler's prerogative.

A related aspect of the characters' status, as it affects the spectator's relationship to them, is expressed by Robortello, writing in 1548:

> The names of all comic characters should be fictitious. This is not done in tragedy, because tragedy uses stories of the more pitiful events that have befallen certain well-known people, whose names must be declared. Comedy, however, feigns in a verisimilar manner and therefore, as Aristotle very clearly informs us in the *Poetics*, invents its names.[4]

And a similar point of view is embodied in the familiar axiom that (to quote Diderot, who formulated it in 1757):

> Comedy deals with general types, tragedy with individuals. . . . The tragic hero represents a certain individual, be it Regulus, Brutus, or Cato, who cannot be mistaken for anyone else. The comic hero on the other hand represents a great many men: if by mistake the playwright were to give him a character which could be identified with that of a recognizable individual, he would

[4] Robortello, 'On Comedy', in P. Lauter (ed.), *Theories of Comedy* (New York, 1964), p. 54.

have failed, and his comedy would have degenerated into satire.[5]

But what are we to say in this connection about Aristophanes? Ought we to say, as has been claimed, that when Aristophanes lampooned Socrates and Euripides he was really satirizing in general terms the calling of the philosopher and the profession of the tragic poet? Or should we acknowledge that some of his plays contain extremely sharp personal satire, and see in this kind of writing one of the boundary lines which help to delimit the nature of comic drama as we are trying to define it?

For, however common they may have been in Athenian Old Comedy, such personal lampoons are not at all typical of the genre as it has developed in modern times (due partly no doubt to the laws of libel and the existence of a vigorous censorship); and the notion that comedy is concerned with general types, not individuals, can be supported by reference to practice as well as theory. Having said that, however, and having isolated, and excluded as atypical, the Aristophanic form of satire directed against a personal target, one is forced to admit that the use of the terms 'type' and 'individual' in literary theory is not very satisfactory. For we seldom, if ever, meet in practice anything corresponding to either concept in its absolute form. It is easy enough, perhaps, to distinguish at the opposite end of the spectrum from the Aristophanic satire a kind of generalized character possessing virtually no individuality: this extreme is to be seen in the abstract allegories of the *Three Estates* or many Tudor interludes, and in the more sophisticated abstractions of the court masque, the *ballet de cour* or the Italian *intermezzo*. But elsewhere, even where we are inclined to pronounce equally confidently on the characters of comedy as abstractions – in the case of those products of the longlived tradition of characterology which stretches from Theophrastus to Joseph Hall and La Bruyère – we are surely dealing with a quite subtle blend of the *type* – that *a priori* conception of the misanthrope, for example, which underlies both Menander's Knemon and Molière's Alceste – and the *individual*, possessing those unique traits which distinguish Alceste from all other misanthropes, or which ensure that Jonson's Volpone is so much more than the embodiment of fox-like cunning.

Nor is it merely the characters proper to *comédie de caractère* or 'comedy of humours' who are based on *a priori* abstractions. Diderot no doubt thought he was being very radical in proposing to replace the 'characters' of classical comedy – the miser, the misanthrope, the

---

[5] Diderot, 'Entretiens sur le *Fils naturel*', 3rd Entretien, in Diderot, *Writings on the Theatre*, ed. F. C. Green (Cambridge, 1936), p. 76.

jealous man – by the socially more relevant 'conditions' of his domestic drama: the judge, the merchant, the soldier. But these professional types can be just as abstract in their conception, if they derive from an *a priori* notion of the essential virtues and vices proper to each calling; and such concepts do not necessarily correspond to observed social reality any more than the slaves and parasites of ancient comedy, or the pedant, the *capitano* or the servants of the *commedia dell' arte*. Here, too, what makes a character come alive is the successful blend of the general type to which he belongs with the individual features that distinguish him from that type. And if the characters of English comedy have often been seen as the products of an inductive process born of our native empirical tradition, while Continental playwrights are thought to have relied more heavily on the tradition of an *a priori* typology, nevertheless Falstaff and Harpagon have this in common, that we think of them both as representative figures. It is not so very unusual for us mentally to pigeonhole the more eccentric among our own acquaintance as 'a Falstaff' or 'a Harpagon', whereas we do not equally readily classify people as 'an Oedipus' or 'an Othello'. This surely means not only that the *situation* of the tragic hero is highly particularized but also that his *character*, while possessing enough common humanity to invite our sympathy, is related to his situation in such a way as to exclude any closer identification with broad human types. (It is also the case, surely, that the nature of tragedy makes it impossible to isolate the tragic hero from the plot to which he belongs. When we think of Oedipus, we call to mind the whole of Sophocles' play, leading up to the final catastrophe; on the other hand, comedy being a matter of instantaneous creation of mood, not of cumulative build-up, we think of Harpagon or Falstaff as characters revealed in any one of a number of situations.)

In the nineteenth century a new form of comedy, owing much to the theories of Diderot and Lessing a century earlier, and based, as those theories had been, on an increased awareness of the social and political interests of a middle-class audience, was to bring about a move away from the generalized 'types' of neoclassical comedy, in favour of individuals with a well-established social identity. The more convincingly we are led to believe in the characters of a play as individuals, however, the greater the strain we put on the concept of comedy. The intimate involvement we feel with Ibsen's Nora or Chekhov's Vanya is difficult to reconcile with the cool detachment that theories of comedy have traditionally required of the spectator. Let us agree that comedy holds a mirror up to nature: not, however, a plain reflecting mirror which shows life exactly as it is, but something not unlike the distorting mirror of the fairground which turns us all into stylized thin men, fat ladies, giants or dwarfs. Comedy must always reflect a certain social reality, but only those plays are in the mainstream of the true comic tradition which do this with enough stylization to prevent emotional involvement, and to facilitate that more objective intellectual approach which is another important characteristic of comedy.

Much has been made of the moral purpose of comedy. When playwrights themselves talk of their moral aim, this is generally in order to defend themselves against accusations of immorality; for comedy has always attracted the censure of the Puritans, and of those stern moralists like Rousseau, who have seen the public theatre as a corrupting force. When Molière asserted that 'the function of comedy is to correct the vices of mankind', or when Biancolelli, the Arlecchino of the Italian players in Paris, adopted the motto *castigat ridendo mores* ('the laughter of comedy acts as a corrective to men's behaviour'), they were reacting against this moral disapproval. Indeed, they were overreacting; for there is little evidence that comedy – that is to say, pure comic drama – ever corrected any of the follies and foibles that it portrays. Satire is a different matter, and the sharper the angle of the satirist's vision – in other words, the more closely his portraits resemble their real-life originals – the more likely it is that his victims may be shamed into mending their ways. In a more general sense, however, comedy may be said to be 'moral' if it is based on a wholesome, positive attitude to life. Though it does not normally set out to change men's attitudes, nevertheless its effect is to reinforce our acceptance of a viable social order, a norm of behaviour based on an unwritten compact between the playwright and his audience. The misfits, the selfish schemers, those who would upset the order of things, are rendered harmless; if they are not converted to a right way of thinking, at least they are excluded from the social microcosm that the dramatist has created. The tricks and deceits, the moral turpitude of the rogues and villains, become part of a larger scheme which flatters the spectator's need for security and sends him home reassured.

Of all the attributes which help to define comedy, the happy ending is perhaps the most unequivocal and the least disputed. Comedy shares with the romance and the fairy-story the element of simple wish-fulfilment: as children we have all looked forward to being told that 'they all lived happily ever after', and the marriage with which so many comedies end represents a similar willingness to suspend disbelief. No matter what trials the hero and heroine may have had to undergo on their way to this happy conclusion, no matter how clear a warning the play may have sounded by showing the conjugal strife of couples already married, such things are forgotten in the euphoria of the happy ending, and we are content to think neither of the past nor of the future, but to participate in a moment of celebration which suspends time. Obstacles and misunderstandings are cleared away, the long-lost relatives are discovered, the antisocial plotters slink away defeated or else, pardoned, themselves join in the affirmation of serene good humour. The end of a comic drama according to this most traditional formula is essentially escapist in character; and however strongly the play may have seemed to be attached to social reality, the playwright helps us to pretend for a brief moment that reality has ceased to exist.

A similar point could be made about those comedies which do not end with the ritual pairing-off of eligible couples, in which, for instance, the principal emphasis seems to be on the retribution dealt out to a character who disturbs the social harmony. What Aristotle, in his brief remarks on the nature of comedy, and the tradition of medieval and Renaissance commentators who followed him, had to say about the relationship between the ugly and the ludicrous is relevant here, if we take moral turpitude to be the counterpart of physical ugliness; for the province of comedy, according to these authorities, is the portrayal of 'some defect or ugliness which is not painful or destructive'.[6] The sacrifice of Celia's virtue to Volpone, the eviction of Orgon's family by Tartuffe, would certainly be 'painful or destructive' if they were allowed to succeed: the fate of innocent, virtuous, sympathetic characters is involved, and both Jonson and Molière, recognizing this, make the representatives of the law step in. The dénouement redresses the balance; and however blatant the artifice by which this is done in the case of *Tartuffe*, however obviously didactic the author's purpose in both of these plays, the reassertion of the moral order is necessary if the tone of comedy is not to be abandoned. There are other cases, however, where the 'ugly' is less pronounced, and its consequences less 'painful': in plays like Gay's *Beggar's Opera* – and the same is true of Machiavelli's *Mandragola*, Wycherley's *Country Wife* and Lesage's *Turcaret* – the rogue or trickster triumphs, and yet our moral sense is not offended, unless we are hypersensitive moralists like Rousseau. In such cases we enter into a sort of complicity with the rogue: our moral judgement is suspended, and we applaud his success – but only if we are sure that his victims' folly makes them a fitting prey for his schemes. And, even then, we must be sure that the offences of the rogue are venial enough not to raise insuperable moral problems once the play is over: when the most notorious trickster of them all, Tirso's Don Juan, has demonstrated his immunity from the processes of human law and order, the dramatist has no option but to extend the normal limits of his comic

[6] Aristotle, *Poetics*, V.

world, and to bring in the Statue as the representative of the divine law his hero has flouted.

So far, our 'minimal definition' of comedy has dealt with the setting proper to the genre, with the kind of plot, with the rank and status of the characters, and with such distinguishing features as the happy ending. Little has been said yet about the nature of the response required from the spectator, and nothing at all about the role of laughter as a characteristic element in that response. In fact, the relationship between comedy and laughter has always been a controversial subject with the theorists. On the one hand, many have taken a close link for granted, and have seen in the laughter of a theatre audience a peculiar aesthetic response which is essential to the definition of comic drama; we may take Meredith's 'The test of true comedy is that it shall awaken thoughtful laughter'[7] as a representative expression of this view (reserving until later the opportunity to examine the value of Meredith's qualifying epithet). On the other hand, there are both practising dramatists and academic theorists who have shown themselves unable to accept the proposition that laughter is an essential feature of comedy. Ben Jonson, for instance, followed Heinsius in misinterpreting Aristotle on the subject: 'Nor is the moving of laughter always the end of comedy: that is rather a fowling for the people's delight, or their fooling.'[8] Steele, a hundred years later, argued that 'Anything that has its foundation in happiness and success must be allowed to be the object of comedy; and sure it must be an improvement of it, to introduce a joy too exquisite for laughter, that can have no spring but in delight.'[9] And a modern critic, L. C. Knights, states quite categorically, at the beginning of his 'Notes on Comedy': 'Once an invariable connexion between comedy and laughter is assumed we are not likely to make any observations that will be useful as criticism.'[10]

It seems to us, however, that this controversy is largely an artificial one, based on a semantic confusion common to the principal European languages. For there exist in comic drama two separate and independent elements. On the one hand we have the aesthetic principle animating comedy, the comic impulse which determines the spectator's peculiar response of laughter; on the other those features – plot, theme, situation – which give dramatic shape to the play and produce a quite different response: one of interest, curiosity, suspense and surprise. 'When this dynamic organization is fully and

---

[7] Meredith, *An Essay on Comedy and the Uses of the Comic Spirit* (London, 1919), p. 88.

[8] Jonson, *Timber, or Discoveries* (1640), in Lauter, op. cit. p. 139.

[9] Preface to *The Conscious Lovers* (1722).

[10] Published 1933; see Lauter, op. cit. p. 432.

most powerfully present in a play,' writes Albert Thibaudet, 'then the comic element itself is forced to take second place.'[11] Indeed, it is possible to imagine a whole range of potential combinations of these two elements. One extreme, at which the comic element plays an absolutely minimal role, could be illustrated by *A Doll's House* or *The Cherry Orchard* (and more generally this is true of nineteenth-century social comedy as a whole); while at the other extreme the revue-sketch, or music-hall turn, represents the comic element in an almost pure state, where it is hardly subject at all to the exigencies of the dramatic form.

It could hardly be maintained that theoretical and critical writing on comedy has always been mindful of the distinction between these two elements; on the contrary, they have usually been confused. Hence the error, so widespread as to be almost universal, of ascribing to the essential comic principle effects that properly belong to the dramatic framework within which that principle is embodied. This failure to distinguish between the comic, or laughter-provoking, component of comedy and what we may term its non-comic or dramatic component, can be seen to be reflected in the inadequacy of our critical vocabulary in this field, and it seems reasonable to suppose that in its turn this inadequate linguistic equipment has been responsible for further confusion. A case in point is the Latin term *vis comica*. Whether or not its traditional interpretation, as 'strength of comic effect', is based on a misreading of the original text (by Suetonius, quoting Caesar on the subject of Terence), in which the adjective *comica* should apparently not be taken as qualifying *vis*, is really immaterial: more important is the fact that it *has* traditionally been used in a certain sense, whose effect has been to confuse the two elements we are seeking to distinguish. When Stendhal, for instance, writes of the scene in *Tartuffe* in which Orgon curses his son and turns him out of doors:

> This is a scene to which classical commentators applied the term *vis comica*, though there is little that is comic about it. The spectator suddenly becomes aware of something profoundly human, but something more thought-provoking than amusing[12]

he may conceivably be right in his interpretation of this scene, but he does not draw the conclusion which seems to us to follow, namely that *vis comica* perhaps ought not to be equated with the 'comic' component of Molière's play, and that a more accurate rendering might well be 'strength of *dramatic* effect'. The romance languages, following on from Latin, have been forced to adopt the derivatives of

[11] 'Le Rire de Molière', *Revue de Paris* (January 1922), p. 332.
[12] Stendhal, *Racine et Shakespeare* (1823; Paris, 1928), p. 308.

comoedia to mean both 'play' and 'comic play'; while English, having taken the word 'comedy' from the French, is similarly handicapped. The resultant confusion is perhaps best illustrated by the semantic paradox which enables Molière to make one of his characters, a pedantic critic, complain that certain material is too comic ('trop comique') to deserve a place in a comedy. Only German, with its terms *Lustspiel* and *Schauspiel*, seems better equipped for the discussion of the problems of comic drama. And whereas the French do use *le comique* to indicate something distinct from (and, as we have just seen, sometimes opposed to) *la comédie*, the corresponding English term 'the comic' still has a rather stilted air about it; the fact that we have had to resort to such artificial coinings as 'the comic element' or 'the comic component' itself indicates the lack of an accepted term. Meredith, for his part, uses the expression 'the comic spirit' to denote this essential ingredient that we have been endeavouring to define; and, this being so, his insistence that all 'true' comedy contains this animating spirit is understandable, and fully justified.[13] The apparently contrary opinion expressed by Knights is not really incompatible with this view: his article makes it quite clear that by 'comedy' he means 'comic drama' in a wider sense, and that he is particularly interested in themes and dramatic structure, not in the spectator's aesthetic response which is Meredith's concern.

That one category of comedy exists, in which laughter plays a minimal part, or no part at all, is quite clear. This is not only established by numerous theoretical and critical writings from the Renaissance onwards, but has also been supported in practice by certain playwrights through the whole of the modern period, even if they do not represent the main tradition of comic drama. Indeed, if the basic minimal definition of our genre is a play mirroring the occupations of ordinary people, in ordinary language, with a happy ending, there might well seem to be little essential connection between such a formula and the arousing of laughter. When Steele, La Chaussée and others catered for eighteenth-century taste by writing 'sentimental comedies' or *comédies larmoyantes*, they were neither wholly innovators nor out to create some monstrous kind of hybrid. Though their combination of moralizing and social propaganda may have been peculiar to their own age, as regards form they were in fact harking back to an earlier type of comedy, well known on the Continent if not in this country, whose object was the realistic imitation of manners, not their caricatural portrayal; and the point is well made by a German critic, that the concept of 'tearful comedy' is not the

---

[13] 'I do not know that the fly in amber is of any particular use, but the Comic Idea enclosed in a comedy makes it more generally perceptible and portable, and that is an advantage' (op. cit. p. 104).

unnatural paradox it might appear to be at first sight: we should understand by it not *weinerliches Lustspiel* but simply *weinerliches Spiel*.[14] Nor was it mere convenience, and the lack of a more appropriate term, that led to the domestic dramas of Diderot and Lessing, and in the following century the social dramas of the Second Empire, being labelled 'comedies'; for these plays represent a further development of comedy of manners in the direction of documentary realism: they merely continue the tradition, established by Renaissance theorists, according to which the function of comedy is to hold a mirror up to ordinary life.

A 'minimal definition' such as we have arrived at is of course no more than a methodological convenience. It is clear that any comedy that made its mark at the time it was written, *a fortiori* any comedy that has survived as an acknowledged masterpiece, must possess something distinctive, over and above the bare minimum. This distinctive quality may be an ethical (or even political) concern, as in the case of Steele; it may be the expression of a contemporary sensibility, as with La Chaussée; it may be a moralizing zeal, such as we find in nineteenth-century social comedy. But these are all examples of a minority tradition: one whose existence it is proper to acknowledge, in view of its historical importance, but nevertheless standing well apart from the mainstream of comic drama. And the characteristic attribute which defines the mainstream of comedy, as it has developed from antiquity down to the modern era, is without a doubt what Meredith calls the comic spirit: the desire to present human experience not plain and unadorned but in a stylized, imaginative or caricatural manner in order to arouse laughter.

When we come to discuss the relationship between comedy and laughter, as the aesthetic response that characterizes the most typical productions in that genre, we are faced with a formidable body of theoretical writing about the nature of laughter itself. Much of this we may leave to one side as irrelevant. Nobody has yet been able to offer a satisfactory explanation of the connection between the psychology and the physiology of laughter, and to show how a mental process, the perception of the ridiculous, translates itself into spasmodic convulsions of the diaphragm and the emitting of one's breath in staccato gasps. Nor are we here concerned, within the narrower field of the psychology of laughter, with the numerous attempts to assimilate the kind of laughter we encounter in comic drama – that is, laughter which appears to have a predominantly intellectual source – to various other kinds with a purely physical cause, such as a dose of nitrous oxide, tickling, or a child's enjoyment of play. Limiting our inquiry,

[14] E. Winkler, *Zur Geschichte des Begriffs 'Comédie' in Frankreich* (Heidelberg, 1937).

therefore, to the kind of laughter aroused by comedy, we find the existing theories fall into two main groups, which we may classify respectively as 'subjective' or 'moral' on the one hand, and 'objective' or 'intellectual' on the other; and a survey of the more notable theories during the post-Renaissance period reveals a general shift of emphasis from the former to the latter. Descartes and Hobbes, writing in 1648 and 1651 respectively, represent clearly enough the moral attitude towards the nature of laughter. Descartes writes of

> . . . a kind of pleasure combined with disapproval, deriving from the fact that we perceive a certain minor imperfection in a person whom we consider to deserve such imperfection. We feel disapproval towards the imperfection, and pleasure because we see it in someone who deserves it; and when this happens unexpectedly, the astonishment we feel makes us break out into laughter.[15]

And Hobbes's well-known passage from *Leviathan* puts forward a remarkably similar explanation:

> Sudden glory is the passion which maketh these grimaces called laughter; and is caused either by some sudden act of their own, that pleaseth them; or by the apprehension of some deformed thing in another, by comparison whereof they suddenly applaud themselves.[16]

Laughter for both these philosophers is the expression of a moral judgement, based on a favourable comparison made by the person who laughs, between himself and the object of his laughter. Such subjective 'superiority theories' can be matched with numerous other theoretical definitions from the seventeenth and eighteenth centuries; indeed, expressions of a more objective view of what happens when we laugh are very rare during this early period. An isolated example from the seventeenth century is Pascal's remark: 'Two faces resembling each other, neither of which makes us laugh on its own, become laughable when they are juxtaposed.'[17] And a century later Voltaire makes a similar observation, with particular reference to laughter in the theatre: 'I have noticed as a spectator that general bursts of laughter are almost always caused by a mistaken apprehension: for example, when Mercury is taken for Sosia. . . .'[18] One of the earliest, as well as one of the clearest, attempts to formulate an objective theory of laughter must be that of the Scottish philosopher Beattie, writing in 1776:

[15] Descartes, *Traité des passions*, V, art. 178.
[16] I, vi.
[17] Pascal, *Pensées*, ed. L. Brunschvicg (Paris, 1921), Vol. II, p. 50.
[18] Preface to *L'Enfant prodigue* (1736).

Laughter arises from the view of two or more inconsistent, unsuitable or incongruous parts or circumstances, considered as united in one complex object or assemblage, or as acquiring a sort of mutual relation from the particular manner in which the mind takes notice of them.[19]

At approximately the same time, in 1781, Kant was formulating a variant of the 'incongruity theory'. For him, laughter is 'an affection arising from the sudden transformation of a strained expectation into nothing'[20] – in other words, the frustration of our expectation by the sudden revelation of incongruity in two things apparently congruent. This formula was to be expanded by Schopenhauer, who may be seen as combining Beattie with Kant:

The cause of laughter is in every case simply the sudden perception of the incongruity between a concept and the real objects to which it has been related in our mind. . . . All laughter then is occasioned by a paradox, and therefore by unexpected assimilation, whether this is expressed in words or in actions.[21]

It is the sort of approach which inspired these 'incongruity theories', as distinct from the theories based on 'superiority', that seems to have predominated in the nineteenth and twentieth centuries; though one of the most influential theorists of the present century cannot be identified squarely with either tradition. Although Freud writes (1905):

A person appears comic to us if, in comparison with ourselves, he makes too great an expenditure on his bodily functions and too little on his mental ones; and it cannot be denied that in both these cases our laughter expresses a pleasurable sense of the superiority that we feel in relation to him[22]

nevertheless the chief emphasis of his views on comedy is on laughter as a relief of tension, an attitude which can be seen to be a development of that of Kant and Schopenhauer. Bergson, however, the author of perhaps the best known of all theories of laughter, which may be formulated as follows:

The attitudes, gestures and movements of the human body cause

[19] Beattie, *Essays on Poetry and Music*, 3rd ed. (London and Edinburgh, 1779), p. 320.
[20] Kant, *Critique of Aesthetic Judgement* (1790), trans. J. C. Meredith (Oxford, 1911), pp. 196–203.
[21] Schopenhauer, *The World as Will and Idea* (1836–54), in Lauter, op. cit. p. 355.
[22] Freud, *Jokes and their Relation to the Unconscious*, trans, J. Strachey (London, 1976), p. 256.

us to laugh whenever they make us think of a mechanical process. . . . We laugh whenever a person reminds us of an inanimate object[23]

remains close to the theories outlined above. Among those who have followed him in this respect is Arthur Koestler, for whom laughter results from our intellectual perception of 'the sudden bisociation of a mental event with two habitually incompatible matrices'[24] – a formula resembling that of the eighteenth-century Beattie; while another proponent of the 'intellectualist' theory, Claude Saulnier, goes beyond those already quoted in his insistence on the gratuitous nature of laughter, which he sees as:

. . . neither an intellectual, nor a moral, judgement, but a phenomenon distinguished above all by its aesthetic character. . . . When the lack of discipline that characterizes playful laughter gives way to the ordered discipline of a work of art, the resultant combination is the triumphant achievement of the human mind conscious of its liberty.[25]

It may be felt that such abstract inquiries into the nature of laughter have little to do with the appreciation of comic drama; and even readers who are not inclined to be sceptical about the central place of laughter in comedy may well think it irrelevant whether such laughter is judged to be moral or intellectual in its reference. For these are the views of theorists, not of practising dramatists; and, even where we are able to attribute certain attitudes to the playwrights themselves, can it be said that this affects the kind of comedy they wrote?

One answer might be that theoretical attitudes current at a given time can tell us something important about the expectations of the spectators for whom a playwright was writing; for one thing that appears to be certain about laughter in a theatrical context is that it is subject to the influence of fashion, inhibiting or liberating as the case may be. Molière, for instance, complains of the difficulty of writing for spectators 'who fill us with respect, and laugh only when they are willing to'.[26] There is plenty of evidence among the fashionable gentry of Molière's time of a disparaging attitude towards laughter and its place in comedy, and this can be seen to be closely bound up with contemporary theories of laughter as a subjective phenomenon expressing moral judgement, rather than as the spontaneous expres-

[23] Bergson, Le Rire: Essai sur la signification du comique (1899; Paris, 1946), p. 22.
[24] Koestler, The Act of Creation, 3rd ed. (London, 1976), p. 59. See also Insight and Outlook (New York, 1949).
[25] Saulnier, Le Sens du comique: Essai sur le caractère esthétique du rire (Paris, 1940), p. 168.
[26] Molière, L'Impromptu de Versailles, scene i.

sion of an intellectual perception. Laughter could only be justified if it was directed to a worthy cause; hence the insistence, on the part of critics of the time, on the difference between 'trivial' and 'dignified' subjects for comedy, and hence the stress they laid on the satirical function of this genre. There is little doubt that Molière himself was more open-minded about the nature of laughter and its function in comedy; but this highly selfconscious attitude on the part of his cultured contemporaries, this genuine reluctance to laugh in public, certainly helps to explain the reception given to some of his plays, and may well also have influenced his choice of subject matter. At all events, one can see a tension on this score between the playwright and the most influential section of his audience – a tension by which Shakespeare, writing for a less homogeneous audience, and one less persuaded of the moral function of laughter, remained unaffected. However, if perhaps not so well established among the typical play-goers of the Elizabethan period, this moralistic interpretation of laughter was certainly expressed by some theorists of the time. In Sidney's definition 'Comedy is an imitation of the common errors of our life, which [the playwright] representeth in the most ridiculous and scornful sort that may be'[27] the assimilation of the terms 'ridiculous' and 'scornful' is surely significant; while, in the case of Jonson, his increasing reluctance to accept laughter as essential to comedy seems to have been due to a similar apprehension that laughter (unless it be the 'high strain of laughter' he refers to in *Cynthia's Revels*) is a degrading activity.

When we reach Steele in the following century, whose preference for a 'joy too exquisite for laughter' we have already noted, we see a reflection of the new sensibility of a highly selfconscious age, which looked down on laughter as a sign of the trivial and the superficial, and regarded public tears as the hallmark of moral superiority. In the early nineteenth century Jane Austen's Mr Darcy embodies a point of view very similar to that of Molière's 'difficult' courtiers, though in this fragment of dialogue it is not difficult to see that the author's sympathies lie with her heroine Elizabeth Bennett:

> 'The wisest and the best of men, nay the wisest and best of their actions, may be rendered ridiculous by a person whose first object in life is a joke.'
>
> 'Certainly', replied Elizabeth, 'there are such people, but I hope I am not one of them. I hope I never ridicule what is wise or good. Follies and nonsense, whims and inconsistencies do divert me, I own, and I laugh at them whenever I can.'[28]

[27] Sidney, *Defence of Poesie* (1595; London, 1931), p. 30.
[28] Jane Austen, *Pride and Prejudice*, ch. xi.

Those whom Meredith calls the 'agelasts', whose education and social standing make them reluctant to laugh, have become progressively fewer in our day. Hostility such as that of Paul Valéry, to whom laughter was suspect as a reflex action in which the intellect capitulates to the physical in man, is nowadays rare indeed. Laughter has become respectable in the twentieth century, and the public display of emotion is correspondingly devalued.

Moreover, there seems to be a clear correspondence between the current predominance of 'objective' theories of laughter as a spontaneous phenomenon without a moral basis, and representative examples of modern comic writing. Theories based on 'incongruity', for instance, have their counterpart in the purely verbal comedy of a play like *The Importance of Being Earnest*; while Bergson's contention that we laugh at human nature when it behaves with a machine-like rigidity finds convincing illustration in the *comédie-vaudeville* tradition that flourished from Labiche and Feydeau to Ben Travers and Brian Rix, before receiving its fullest justification, perhaps, in the Marx Brothers films. Examples of 'aesthetic' laughter at its most gratuitous may be seen in our response to the plays of N. F. Simpson or to much of Tom Stoppard's work, as well as to the comedy of *The Goon Show* or of *Monty Python's Flying Circus*. Here, however, we touch the extreme limits of our subject. This is comic drama in its purest and most absolute state, stripped of virtually all those features of plot, characterization and theme which help us to identify a work as 'dramatic'. The works cited may exhibit, as Saulnier suggests, one kind of discipline: that imposed by art on the spontaneous nature of laughter seen as play; but they are conspicuously lacking in the kind of formal discipline we are accustomed to look for in a dramatic work. Nevertheless, in that they enable us to isolate this element of aesthetic laughter in something like a pure state, such extreme cases may help us to recognize the gratuitous nature of this element in all comic drama. For if we can mentally isolate the purely comic, or laughter-producing, component of plays as diverse as *Volpone*, *L'Avare*, *The Importance of Being Earnest* or *One-Way Pendulum*, it may be argued that what we laugh at in each case is essentially a variation on the same basic formula, and that the differences between such very dissimilar plays derive above all from features like characterization, ethical purpose and the degree of social reference.

The fact that we have chosen modern plays to illustrate the kind of comedy in which comic writing with a spontaneous intellectual appeal, dependent on verbal humour, predominates does not mean that comic drama of earlier ages possessed no such writing. It abounds in Shakespeare, it is to be found in Plautus and Molière, and it gives a distinctive flavour to the work of Congreve and Farquhar.

Moreover, the *commedia dell'arte* may be seen as offering a visual counterpart, in the form of a comic action largely based on gesture and mime, which is equally gratuitous in its nature. On the other hand, it is surely true that at certain periods playwrights themselves, the educated part of their audiences and the most influential of their critics have shown by their heavy emphasis on comedy as a moral corrective, their insistence on the social reference of comic drama, and their tendency to confuse comedy with satire, that in their eyes the only dignified use of laughter was to harness it to some moral purpose. At such periods 'gratuitous' comic writing with a purely aesthetic purpose has tended to be correspondingly depreciated; and, by the same token, it is only recently that a liking for pure farce has been regarded as compatible with good taste.

A variant form of the old prejudice is the attitude which prefers smile to open laughter. Molière was praised, at the time of *Le Misanthrope*, for appealing to the 'laughter of the mind';[29] Voltaire recommends 'that interior smile, so much to be preferred to open laughter';[30] and Meredith's 'thoughtful laughter' is surely a further instance of the same attitude. Here, we are on very delicate ground. It would be impossible to maintain that the difference between laughter and smile has no basis in fact, or that there is no distinction to be drawn between moderate and immoderate laughter; but whether these are differences of kind, or merely of degree, is more difficult to determine. The question belongs as much to the province of psychology as to that of aesthetics, and if on the one hand there seems to be a real difference between the uproarious laughter aroused by *Charley's Aunt* and the discreeter smile evoked by *The Cocktail Party*, on the other hand it is undeniable that social fashions and prevailing habits of thought have an influence on the manner in which we laugh. As a social phenomenon, laughter in the theatre is peculiarly subject to changes in fashion, and the difference between laughter and smile may often be due less to the contents of the play itself than to other factors affecting the audience. And there is of course an important distinction to be made between laughter (or smile) as the peculiar aesthetic response we have been endeavouring to define, and that kind of smile which expresses euphoria, pleasurable expectation or satisfaction at the fulfilment of our wishes. Any comedy, even one whose 'comic' content is minimal, should take us out of ourselves, entertain us and delight us; and, whether we laugh immoderately or not at all, we may well smile with anticipation as we identify with the sympathetic characters, with relief as we applaud the discomfiture of

---

[29] 'Rire dans l'âme'; cf. Donneau de Visé, 'Lettre sur le Misanthrope', in Molière, *Œuvres*, ed. Despois and Mesnard, Vol. V (Paris, 1880), p. 440.

[30] Voltaire, Preface to *L'Écossaise* (1760).

their opponents, or with relaxed wellbeing as we enjoy the happy ending.

Although it has been necessary, for the purpose of this analysis, to treat the two components of comic drama as if they were quite separate elements, it would be wrong to give too much emphasis to what is after all a largely theoretical distinction. 'Comedy', Christopher Fry reminds us, 'is not a drama with the addition of laughs. It is a world of its own . . .';[31] and it is surely the case that in all true comedy the laughter-producing element is integrated into an aesthetically satisfying whole which reflects the author's comic vision, so that laughter is complemented by the euphoric smile, and perception of the comic by pleasure of a less specific nature. The richer these complementary dramatic features – theme, plot, characterization – the more complete the audience's appreciation of the play will be (and, parenthetically, if on the whole we find farce less rewarding than types of comedy with higher literary aspirations, this is surely not so much due to any difference in the quality of the laughter aroused by the two kinds of play – or to the difference between laughter and smile – as to the relative poverty, or lack of variety, of dramatic invention in the case of farce).

What do we mean when we talk of 'the author's comic vision'? What is this imaginary world that he creates, and how is it related to the real world in which we live? The comic dramatist's view of the world is an intellectual rather than an emotional one: laughter may be able to maintain an uneasy coexistence with a shallower form of sentimentality, but it cannot exist together with genuine emotion. The fantasy, the exaggeration, the whole make-believe aspect of the playwright's invention, combine to prevent the audience's emotional involvement with the characters he has created. We may sympathize in a sentimental way with the fortunes of the young lovers, but we identify more fully with the jokers and scheming servants whose ingenuity we applaud; and, if ever we begin to feel sorry for the victim of the jokes and schemes, the comic perspective has miscarried. Comedy almost always persuades us to 'laugh with' certain characters and to 'laugh at' others; and by our laughter we spontaneously concur in the dramatist's critical judgement. The only kind of comic drama in which this judgement relates directly and unambiguously to the real world, however, is satire. When Molière introduces recognizable contemporaries into his plays as doctors or as pedantic poets, when Jonson indulges in a similar kind of personal polemic in his *Poetaster*, or Fielding in his *Pasquin*, reality breaks in and overthrows those barriers which pure comedy sets up, and which preserve it as a

[31] Fry, *An Experience of Critics* (London, 1952), p. 26.

world apart. Here, and only here, can we speak confidently of the 'corrective' force of comedy, for we can well imagine such plays creating in the spectators for whom they were written a more critical attitude towards the individuals they lampooned. The definition of satire as ridicule directed against a specific target would also apply to the related genre of parody, which has been a fertile source of dramatic comedy from Aristophanes in the *Thesmophoriazusae* down to Gilbert and beyond. In parody, however – as in the burlesque and the mock-heroic – the element of personal malice is normally lacking; here, the original work, the object of the satire, serves as a pretext for a more gratuitous form of cultured joke, shared between the parodist and his audience.

True dramatic satire is in any case relatively uncommon; and, while there are many comedies that we call satirical, the term is often used very loosely. The practice in this respect of Shaw, one of the master satirists of his day, is instructive: if we consider plays like *Major Barbara* or *The Doctor's Dilemma*, we shall see that they are not satires in this sense at all, and that, whereas the same themes are treated in a recognizably satirical manner in his prefaces, the plays themselves lack the very specific identification with the real world that the strict definition of satire seems to require. Such plays are satires, if at all, in a much more general sense – and they are no doubt better plays because of that: we need only look at the example of Shaw's later plays, in which the comic dramatist seems to have given way to the satirist.

The fact that it lacks this specific identification with reality does not mean that comedy has nothing constructive to offer to the world we live in. 'Comedy . . . is a world of its own,' writes Fry; but he continues: '. . . when we leave it again, it can have given to the world of action we rejoin something of a new cast.' Shaw's caricatures of fashionable doctors, though too generalized to permit of individual identification, as well as Molière's, which even if they could once be so identified have long since lost their satirical point, nevertheless illustrate the ability of all great comedy not only to entertain us but also to send us home at the end of the play in reflective mood. And if we are prepared to accept the intellectually based 'incongruity' theory of the function of laughter, then when we laugh at the comic portrayal of pedantry, pretentiousness or vanity in the theatre we are moved less by the moral censure of such traits as we apply them in our minds to our own doctors, our own teachers or our own next-door neighbours than by a much more gratuitous intellectual appreciation of the absurdity of all folly, as it exists in ourselves as well as in others. When Meredith, discussing the philosophical scope of comic drama, writes of 'the uses of comedy in teaching the world to understand what ails it', he clearly has in mind a more direct, specific effect such as we have associated with satire. Lane Cooper, however, attempting to reconstruct Aristotle's missing treatise, suggests that the philosopher would have claimed for comedy a cathartic effect similar to the 'purging of the passions' he postulates for tragedy.[32] As the tragic poet arouses the emotions proper to tragedy (that is, pity and fear) in order to purge the excess of such emotions, so his comic counterpart arouses the appropriate emotions of pleasure and laughter, with the object of purging them of harmful excess. The cathartic process, so defined, depends on both the comic and the non-comic, or dramatic, elements of comedy; and, as with tragedy, disruptive analysis gives way to harmonious synthesis. The comic exposure of folly – what Aristotle calls the 'ugly' – to the critical analysis of our laughter produces discord and incongruity; it corresponds, *mutatis mutandis*, to the violence and the shock of the tragic catastrophe. But in both cases the dénouement brings reconciliation and restores harmony; and, just as a positive reassertion of moral order characterizes the closing lines of *Hamlet* or *Phèdre*, so a stable social order is restored to the little world of comedy by the weddings, the feasts and the celebrations which end so many plays.

It would be rash to try to theorize about comedy with the same rigour as is common in the case of tragedy. There is a sense, as Helen Gardner has said, in which 'tragedy that is not great is not tragedy, but failed tragedy',[33] and this is what justifies prescriptive generalizations based on one's reaction to the acknowledged masterpieces of that genre. With comedy such generalizations are impossible; and a similarly exclusive prescription based on selected plays by (let us say) Terence, Molière, Shakespeare and Jonson – a formula that might well include the equivalent of tragedy's purging of the passions – would involve neglecting whole areas of comic writing, from farce to satire, and whole periods during which the comic tradition has flourished. In particular, it would mean neglecting the important modifications that the concept of comedy has undergone in the century and a half since the Romantic revolution, and which will be studied in certain chapters of this volume. For the Romantic sensibility was essentially hostile to the traditions of comedy that the Renaissance had inherited from classical antiquity. The individualists, the social misfits, were no longer to be seen as material for comic portrayal: instead, they were glorified as examples of the Romantic hero. If the Romantic hero was himself to suffer a setback in the second half

---

[32] Lane Cooper, 'as for the end or function . . . it is to arouse, and by arousing to relieve the emotions proper to comedy', *An Aristotelian Theory of Comedy, with an Adaptation of the Poetics* (New York, 1922), p. 179.

[33] Helen Gardner, *Religion and Tragedy* (London, 1971), p. 17.

of the nineteenth century, he has come into his own again in our day: the dramatist's standpoint increasingly tends to be that of the individual rebelling against a social norm, which has itself become a much more fluid concept. Meanwhile, the surrealist cult of the subconscious, developing into the postwar Theatre of the Absurd, has put a further strain on conventional notions of well-defined and mutually exclusive genres. If the traditions of Western European comedy can be said to have developed as the artistic expression of a lucid critical intelligence, perhaps an age in which lucid intelligence is increasingly devalued in the arts may offer a suitable opportunity to attempt a retrospective survey of that tradition.

1

The comedy of Greece and Rome

MICHAEL ANDERSON

THE COMIC SPIRIT may be defined as something so indigenous to our species that any attempt to pin down its essence by the scholarly tracing of sources and influences is bound to be wide of the mark; comedy itself may be investigated as a specific dramatic genre with clearly defined boundaries and an interesting history. From either vantage point, the comic authors whose work has survived from Greece and Rome will repay our attention. For the word 'comedy' itself we are indebted to the ancient world or, to be more precise, to Athens, where κωμῳδία was presented alongside tragedy at the City Dionysia from around 487 BC onwards; the word entered the European vocabulary in its latinized form *comoedia*, and scholarship is now agreed that the derivation is from κῶμος, 'a revel', and not κώμη, 'a village'. With the word is associated a theatrical form and, perhaps more important, a particular perspective in which to view man and his misdemeanours; and this, too, can be traced back to classical antiquity. The Roman dramatists Plautus and Terence were the chief agents of transmission, but the creative impulse was almost exclusively a product of Athenian civilization. Democratic Athens of the fifth century BC, with its tradition of free speech and popular politics, was the home of the Old Comedy of Aristophanes; two generations later an Athens shorn of most of its military and political power remained the intellectual centre of the civilized world, and saw the first performances of the New Comedy of Menander and his contemporaries.

It is not quite clear when the literary critics of the ancient world began attaching the labels Old, Middle and New to Greek comedy, and it is probable that the authors themselves were not always conscious of making decisive breaks with tradition precisely where the later grammarians placed these divisions; nevertheless the terms have proved convenient and remain in general use. Perhaps the most difficult, and yet the most rewarding, of the three for the modern reader or audience is Old Comedy, with its inexplicable form, its indescribable atmosphere and its often unrepeatable jokes.

For us, despite a sizeable collection of fragments by other authors, Old Comedy means Aristophanes, since his are the only complete plays in the genre to have survived. Although some generalizations may fairly safely be made, it is also worth remembering that what seems to be a distinctive feature of Old Comedy may in fact be peculiar to Aristophanes' inventive genius. Accustomed as we are, by later developments in the comic form, to distinguish between comedy and farce, between moments of pure entertainment and of more thoughtful moralizing or character study, it may at first be difficult for us to come to terms with a form of comedy in which such distinctions hardly exist. Certainly Aristophanes has posed some problems for critics and playwrights seeking a model for their own day. He was not much imitated during the Renaissance: this was due partly to his inaccessibility, as a writer in Greek whose plays were packed with puzzling contemporary references, and partly, no doubt, to the dangerous principles of free speech, obscenity and untrammelled satire which the comedies flaunted. Aristotle seems to have rated Aristophanes below his less exuberant successors, and in later theories of comedy, from antiquity itself to neoclassicism, Old Comedy continues to be regarded as an Athenian idiosyncrasy outside the main development of the comic genre. It may be that the twentieth century has equipped us better than some of our predecessors to come to terms with the nature of Aristophanic comedy. Freud's investigation of the relationship between jokes and dreams and the working of the unconscious mind can throw a great deal of light on the imaginative processes of an artist like Aristophanes, while surrealism and its heirs (not excluding *The Goon Show* and *Monty Python*) have refreshed our appetitite for his kind of comic technique. In *Homo Ludens* (1938) Johan Huizinga argued that man's play is as important to his culture as his work, and theories linking 'play' to the essence of drama, together with a growing understanding of the festive element in Shakespearian comedy, have shown the way towards a more fruitful approach to Aristophanic comedy than is possible along the well-trodden paths of more formal dramatic theory. Studies of imagery, after establishing themselves as a useful (if sometimes overworked) approach to Shakespearian drama, have been productively applied both to Greek tragedy and to Aristophanes, and permissiveness itself has made its contribution to Aristophanic studies in a more open approach to his obscenity, never a negligible factor in his artistry.

'All Comedy', wrote Gilbert Murray in 1933, 'involves what modern psychologists call a Release';[1] and this element of 'release', which appears in its most unmistakable form in Old Comedy, is probably as important a legacy of the ritual origins of comedy as the pattern of combat, mock death and regeneration so zestfully traced by Cornford and Murray himself, and canonized by Northrop Frye. This release or liberation from everyday restraint can be traced, certainly, in the scurrility and abuse in which Aristophanes so clearly delights, but more importantly in the freedom from everyday logic which marks the language, plots and staging conventions of his drama. But 'release' for an artist of Aristophanes' stamp did not mean loss of artistic control or moral perspective, and despite the loose structure of Old Comedy, particularly in the early plays, a firm unifying vision can almost always be detected.

The Acharnians (425 BC), Aristophanes' first extant comedy, opens with one Dikaiopolis, alone and cogitative, waiting to heckle at the Assembly in favour of peace. He is, the audience soon learns, a countryman, confined (like all his fellows) for strategic reasons within the walls of Attica for the duration of hostilities with Sparta. The contrast between rustic simplicity and urban sophistication is a constant theme of New Comedy, but in this Aristophanic peasant, up early and gazing

> Out over the fields, craving for peace,
> Hating this city, aching for my village,[2]   (ll.32–3)

one senses a kind of authenticity missing from the roughest of the gentleman farmers of the later comedy, and the enforced separation from his smallholding invests him with a sense of deprivation that, for all his buffoonery, is genuinely felt. Aristophanic comedy always begins with a real problem and, unlike the thwarted love affairs which, we shall find, are characteristic of New Comedy, it is one with public reverberations. Dikaiopolis' need for peace is the city's need for peace; but, when he realizes that orderly protest will get him nowhere, he exercises the prerogative of the 'comic hero' (Whitman's term) and sidesteps from reality into a metaworld of immediate wish fulfilment. He signs a private peace treaty with the Spartans and luxuriates with his family inside an isolated paradise of prewar self-indulgence. Dikaiopolis savours his peace treaty like a rare wine (ll. 195 ff.), and in fact the treaty was probably represented on the stage by a wine flask, since σπονδαί is the word standing both for 'treaty' and for 'libation' or 'drink-offering'. This visual pun provides the key to the imagery of *The Acharnians* associating peace with the Dionysiac qualities of drinking, feasting and lovemaking. 'O Dionysia!' cries the

---

[1] Gilbert Murray, *Aristophanes* (Oxford, 1933), p. 2.
[2] The translation is Patric Dickinson's.

hero, smacking his lips, and before long he is celebrating his private festival of Dionysos – a feature of the rustic calendar in reality made impossible by the war. Each play is rich in its own distinctive imagery. *The Birds* (414 BC), whose heroes find solace in Cloudcuckooland, is a masterpiece woven around the airy, insubstantial, winged province of the birds. *Lysistrata* (411 BC), with its famous sex-strike for peace, contrasts the masculine ethos, bawdily ridiculed in the play's phallic imagery, with the comfortable sanity of domestic life – in a long and noble simile, Lysistrata explains how extricating Greece from its war is no more difficult than the woman's work of cleaning, carding and drawing the wool for weaving (ll. 567 ff.).

It is never long before the hero of Old Comedy encounters the chorus, and it is in the chorus that Old Comedy remains closest to the primal κῶμος or revel in which lie its origins. The chorus may be in animal disguise; just as likely it will be composed of old men, their dance movements as they enter the theatre expressing excitement and agitation at the enterprise of the hero. Rarely do they support the hero from the beginning (*Peace*, 421 BC, is an example; no one wanted a continuation of war in that year): usually strident opposition has to be overcome in a series of scenes that begin in bustling activity and end in a presentation of opposing views with some degree of formality. Dikaiopolis, for example, must convince the Acharnians – old warriors whose vines have been destroyed by Spartan troops – that their patriotism may be a little narrow. Luckily, the logic of comedy allows him to dress up as a tragic hero out of Euripides and, with the nonsense of his borrowed rhetoric, win them over to a man (ll. 497 ff.). The chorus of Old Comedy, apart from being endowed with the finest poetry to be found in any comedy until the time of Shakespeare, reinforces the central fantasy of the play and inevitably escorts the hero off the stage in a triumphant finale: equally importantly, perhaps, by ensuring that the great issues of peace and war, old and new ways of thought, the poet and his responsibilities, in which Aristophanes deals, are played out in front of them, the chorus reinforces the public nature of Old Comedy's themes. The decline in the importance of the chorus (in Menander's day it simply performed interludes unconnected with the play, and in Roman comedy it was not there at all) emphasizes the shift in balance from public to private, from political to personal, from the actual to the general, which can be traced in the comedy of the ancient world.

Aristophanes' humour progressively reveals a darker underside. The very fact that in *Lysistrata* the women, whose springtime is short (l. 596), must check the irredeemable folly of their men suggests that the dramatist did not see things as simply as when he had written *The Acharnians*. In *The Frogs* (405 BC), performed before an Athens bewildered and close to capitulation, many critics detect a tone of near-tragedy behind the skilled, affectionate and hilarious parody of Euripides and Aeschylus. Instead of the joyful imagery of fertile sexuality of the earlier plays, here in the parody of a quest to the underworld the wintry landscape of death asserts itself as a motif. Dionysos, the very god of drama whose arrival on the shores of Greece was celebrated each new spring, when his image was triumphantly escorted inland on a wheeled ship, now sets sail in the opposite direction (again, doubtless, circling the *orchestra* in a wheeled ship) seeking his lost Euripides to the grotesque accompaniment of the marsh-frogs' *brekekex coax coax* – to which the god, unable to be wholly tragic even in this extremity, answers with a resounding fart (ll. 209 ff.).

Aristophanic comedy thrives on parody: Dikaiopolis delivers his speech in favour of peace with Sparta dressed in the tragic rags of a Euripidean hero, declaring that even comedy can tell what is right (l. 500).[3] With the death of Euripides and Sophocles, the great age of tragedy had passed, and *The Frogs* is its lament; but it is also, perhaps unconsciously, a lament for comedy itself. For there is an organic connection between tragedy and the kind of comedy which has an Aristophanic or Shakespearian amplitude; the very contest between Aeschylus and Euripides in *The Frogs*, with its emphasis on the role of the poet's imagination in shaping the moral and political life of the city, helps to show why. Euripides, tingeing his myths with realism and his poetry with logic, had helped to destroy the traditional basis of drama: henceforth thought, clothed in rational language, was to become increasingly the province of the philosopher while the horizons of poetry and drama became steadily more limited.[4] It may be that in this final example of Old Comedy, with its portrait of a city confused by intellectual subtlety and hankering after the grandeur and simpler certainty of Aeschylean days, there are some uncomfortable parallels with modern times to be drawn. Fifth-century Athens, like twentieth-century Europe and America, saw its heroic ideals shattered in the long-drawn-out processes of war; it saw the self-confident optimism of new philosophies based on reason and the

---

[3] Τὸ γὰρ δίκαιον οἶδε καὶ τ ρυγῳδία. In *to dikaion*, 'what is right' or 'just', there is an allusion to Dikaiopolis' own name (he is 'Mr Justseeking-Citizen'); but Justice, or *Diké*, was the perennial theme of tragedy. Aristophanes uses the obscure word *trygoidia* for 'comedy', partly for its festive connotations (in origin it seems to have meant a 'vintage-song'), linking it to the Dionysiac undercurrent of the play, and partly for its punning similarity to *tragoidia*, 'tragedy', appropriate enough at this moment when Dikaiopolis is travestying an Euripidean hero.

[4] Cf. Bruno Snell, *The Discovery of the Mind* (Cambridge, Mass., 1953), ch. 6 ('Aristophanes and Aesthetic Criticism').

intellect eat away at the traditional foundations of social and political morality; and, like our own society, in the process it saw the established boundaries between tragic and comic experience become blurred, confused and no longer appropriate.

The last two surviving comedies of Aristophanes are the only complete comedies which belong to the transitional genre of Middle Comedy. In formal terms, it is the declining role of the chorus, signalled by the absence of a *parabasis* – a curious moment when the chorus lays aside its dramatic *persona* to address the audience directly – which marks off Middle from Old Comedy; more generally, there is a decline in the specific references to the actual Athens of the day in favour of a more generalizing quality in the comedy. In *Ecclesiazusae* (*Women in the Assembly*, c. 393 BC) the women of Athens trick their menfolk into handing over political power to the female sex: what follows, described by the play's Victorian editor as 'a scheme of naked socialism',[5] involves the end of marriage and the reversal of sexual roles in courtship as well as the abolition of private property. In *Plutus* (*Wealth*, 388 BC) the god of wealth's traditional blindness is cured and there is a general redistribution of cash in favour of the deserving. The action of both plays is coloured by the background of poverty and distress in which Athens was forced to come to terms with her reduced role in the world. The unladylike communism of *Ecclesiazusae* is generally taken to be a parody of ideas later to emerge in their definitive form in Plato's *Republic*; the gaunt figure of Poverty herself strides on to the stage in *Plutus* to remind us that the hard years following Athenian defeat in the Peloponnesian war give particular significance to the comedy's wishful financial thinking (ll. 415 ff.).

Albeit from the safe distance of fantasy, the two plays that initiate the period of Middle Comedy reflect a period of profound intellectual and social change. It is doubtless a coincidence, but perhaps a significant one, that they deal with the two themes that lie behind most later comedy – sex and money – but in a way that, by and large, was not to appear in comedy again until the confusions of our own century. The suggestion that women may change their conventional social or sexual roles at will, or that money need not fix the individual immutably on his rung of the social ladder, is perhaps indicative of the unstable nature of Athenian society at the time of these two plays; at any rate the contrast with New Comedy, which dates from the last quarter of the fourth century BC, is almost complete. In the world of New Comedy social disturbance is unthinkable: *Tyche*, Fate or Fortune, has allotted everyone their part, from slave to wealthy landowner (and the stage manager has a stock of masks appropriate to these charac-

[5] Rogers, p. xxii.

ters – hence the phrase *dramatis personae*);[6] and although the mutabil-
ity of that same Fortune may lead to minor readjustments in the
pattern – an unexpected legacy here, a rescue from servitude by a
long-lost father there – the general structure of society is the datum
from which the comic action springs. In sexual matters, too, New
Comedy celebrates a strictly limited anarchy. Young men may fall
head over heels in love – as long as they are freeborn and can afford it;
Gorgias in *Dyskolos* admits that he can't (ll. 341 ff.). Old men, for ever
scurrying to and from their estates in the country, or returning unexpectedly from business trips abroad, may look indulgently or jeal-
ously upon the escapades of the young hero, according to their
allotted character and the needs of the plot: their own love affairs are
bound to be ludicrous. The heroines fall into two categories: there is
the freeborn maiden, separated from her lover by some ingeniously
devised circumstance or moral dilemma, and there is the *hetaira*, an
elegant courtesan whose love is available at a price and whose heart,
perhaps, belongs to a handsome client. The slaves, who have no
property, may aid the affairs of their masters, acting as confidant or
trickster, but have no amours of their own. It is not unknown for a
young man to disguise himself as a slave in pursuance of an affair
(witness *Eunuchus*) but it was unheard of, because no joking matter,
for a slave to make advances to a freeborn woman.[7] And the heroine,
too, may have her trusty confidante, Horace's *sedula nutrix* ('fussing
nurse', *Ars poetica*, l. 116) or, for the *hetaira*, an ageing bawd with vast
experience in the tricks of what, to her, is the trade; she too steers clear
of personal involvement in love.

It was Nietzsche who saw in New Comedy – 'that chesslike species
of play' – the triumph of the 'bourgeois mediocrity' first encouraged
in tragedy by the rationalizing innovations of Euripides;[8] a modern
critic, in less extravagant terms, sees in the genre the reflection of 'a
middle-class world with narrow limits':

> Gain and the security of gain dominate; the great political deci-
> sions are made elsewhere and people are pleased when they do
> not notice their effect. . . . Each individual with his circle created a
> world for himself with its own wants, desires and passions.[9]

---

[6] Literally, 'the masks of the play'; it, and its Greek equivalent, headed the
lists of characters in the MSS of Greek and Latin plays.
[7] But what was forbidden in comedy could appear in the mime: a mistress's love for her slave is the subject of a literary mime by Herodas (third
century BC, V) and of the debauched 'Oxyrhyncus Mime' (second century AD, translated by Beare, *The Roman Stage*, 3rd ed. (London, 1964),
pp. 314 ff.).
[8] Nietzsche, *The Birth of Tragedy* (1872), Ch. XI.
[9] Albin Lesky, *A History of Greek Literature* (London, 1966), p. 643.

In the stability of this *milieu* – an idealized stability, to be sure, for the Athens of the fourth century BC suffered its fair share of political turbulence – money and sex stand at opposing ends of experience. One is the most abstract medium of transaction in the human world, and the other the most personal one. Comic dramatists have never ceased to find it amusing that, within limits, one can be substituted for the other.

By the time that Menander (342/1–293/89 BC), the greatest exponent of New Comedy, made his début on the Athenian stage, Aristotle's *Poetics* had been written; if, as is generally supposed, there was a now lost portion of the work containing the philosopher's treatment of comedy, it would have been familiar to Menander, who was in all probability a pupil of Aristotle's successor Theophrastus. And in fact the general principles of Aristotle's theory of drama as they emerge from the remaining portion of the *Poetics* accord rather better with Menander's comedy than they do with most of the tragedies with which they are ostensibly concerned. Menander, like Aristotle, approves of an intricate plot that banishes the irrational (usually in the form of an omniscient deity) to the prologue, even if the action has to rely heavily for its effect on improbable coincidence; he lays great emphasis on consistency of characterization, reminding us not only of Aristotelian precepts but also of the shrewd semiology of human nature found in his mentor Theophrastus' *Characters*; much depends, in play after play, on a skilfully prepared climax embodying the reversals and recognitions which are so important a feature of the Aristotelian complex tragedy. Menander, in short, wrote with self-conscious artistry and was fully capable, we may imagine, of wielding the technical terms of the theorists in defence, if defence were needed, of his comedies.

But Menander is more than an apt interpreter of theory. His reputation throughout antiquity was high, both as a master of the epigram and as a shrewd observer of the world around him. Until the beginning of this century scholars and critics had not much opportunity of putting this reputation to the test: the fragments that remained bore testimony to his gift for a happy phrase but cast little light upon the larger matters of plot and characterization. From then on the discovery of papyrus fragments containing substantial portions of Menander has thrown increasing light upon his work. It was not until 1958, however, that a complete play, its text suffering only from minor gaps, was published. The first reaction to the appearance of *Dyskolos* (*The Bad-Tempered Man*, 316 BC) was, outside the scholarly world, one if anything of mild disappointment: by an irony which he might have appreciated, Menander became available for study at a moment when the form of drama he had initiated was decisively on the wane. But analysis of the play reveals, I believe, a masterly understanding of what must still have been a novel genre in 316 BC.

'There is no play of Menander's without love', grumbled Ovid (*Tristia*, ii. 369), and, although the course of true love never did run smooth, in Greek New Comedy it follows certain fairly well-worn paths. Between the heroine and her lover stand the countless unfortunates who try to prevent the inevitable – rival lovers, strict or jealous fathers, pimps reluctant to lose their source of income – and in *Dyskolos* the bad-tempered man of the title is the obstacle. The difficulties the lovers have to overcome may be the result of a genuine mistake about facts or identities (in *Perikeiromene* or *The Girl Who Has Her Hair Shorn*, c. 313 BC, the trouble starts when the girl's brother is mistaken for a lover) or, as is eminently the case in *Dyskolos*, they may spring from a mistaken attitude towards life on the part of one of the major characters involved.

One glimpse of Knemon's daughter is enough to set Sostratos alight with amorous frenzy (the rustic deity Pan claims responsibility in his prologue, but this, as everyone knows, is only a pleasant dramatic convenience to help along the necessary network of coincidence). But Menander handles Sostratos' character so as to make more than a simple stage lover of him. He rejects the offer of Chaereas the parasite, who is always ready to aid and abet amorous adventures (ll. 57 ff.), and makes it clear that he wants to win the girl's hand by honourable means (ll. 301 ff.). Sostratos' character defines the kind of comedy *Dyskolos* is to be, for his intentions ensure that Knemon's surly nature has to be confronted directly, not evaded by some trickery, and before the play can reach a happy resolution the old man must be persuaded to abandon his churlishness.

The chain of events leading up to the aged misanthrope's revision of his life, followed by a grudging approval of his daughter's betrothal, is handled with delicate yet at times robust humour. Menander shows his understanding of one of the presiding principles of comic structure – that enormous confusion should spring from an initially minor incident. When a bucket falls down a well in the first act of a comedy, theatrical logic demands that before the end of the play one of the characters should follow it with a splash; and this is to be the fate of Knemon, outraged at his family's incompetence and determined (quite in character) to put the mishap to rights without anyone's help. An ideal opportunity for Sostratos to dash into the house and rescue the old man, winning his daughter's hand in gratitude; but that is not quite what happens. The man who has least to thank Knemon for, the stepson Gorgias living next door with his mother (now estranged from the old man), is the one who gallantly conducts the rescue operation while Sostratos, with the opportunism of the enamoured, enters the house simply to gaze upon the daughter, perfunctorily and none too efficiently aiding the virtuous Gorgias. Thus Knemon, dripping wet and chastened, is constrained to admit the existence of altruism, and adjust his world-view accordingly (ll. 713 ff.).

Dyskolos is a good example of drama in which the comic action is linked firmly to an ethical pattern: a miscreant is forced to recognize the error of his ways. A much-imitated play of the same type, which may well hark back to a Menandrian original, is Plautus' *Aulularia* (*The Pot of Gold*), in which a miser's obsession with his secret treasure is ingeniously tangled with a sex plot involving his daughter's seduction. In some comedies this figure is punished for his foolishness; but quite as often a general amelioration of his character is the result of the enlightenment and forms the celebratory climax. A good example of the latter is *Adelphoe* (*The Brothers*, 160 BC, Terence's adaptation of a Menandrian original) where Demea, having revised his own intolerant ways, arranges a surprise marriage for his urbane bachelor brother.

But *Dyskolos* is not simply a dramatization of the lesson that Knemon learns: that stands at the centre, so to speak, of a whole spectrum of comic concerns. At one extreme is the rough and tumble of the farcical action in which, apart from Knemon himself, only slaves and servants are involved; then there is comic trickery of a traditional kind (Sostratos is persuaded to spend a day working in the fields, ll. 366 ff., a joke upon the elegant city-dweller which rebounds to his credit when his willingness to work hard wins him the vital friendship of Gorgias, ll. 766 ff.); and the play includes an extended treatment of the theme of wealth versus poverty. The spontaneous friendship that springs up between the poor farmer Gorgias and the rich young man-about-town is touching and convincing; and when Sostratos' father arrives, in another of those convenient coincidences engineered by Pan, he demonstrates the relative values of wealth and friendship by agreeing readily and liberally to accept the penniless Gorgias for a son-in-law (ll. 784 ff.).

It may well be claimed that Menander is an observer of society; but this claim, once made, must be hedged about with caution. For comedy, throughout its long development, has been pre-eminently a genre built up from tradition and artistic convention: the audience will know the conventions, accept them as such and even look forward to them. New Comedy teems with stock characters, some of them, like the crafty slave, the boasting soldier and the aged crone, growing out of the familiar characters of Old Comedy, others, like the hero and the freeborn heroine, transposed (and a little transformed) from the tragic genre. Probably only a minority – like the parasite who feeds at the tables of the rich or the *hetaira* with her magnificent establishment – owed their particular and distinctive form to the social conditions of the day. The characteristic themes and situations of New Comedy have a similarly varied origin, and it is tempting but dangerous to accept them too literally as social documents: 'foundling children, kidnapped daughters, and scheming slaves cannot have been the experience of many Greek households,' F. H. Sandbach reminds us;[10] the same goes for a host of recurring features, from the pseudo-military raids upon the houses of *hetairai* to a fond father's discovery that his unmarried daughter is in an advanced state of pregnancy resulting from momentary unwisdom at a religious festival. Theatrical conventions – the aside, the overheard conversation, the confidential conference in midstreet – jostle happily in New Comedy with realistically observed behaviour and speech.

If the relationship between actual society and its comic representation is subtle in Athenian New Comedy, in the Latin comedies of Plautus and Terence (which, until the beginning of this century, were the only surviving examples of classical comedy after Aristophanes) it is almost indiscernible. For the Roman comedies were not wholly original works, like those of Menander and his contemporaries; they were copies, somewhere between an adaptation and a translation, of Greek plays. They were called *fabulae palliatae* by token of the fact that the characters wore the Greek *pallium* or cloak. (The attempt to create a similar but more edifying type of comedy with native Roman characters, the *fabula togata*, seems to have met with limited success; the older and more farcical native *fabula Atellana*, replete with stock characters who may have lent some of their vigour to the early *palliatae*, sounds to have deserved its longer run.) The characters of the *palliatae* retain Greek names and appear in Greek settings; but there is a flavour to the characterization which, in Plautus at any rate, is distinctly Roman: *pergraecari*, 'to play the Greek', is a word that characters, supposedly Greek themselves, use more than once in Plautus to describe unwarrantably luxurious living. The general effect is to translate the comedies into a world that is neither Greece nor Italy, where lovers pursue their aims with inextinguishable ardour, slaves devise the most incredible plans, soldiers are inevitably boastful, and parasites outbid one another in their claims to Gargantuan hunger. Plautus, we may guess, revelled in this fantasy world, while Terence deprecated its extremes and tried to return to the more moderate tone of his Greek models.

The extent to which the Roman dramatists were at liberty to depart from their Greek originals is a question that has been much debated.

---

[10] *Oxford Classical Dictionary*, 2nd ed. *s.v.* Menander.

In its detail, the argument is both technical and highly speculative, but one fact is undeniable: the difference between Plautus and Terence is so marked that their work cannot be simply derivative. What little we know of the life of Plautus (?254–?184 BC; there is not even complete agreement about his name) suggests that he began his working life as an actor or stage manager (quite possibly as a slave in a troupe performing Atellan farces) and turned relatively late in life, after financial misadventures, to writing comedies for a living. The *comoedia palliata*, along with the tragic drama, had been introduced to Roman audiences in Latin adaptations by Livius Andronicus in 240 BC; Plautus, perhaps the first commerical dramatist, catered successfully for the growing interest in this new form of entertainment. Terence's short life (*c.* 190–159 BC) was cast in a different mould. Probably born a slave in Carthage, but evidently well educated, he came to Rome, was freed, and enjoyed the patronage of the younger Scipio Africanus (185–129 BC) and his circle of philhellenic friends. Admired by an intellectual élite, he was less successful with the public and became involved in controversy about his manner of adapting Greek originals (the precise grounds of the accusations are obscure). He is said to have died on a visit to Greece in search of new manuscripts. If these biographical titbits (each a battleground of scholarship) did not exist, it might have been possible to invent them, so clearly do Plautus' comedies show him to be a professional man of the theatre with a sense of what will please an audience, while the polished elegance of Terentian comedy, equally clearly, is more calculated to elicit respectful admiration from literary critics aware of the standards of dramaturgy set by Greek New Comedy.

To illustrate the characteristic styles of Plautus and Terence, I have chosen two plays which have been so much imitated from the Renaissance onwards, in detail as well as in broad outline, that a comparison of the techniques of the two Roman dramatists may almost be said to serve as an introduction to some of the major themes and artistic problems of later comedy. Plautus' *Menaechmi* (*The Menaechmus Brothers*; like much Plautine drama, it cannot be dated) is a comedy of mistaken identity, with a visual theme and physical action on stage as its keynote. In *Eunuchus* (*The Eunuch*, 161 BC) Terence introduces one of the most ingenious devices in ancient comedy for smuggling an ardent lover into the presence of the girl who has captured his heart – a device which later dramatists rarely copied directly, although it served as the inspiration for countless plots of sexual intrigue.

From the very beginning of each play, the differences are in evidence. In *Menaechmi* there is, as so often, a complicated story of a child separated from his family when young; in this case twins are involved, and one has been renamed after the loss of the other. The extended joke of the play depends almost exclusively on the fact that two individuals, identical in appearance and both answering to the unusual name of Menaechmus, are abroad in the streets of Epidamnus. Accordingly the main job of the Prologue, after a few jokes to capture the audience's attention and a summary account of the story of separation, is to hammer home the point that the twins *have the same name* (l. 43); it is repeated for good measure a moment later, 'so that you won't go wrong' (l. 47). Throughout the Prologue, delivered in direct address to the audience, there is no pretence that the performance is not a performance, that the stage setting is not a stage setting ('This is the city of Epidamnus,' it is explained, 'while this play is on', l. 72), that a noisy audience, capable of impatience and bad behaviour, is not a few feet from the stage; in short, the whole story of the separated twins and the confusion awaiting them is cheerfully accepted as a fiction designed expressly for entertainment.

Eunuchus, if lack of serious moral concern in the plot is the criterion, is as farcical as *Menaechmi*, but the popular techniques of the earlier play have been almost banished from the stage. Rejecting the simple Prologue which had satisfied Plautus (and for that matter his Greek predecessors), Terentian comedy conveys the information through an exposition scene fully integrated with the play:[11] even when, as in *Adelphoe*, the play opens with a lengthy direct address to the audience, it is delivered by someone reacting, in character, to the opening situation. In *Eunuchus*, the opening scene is a masterpiece in miniature:

> What should I do then? Not go, even when she invites me of her own accord? Or should I stand firm and take no insults from whores? She shut me out, she calls me back: should I go? No, not if she begs me to!   (ll. 45–9)

The first lines of the young hero Phaedria plunge us, as Horace recommends, *in medias res* – straight into the action: indignant because another has apparently received preferment from his mistress, he debates in front of the door whether he should swallow dignity and pay her another call. Soon Thais, the woman in question, appears and reveals her reasoning: it is a familiar story of a girl carried off into slavery, whom Thais now wants to restore to freedom and her family; and so she has to be accommodating to Phaedria's rival to get the girl away from him. But is the story true? Phaedria, encouraged by the impudence of his slave Parmeno, is bound to doubt:

> As if I didn't know where your words were leading! 'She was

---

[11] And Terence finds a new use for the formal prologue, employing it, like a Shavian preface, in defence against his critics.

carried off from here as a child, my mother adopted her, she was
called my sister, and I want to get her away to hand her back to her
family.' And all these words come back to this: I'm shut out, he's
let in!   (ll. 155–9)

Ingeniously, Terence has done exactly what Plautus did – repeat the
main line of a complicated plot for the benefit of the audience – but
this time as part of the action, arising naturally from character in
Phaedria's ironic mimicry of his mistress's protestations.

Thais' strength of character (as soon as she is alone she lets the
audience know that she was telling the truth, ll. 197 ff.), Parmeno's
impudence, Phaedria's distrust and irresolution (two more characteristics of love in a comedy): the psychological interaction of these
personages is as important to Terence as the events of the plot, and it
is delicately established in the exposition scene. Now Terence is ready
to move on to the next strand of the plot: enter Gnatho the parasite,
escorting the beautiful Pamphila to Thais' house.

A parasite appears in both *Menaechmi* and *Eunuchus*; it is interesting
to compare the treatment of the two. In *Menaechmi* the long speech of
Peniculus ('little brush', so called because he sweeps the table clean)
in which he introduces himself, his life philosophy and the self-
interest that attaches him to Menaechmus, coming as it does immediately after the Prologue (ll. 77 ff.), suggests that he is to be an
important character – and so in a sense he is: he is one of the first to
meet the wrong Menaechmus and in return for a supposed injury (in
fact a consequence of confusing the twins) stirs marital discord by
denouncing his patron's peccadilloes. Once the wife is involved, the
theme of mistaken identity moves on to its grand climax; but Peniculus
himself, his contribution to the mechanics of the plot performed,
simply abandons the stage, grumbling because no one in that household will reward him (l. 667). In performance, as the action becomes
increasingly frenzied, the audience is unlikely to be bothered by his
abrupt dismissal; but to Terence it must have seemed crude and
unsophisticated, and indeed in *Eunuchus* Gnatho is given virtually
the last word. Like Peniculus, he introduces himself by boasting of his
art, claiming to be different from the run of his profession. While
others make a living out of their gift for repartee, he has discovered an
important labour-saving fact: there are many who are satisfied simply
by hearing their own witticisms applauded, and when no one else
will praise them he will (ll. 232 ff.). This is a necessary introduction to
his relationship with Phaedria's rival Thraso (who is himself a new
kind of boasting soldier, a military man who thinks himself a wit), but
it also contributes to the final resolution of the play when Gnatho,
hypocritically praising his patron's table talk, persuades Phaedria to

allow his rival to continue to pay court to Thais, so that his own greed ensures a happy outcome for all the characters (ll. 1067 ff.). Terence never likes to let the action pause: while Peniculus arrives on an empty stage for his first speech, Gnatho is overheard by Parmeno from the rival camp; and while Peniculus more or less aimlessly plans a visit to his patron, Gnatho is employed on the all-important mission of delivering Pamphila (the cause of the controversy in the opening scene) safely into Thais' hands. The fact that she has been glimpsed along the way by Phaedria's brother sets the main device of the play in progress, and it is not long before Parmeno is helping young Chaerea to disguise himself as the eunuch whom Phaedria has promised Thais, and thus gain access to the unsuspecting household. A magnificently complicated series of events in *Eunuchus* turns out, as Aristotle recommended (for tragedy, of course, *Poet*. 9.1452ᵃ4), 'unexpectedly, but in consequence of what has gone before'.

It is not that Terence does not make full use of the conventions of the Graeco-Roman stage; like Plautus, he fills his plays with soliloquies, asides, eavesdropping, opportune exits and entrances from the two doors on stage, foreshortening of time for dramatic purposes, and a variety of other devices. But Terence discreetly does his best to subordinate the conventions, as far as may be, to reason and probability. Plautus, for instance, has few scruples about acknowledging the presence of the audience: *sitiunt qui sedent* ('they're getting thirsty'), an expansive character is warned about them towards the end of one play (*Poenulus*, l. 1224). Terence is unwilling to break out of the dramatic situation in this way. One example must suffice. The stage arrangements in the Graeco-Roman theatre made it almost inevitable that one of the main sources of humour should derive from the proximity of two houses, with their separate entrances giving on to the street that forms the acting area. In *Miles gloriosus* (*The Boasting Soldier*, *c*. 205 BC; the title indicates a character who was to become one of the most important stock figures in later drama), Plautus' plot depends on a love affair made possible because a secret passage has been built between the house of the boasting soldier of the title and his neighbour's. The first half of the play is a sort of *Menaechmi* in reverse, in which a lively heroine, by appearing in rapid succession at two separate front doors, convinces a gullible slave that she is her own twin sister; but towards the end Pyrgopolynices, the grandiosely titled warrior, falls the victim of a duplicity in which he is easily persuaded that his neighbour's wife, under the fascination of his charms, is prepared to elope with him (ll. 969 ff.). Useless to argue that by all the laws of probability he should have known that his neighbour was a bachelor of long standing and firm commitment (ll. 679 ff.): logic of that kind is foreign to Plautine comedy. In *Eunuchus*, on the other hand, with the slightest of touches, Terence removes the improbability that Chaerea's disguise as the eunuch should not be penetrated instantly by his next-door neighbours: Thais, it is casually declared, has only recently come to live in the house (l. 359).

'The difference between the *Menaechmi* and the *Adelphi*', wrote Beare, 'is the difference between farce and comedy.'[12] We might attach varying meanings to the terms 'farce' and 'comedy'; we might recognize that Plautus sometimes deepens his dramatic tone, if never enough in earnest to satisfy a Leavisite (*Captivi* or *The Prisoners* demonstrates a noble friendship between slave and master; in *Amphitruo* the duping of a faithful wife by Jupiter in disguise produces some moments of pathos), and conversely that Terence, as *Eunuchus* so amply testifies, does not always shun the lively amorality of pure farce. But Beare's distinction holds: Terence could never have written *Menaechmi*, with its physical confusion denying reason and culminating in a grand fight on stage (ll. 990 ff.), nor could Plautus have written *Adelphoe*, in which an elegantly balanced double plot explores the effect of contrasted upbringing upon a pair of brothers. The distinction between farce and comedy, as I have suggested, is one that can be made only after the decline of Old Comedy, although it was a dividing line that was to become increasingly recognizable from the Renaissance onwards, as comedy developed in an age when *decorum* was one of the artist's guiding principles.

One reason, I suspect, why Renaissance dramatists turned so eagerly to Plautus and Terence was that, taken together, they offered a kind of sliding scale of seriousness in comedy, with the farcical knockabout of a *Menaechmi* (not to mention the transvestite indecencies of a *Casina*) at one extreme, and the subtle humanity of an *Adelphoe* at the other. The literary theorist may have been obliged to stress the moral value of the genre; the dramatist found greater freedom.

Terence's early death marks the end, for us, of classical comedy: other dramatists have left us only their names, a few titles and a collection of fragments. But the Italians, then as now, were lovers of spectacle, and the impressive remains of theatres preserved in the great cities of the empire testify to the importance of the performer's art in Roman civilization. The first stone theatre was built in Rome just over a century after Terence's death: Plautus and Terence, unlike their Greek predecessors, had had to content themselves with makeshift wooden stages; and the writing of *fabulae palliatae* seems to have fallen into decline soon after the death of Terence. Indeed, it has been argued that the surviving theatres never saw the full perform-

---

[12] Beare, op. cit. p. 350.

ance of a regular tragedy or comedy but, with the growth of mime companies subject to no rules of moral or artistic decorum, were given over to what one scholar characterized as 'smut, satire and slapstick'.[13]

The golden age of Roman letters and civilization was to follow Plautus and Terence, and no plays have survived from the period, but we do have something perhaps as valuable, and certainly as influential, in Horace's *Ars poetica* (*Art of Poetry*, 65–8 BC). The poet's advice to the playwright is civilized and eminently sensible: the prizes go to the one who has combined profit with pleasure, *qui miscuit utile dulci* (l. 344); comedy must keep away from the style and matter of tragedy, although it too may have its solemn moments (ll. 90 ff.); language and action should be suited to a character's age and station (ll. 114 ff., 153 ff.); action on the stage is preferable to narrative, except for scenes of violence or the supernatural, which occasion disgust and disbelief (ll. 179 ff.); and, of course, every play should have five acts (ll. 189 f.). Horace, no doubt borrowing and adapting the commonplaces of Hellenistic literary criticism, laid the foundations for the neoclassical doctrines of decorum and verisimilitude, and the *Ars* was regarded as a kind of supplement, especially in relation to comedy, to the weightier pronouncements of Aristotle. Despite the colour lent to his work by references to actors and audience, Horace's poetic has a literary rather than a theatrical bias, evidenced by his implied preference of Terence to Plautus:[14] already in Horace's day we can see the divorce between text and performance which has bedevilled dramatic criticism ever since.

Horace, deservedly, is still studied and admired while, equally deservedly, the fourth-century grammarian Donatus is almost forgotten; yet it was his treatise on comedy (or rather the treatise attributed to him, for it was later established that the true author was an equally obscure, though Greek, grammarian called Euanthius) which prefaced almost all the early printed editions of Terence and helped more even than Horace to fix the Renaissance conception of comedy. Here we find the confusing early history and misleading etymology of comedy (i.3) repeated endlessly in Renaissance poetics; it contains the famous definition of comedy as a representation of private affairs, differing from tragedy in certain prosaically enumerated respects, 'in which one learns what is useful and what is to be avoided in life' (iv.2, v.1); it defines the four parts of the comic plot – prologue, protasis, epitasis, catastrophe (vii.1) – so difficult for commentators to align

---

[13] Sir Mortimer Wheeler, *Roman Africa in Colour* (London, 1966), p. 37; for a different view, see M. Bieber, *The History of The Greek and Roman Theater*, 2nd ed. (Princeton, NJ, and London, 1961), p. 227.

[14] *Ars P.* 270 ff.; *Epist*. II.i, 55 ff., 170 ff.

with the five-act prescription; and it is our source for Cicero's famous definition of comedy as 'an imitation of life, a mirror of custom, and an image of truth' (v.1).

One oddity remains to be recorded, an anonymous play *Querolus*, written in Latin in the fifth century AD and owing something to Plautus' *Aulularia*; it even has its stageworthy moments. The next survivors to claim the attention of the student of comedy, the so-called 'Christian comedies' composed by Hrotswitha, the devout tenth-century nun of Gandersheim, and combining bemused imitation of Terence with strenuous advertisements for the Christian virtues, properly belong to the post-classical world.

Viewed in its general outlines, the course of Greek and Roman comedy may seem to be one of uninterrupted decline: from the abundant imagination of Aristophanes to the urbanity and detachment of Menander, from the *vis comica* of Plautus to the divorce between theory and practice (pointing to decadence in the theatre itself) in Horace's day, and from all that to the pedantry of the late grammarians in a world on the brink of barbarism. But this is not how it always seemed: the influence of Donatus upon the Renaissance was profound, and Lessing admired the *Captivi* of Plautus above any other play, ancient or modern. Perhaps our own preferences say as much about ourselves as they do about the works we profess to admire.

2

Medieval comic traditions and the beginnings of English comedy

GLYNNE WICKHAM

I T I S difficult to speak meaningfully about comedy in the Middle Ages in any of the senses that that word has come to possess for Western society since the sixteenth century.

Comedy was not recognized formally as a dramatic genre in the sense in which Sir Philip Sidney, Ben Jonson and their successors defined it: it was not recognized theatrically as something different in kind from tragedy or pastoral in the sense in which Italian scenic designers from Serlio onwards distinguished it visually; yet it was recognized as early as the fourteenth century – at least by Dante and Chaucer – as possessing distinctive qualities in terms of literary narrative. John Lydgate is succinct:

> My maister Chaucer, with his fresh comedies,
> Is ded, allas, cheeff poete of Breteyne,
> That whilom made foul pit(e)ous tragedies;
> The fall of pryncis he dede also compleyne . . .
> *(Fall of Princes*, ll. 246–9)

In his own *Troy Book* he elects to define his own understanding of both terms:

> And to declare, schortly in sentence,
> Of bo(th)e two (th)e final difference:
> A comedie hath in his gynnyng,
> At prime face, a manner compleynyng,
> And afterward endeth in gladnes;
> And it (th)e dedis only doth expres
> Of swiche as ben in povert plounged lowe;
> But tragidie, who so list to knowe,

It begynneth in prosperite,
And endeth ever in adversite;
And it also doth (th)e conquest trete
Of riche kynges and of lordys grete,
Of my(gh)ty men and olde conquerou(ri)s,
Whiche by fraude of Fortunys schowris
Ben overcast & whelmed from her glorie . . .

(Book Two, ll. 845–59)

Both the shape of the story and the persons appropriate to it are thus sharply and clearly distinguished in each case; nor do Lydgate's distinctions depart from those respected by Terence, Plautus, Seneca and Horace in a dramatic rather than a literary context.

That Lydgate was himself prepared to lift his own definition of a comedy out of the literary context within which he had inherited it and restore it to a theatrical one is clear from his own *Mumming at Hertford*, of which more will be said later (pp. 51–2 below).

Although little evidence survives in England before the fifteenth century of any concept of comedy as explicit as Lydgate's, there can be no doubt that the spokesmen of the Roman Catholic church, in Britain as elsewhere in Europe, recognized the difference between the serious and the comic in theatrical representation of scripture as early as the twelfth century. This is apparent in the shift of nomenclature in the rubrics of service books of the liturgies for the principal feast days of the church's calendar, first from *Ordo* and *Officium* to *Representatio*, and then to *Ludus*; for these changes indicate selfconscious recognition of a measurable shift from the gravity proper to adoration of the deity to a levity more appropriate to recreation.

I have argued elsewhere that this recognition among clerics of a distinction between the serious and the comic derives directly from the dualism implicit in Christianity itself.[1] In Christian society the comic thus finds its source along with tragedy in the Fall of Lucifer and the Fall of Adam. In both these cases an error of judgement brings about a catastrophic reversal of fortune that corresponds to Aristotle's description of the tragic hero. Chaucer states that case eloquently in the opening stanzas of the Prologue to *The Monk's Tale*; there, the narrator says he will 'biwayle in maner of Tragedie' tales of those illustrious men of high degree whose prosperity was suddenly shaken and who were overtaken by calamity:

---

[1] This dualism between the Kingdom of Heaven and Hell-Castle came to be spelt out in stage terms musically and visually as well as verbally; see pp. 53–5 below, and G. Wickham, *The Medieval Theatre* (London, 1974), pp. 37–43.

At Lucifer, though he an angel were,
And nat a man, at him I wol biginne,
For, thogh fortune may non angel dere,
From heigh degree yet fel he for his sinne
Down in-to helle, wher he yet is inne.
O Lucifer! brightest of angels alle,
Now artow Sathanas, that maist not twinne
Out of miserie, in which that thou art falle.

Lo Adam, in the feld of Damassene,
With goddes owene finger wroght was he,
And nat bigeten of mannes sperme unclene,
And welte al Paradys, saving o tree.
Had never worldly man so heigh degree
As Adam, til he for misgovernaunce
Was drive out of his hye prosperitee
To labour, and to helle, and to meschaunce.

The conduct of both Lucifer and Adam, however, tragic as its consequences were for them, was regarded by the Christian fathers as
absurd, ludicrous, almost laughable because it was so unnecessary:
both of them had rebelled by *choosing* to disobey the protective
instructions supplied by God.

This polarization between the good and serious, and the bad and
ridiculous, establishes a contrast in behaviour which any actor must
necessarily copy and embroider in the manner that best befits that
character he is required to represent, once biblical characters start to
appear on the stage. Thus in the earliest Christian liturgical drama of
the tenth and eleventh centuries, the behaviour demanded of the
actors in the dialogue (which was chanted) and in the rubrics of the
service books (which served as stage directions) is uniformly serious,
since all the characters are themselves serious and devout believers:
the three Maries and the angel at Christ's sepulchre, and the
shepherds and the Magi at Christ's crib. It is only when the narrative
content of this lyrical drama is extended to include Old Testament
characters like the prophets and their enemies, or New Testament
characters whose purpose is to frustrate God's will, that trouble
begins, for their behaviour patterns must be the opposite of devout,
and instantly recognizable as inspired and guided by Lucifer. Two of
the earliest examples are Belshazzar in *The Play of Daniel* and King
Herod in *The Massacre of the Innocents*: both of these characters are
diabolic in their intentions and are required to behave in an appropriately indecorous and barbaric manner; vanity informs their
actions, and in their tyrannical boastfulness they earn – and are
required to earn – their audience's contempt. Malignity is here bal-

anced against absurdity, and the result, as far as the spectator is concerned, is fear, counterbalanced by mirth. In short, we are invited to reject them, and such thoughts as motivate their actions, by laughing at them. Thus believers are made to triumph through their faith, courage and good works; unbelievers are overthrown and dismissed in ridicule. This technique is fully explicit in *The Play of Anti-Christ* from Tergensee of the late twelfth century.

The balance between the malign and the comic in theatrical characterization was at best a precarious one and likely, in a liturgical environment, to open dramatic representation to question – at least as an integral part of a particular 'order of service'. The danger lay in the threat to the gravity of the occasion being celebrated by recourse to re-enactment, since no obvious frontiers existed to limit the degree of indecorousness in which non-Christian characters might indulge. Thus the Abbess of Hohenburg near Strasbourg (*c.* 1180) laments the contamination of the *Officium Stellae* by unruly priests, claiming that this noble liturgy has been translated into an act of 'irreligion and extravagance conducted with all the licence of youth'.[2] Devils provide the extreme example, eclipsed only by Antichrist himself.

Another feature of early liturgical music-drama that warrants attention is that all of it, despite the seriousness of the idea informing it, was festive in character. It owed its very being to the major feasts of praise and thanksgiving in the Christian calendar, Easter and Christmas. Re-enactment of the central events, Christ's Resurrection and birth, served only to enhance and explain their abiding significance; and the shape of the narrative relating these events conformed in both instances to that of comedy as articulated in classical antiquity, not tragedy. It was only much later, at the close of the thirteenth century, that Christ's Passion came to be treated dramatically; and even then it was normal to frame it – invariable in the vernacular Corpus Christi plays of the fourteenth and fifteenth centuries – with Adam's Fall, Christ's birth and Resurrection, and thus once again to place it within a comic rather than a tragic narrative structure as defined by Chaucer and Lydgate. Once a Judgement play is added, the conclusion becomes ambiguous since the souls on trial may as easily be assigned to perpetual damnation as to everlasting joy.

This ambiguity in point of structure was substantially increased through the centuries by the church's own attitudes to, and treatments of, the person of Christ himself. Worshipped as emperor and king in the early liturgical drama, He comes to be presented as the most humane of men in the vernacular cycles of the gothic era. The

---

[2] See C. M. Engelhardt, *Herrad von Landsberg* (Stuttgart and Tübingen, 1818), p. 104. See also Robert Mannyng of Brunne, *Handlyng Sinne (1303)*, ed. F. J. Furnival for *E.E.T.S.* (1901), pp. 154–5.

Bible, too, imposed its own *diktats* upon the characters assembled in any given scene or play. Thus, while Christ himself was unquestionably an epic figure and placed in a specific, and virtually unalterable, environment as had been considered appropriate to tragedy, neither He nor King David, Herod nor Pontius Pilate had so restricted their acquaintance as to exclude 'swiche as ben in povert plounged lowe', the folk appropriate to comedy.

Finally, it must be remarked that it was the whole purpose, at least of gothic drama, to prove that man's 'adversity', occasioned by Adam's Fall, was no longer an everlasting impediment to final 'prosperity' thanks to Christ's redemptive atonement and His gifts of contrition and repentance through Grace and penance: only those who wilfully declined these gifts and ignored these signs should anticipate the full tragic fate of everlasting separation from the Godhead. Reconcilement through love thus supplied a new, and specifically Christian, reason for the change of fortune from adversity to prosperity stipulated within the inherited classical formula as the structural basis of comic narrative. In other words, a romantic approach had come to be added as an alternative to the purely corrective or punitive approach formulated in the drama of classical antiquity.

'Prosperity' and 'adversity', however, had meanings for all walks of society in the Middle Ages other than those developed by the church within Christian philosophy and Christian drama. Chief among these during the tenth and eleventh centuries were the social ones: those differences of lifestyle between the baronial landlords and their serfs in a feudal society, and between the lords spiritual and the majority of their flock throughout Christendom. With the growth of banking, commerce and cities during the twelfth and thirteenth centuries a new class of wealthy merchants and shopkeepers came, by their way of life, to place the words 'prosperity' and 'adversity' in yet another light: that of money and material possessions. Initially, such jealousy and resentment as may have accrued in the lower levels of society from these glaring discrepancies of social status was harmlessly released through occasional, but regular, festivals dedicated to the inversion of normal social order. The Feast of Fools, Shrovetide and Carnival provided the principal occasions for this release of emotion, and the Lord of Misrule, the Boy Bishop, the French *sot* and the German *Narr* represent in their names and persons the degree of licence accorded to it. In France, the Feast of Fools – a servants' hall parody, as it were, of sacred offices – although never legitimized as a formal liturgy, was widely tolerated on 26 December and served to introduce secular, goliardic, comic incident, music and characterization into liturgical dramatic practice which could never again be wholly extirpated. The Feast of the Boy Bishop (28 December) was open to similar abuse; but where, in England, the senior clergy succeeded in banning the former festival, while encouraging a more disciplined celebration of the latter, both in France and Germany episcopal attempts to purge and control the Feast of Fools went largely unheeded.[3] The spirit of these celebrations was thus broadly anti-feudal and anti-clerical to start with; but it came with time to embrace specific anti-bourgeois elements, as we shall see.

At least as important a component of this 'fooling' from the outset, however, was a more generalized attack on hierarchy and on the spirit of order itself: in other words, an assertion of man's natural condition in the face of society's attempts to regulate and tame it. All these expressions of what at an unselfconscious or natural level we may call 'release', and of what at a more selfconscious level we should term 'rebellion' or 'assault', occasioned mirth, merriment and laughter. In short, they were both purgative and comic. Thus a form of comedy grew up in the Middle Ages that relied far more heavily upon incident and improvisation which carried caricature to the point of the grotesque than upon any particular form, style or structure as postulated by the Latin grammarians and their medieval successors. Lack of texts and other written records prevents us from knowing with any precision how much of the comic licence that confronts us in the banquet halls and taverns and on the village greens of the Middle Ages was a direct survival of similar festivities within the Roman Empire; but there is sufficient correspondence between both the nature of the fooling and the seasons of the calendar when it was permitted for it to seem that these links derived from connections stronger than mere coincidence. Whatever else may be dim and speculative, the existence of actors plying their talents for reward is firmly substantiated by documentary record, from the supposed epitaph of Vitalis, the mime (c. 800), to John, Bishop of Salisbury's description of the impersonation of animals (c. 1300).[4]

Yet however these links may be viewed, the fact of consequence in the present context is the incontrovertible existence in the thirteenth century of a tradition of mimicry and drollery lively enough to have attracted writers to script some of it, and owing little or nothing to religious drama for its themes and methods. Here it must be noted that an important correspondence in date exists between the appear-

[3] See Karl Young, *The Drama of the Medieval Church* (Oxford, 1933), Vol. I, pp. 104 ff.; and E. K. Chambers, *The Mediaeval Stage* (Oxford, 1903), Vol. I, pp. 274 ff.

[4] See Richard Axton, *European Drama of the Early Middle Ages* (London, 1974), pp. 17–32; also Allardyce Nicoll, *Mimes, Masks and Miracles* (London, 1931), pp. 135–75, and E. K. Chambers, op. cit. Vol. I, pp. 23 ff.

ance of these texts and the founding of Europe's first universities; for it was in Paris, Oxford, Padua and Bologna that large numbers of young clerks began to support themselves in their studies by such rewards in cash and kind as they could earn from their own skills as minstrels and entertainers.[5] The perennial concern of youth with sexual prowess and opportunity, and youth's irritation with the irksome controls of authority, inevitably became the principal subjects of the ballads, dialogued debates and mimetic games in their repertoire. One of the earliest of these entertainments is English, *The Interlude of the Student and the Maiden* (*Interludium de Clerico et Puella*), c. 1300. Only two brief scenes of this play, written in East Midlands dialect, survive in a MS now in the British Museum (Add. MS 23986): in the first, the student pleads with the girl to accept him as a lover, while she, contemptuously, refuses:

> By Christ in Heaven and St John
> I don't care for any student,
> For many a good woman have they brought to shame.
> By Christ, you should have stayed at home!

In the second scene the student visits an old procuress whose help he hopes to secure in return for lavish promises of cash. Of approximately the same date – probably earlier – is *The Dialogue of the Blind Man and the Boy* (*Du garçon et de l'aveugle*) from Tournai in northeastern France. An old, lecherous and far from penniless blind man appears before an audience, begging for alms; help is offered by a feckless youth who joins him, and then sets about stripping his shameless but helpless victim of his wench, his wealth and his clothes.[6]

In both these short trifles, command of dramatic action, of comic mood and of method is so deft as to make it well-nigh unbelievable to the modern reader that either play could have been the first of its kind in either French or English. Moreover, it must be remembered that French at this time was still widely spoken in England: this makes the group of four plays from Arras in Picardy of even earlier date just as relevant in this context. Of these Richard Axton writes as follows:

> Arras, a manufacturing town with a thirteenth-century population in the region of twenty thousand inhabitants, had enough

---

[5] See G. Wickham, *The Medieval Theatre*, pp. 105–8, and Helen Waddell, *The Wandering Scholars* (London, 1927), esp. ch. 8, 'The Ordo Vagorum'. No less influential were the *trouvères* with the secular amusements of the banquet halls.

[6] *Du garçon et de l'aveugle*, ed. Mario Roques, C.F.M.A. 5 (Paris, 1921); *Interludium de Clerico et Puella*, in G. Wickham (ed.), *English Moral Interludes* (London, 1976), pp. 200–3.

prosperous and educated burgher-patrons to support a group of resident poets and *jongleurs*. Some of these entertainers were practitioners of the traditional mimic skills; many had clerical schooling; some had acquired a knowledge of ecclesiastical drama as well as of the epic and love-poetry of the feudal courts in northern France. Their own dramatic compositions were . . . suited to the practical interests of their business-minded audiences and usually had a firmly 'realistic' basis in the mimic style.[7]

All four plays are moralistic in intention, but by recourse to farcical situation, irony, wit and festive ritual each makes its point by distinctively comic methods. In two of them – Jean Bodel's *Play of St Nicholas* and the anonymous *'Courtois' of Arras* – a tavern is used as a setting to exemplify vicious aspects of life: the evils attendant upon drinking and gambling, and the fate that boastful and pretentious youths are likely to meet at the hands of sophisticated and unscrupulous prostitutes. Another, Adam de la Halle's *Robin and Marion*, is a pastoral which, idealized as its shepherds and shepherdesses may be, succeeds in contrasting, by comic irony, the social differences between leisured and labouring classes. The fourth, *The Play of the Green Canopy (Jeu de la feuillée)*, is sharply anti-clerical and more farcical in its use of incident; it also relies heavily on both local and topical targets for its humorous effects.[8] In this context use of the words 'France' and 'French', however, can be very misleading, since during the late thirteenth century and early fourteenth so much of France was ruled by the Kings of England, and since French was still so widely spoken in literate circles in England.

What, then, are we to make of this varied and vigorous secular comic tradition in the thirteenth and fourteenth centuries, literary as well as mimetic and separate from, if not wholly independent of, the religious drama of the early Middle Ages?

First we must recognize the combination of caustic realism, ribaldry that often verges upon the obscene, and the predominance of characters 'in povert plounged lowe' that gives the surviving texts their special quality and sets them apart from the more stylized 'laughable' conduct and 'ridiculous' language that attaches to non-Christian characters and their actions in the liturgical music-dramas of Christian worship. Next, we must remark the singular conjunction of physical dramatic techniques and conventions characteristic of pro-

---

[7] Axton, op. cit. p. 131.
[8] *Courtois d'Arras*, ed. Edmond Faral, C.F.M.A. 3 (Paris, 1922); *Jeu de la feuillée*, ed. Ernest Langlois, C.F.M.A. 6 (Paris, 1923); *Jeu de Robin et Marion*, C.F.M.A. 36 (Paris, 1924). See also Grace Frank, *Mediaeval French Drama* (Oxford, 1954), pp. 211–16.

fessional mimes and minstrels, with the advent during the thirteenth century of university students as authors and performers of dramatic texts that rely heavily on irony, satire and verbal wit for their effect. Third, we must note that both of these changes occur at a point in time when medieval society was having to accommodate itself to the rapid growth of a third class of individuals – the merchant burghers and shopkeepers of the new towns – who occupied the middle ground between the landed aristocracy (baronial and ecclesiastical) and the peasantry. This class of spectator was still close enough to the hewers of wood and drawers of water from whose ranks it had emerged to sympathize with the earthy realism of their humour, and yet still sufficiently distanced from the feudal landlords to regard them as rivals in wealth and power, if not actually as enemies. Such an audience could hardly fail to respond warmly to a form of entertainment that served to flatter it by securing it in its own sense of superiority over less able, industrious or physically fortunate members of society, while mocking the pretensions of their rivals in the higher ranks of the social, political and religious hierarchies.

By the close of the fourteenth century these men and their wives had become the regular patrons of this secularly orientated comic drama, able to commission it and reward its executants. Nor should it be forgotten that it was these same merchants and their families who founded the *compagnie* in Italy, the *confradiás* in Spain, the *confréries* and *puys* in France, the Chambers of Rhetorick in Flanders and the guilds in England: for when a new feast in the Christian calendar came to be instituted in the fourteenth century – the Feast of Corpus Christi – these men with their trade associations, their charitable brotherhoods and their quasi-religious guilds were already firmly enough established to be able to offer the church their assistance both in organizing and in founding the new feast, or to make them the most obvious source of help on which the church might call. When, therefore, a new style of drama, religious but vernacular, was initiated specifically to celebrate this feast – the *Play Called Corpus Christi* – its scriptwriters were likely to have to make some moves to accommodate the tastes of this bourgeois class by drawing upon comic forms and techniques of secular origin, if the new drama was to hold its audiences.

It is not possible to *prove* this proposition; I merely offer it as the most probable of explanatory hypotheses, since it is one that acknowledges and contains *all* the surviving evidence in a comprehensive yet unforced manner. What it argues is that a sense of contrast and incongruity developed simultaneously but independently both in the worship of the Christian church and in the recreational activities of lay society. The chance to give expression to both, espe-

cially in dramatic form, occurred at calendar festivals when Holy Days
and holidays were one and indivisible. The sense of occasion promoted the drama, and the drama sought, if not always to explain, at
least to hold the occasion up to public view and to comment on its
significance. Whenever and wherever this awareness of contrast was
sharpened and formulated in images that defined and pointed up
incongruity of situation, conduct and language, comedy resulted. It
could be crude and farcical with slapstick predominant; it could be
subtle with wit and irony as the principal instruments of mirth: either
way, the sense of the comic grew and fed upon itself, borrowing,
stretching, parodying and classifying until a stock of examples, types
and formulae became the common property of actors, authors and
audiences alike. The old man with a young wife, the priest who is
both greedy and lecherous (made all the more conspicuous by the
preaching of Wycliff and his Lollards); pastoral innocence contrasted
with courtly corruption; tyrannical barons outwitted by timorous
bumpkins; the braggart who is a coward; puns, double-meanings and
burlesque: it was out of this material in real life that the monologues,
debates, farces and other comic games of social recreation were
fashioned. The titles of many French fifteenth-century farces in particular bear eloquent witness to this development: *Le Grandisseur et le
sot* (c. 1450), *Pathelin* (1464), *Le Fol, le mari, la femme et le curé* (c. 1465),
Hubert, la femme, le juge et le procureur (1476) and *Robinet badin, la femme
veuve, la commère, et l'oncle Michault* (c. 1490) may serve here as
examples.[9]

It was of course this same sense of contrast and incongruity with its
manifest ambiguities, as we have already noticed, that two centuries
earlier had become a source of acute discomfort and anxiety to clerical
philosophers whose task it was to control the development of liturgical music-drama within the overriding principles of a monastic neo-
Platonism. Since life for such men could never be regarded as more
than an imperfect and deceptive image of spiritual actuality, it was
necessary at all times to preserve a clear distinction between the 'idea'
and the 'sign'. Signs (the facts and figures of daily life), as St Augus-
tine had postulated, had their uses; and, as pointers that might lead
men in their thinking towards the idea, they were to be commended –
if with due caution. The dramatic, however, depending as it did upon
exhibition, impersonation and re-enactment, dealt directly and
almost exclusively in signs, and was on that account especially
untrustworthy. If the idea of Christ's Resurrection could be explained
and made memorable by recourse to signs and symbols, whether

[9] For a full list of titles, editions and approximate dates, see Ian Maxwell,
French Farce and John Heywood (Melbourne, 1946), pp. 123–34; also Grace
Frank, op. cit. pp. 243–64.

visual, musical or mimetic, employment of such signs could be authorized and encouraged; but if the signs themselves became ambiguous – as is clearly the case when a serious liturgy becomes confused with an entertainment in the minds of those attending it – their value, as promoters of the idea, is at once open to question.

Yet, while all men and women are capable at times of transcending the ephemeral (the sign) and grasping the serious (the idea), very few of us possess the strength either of mind or of will to do this constantly and at all times: for most, the flesh rebels and prefers to revert to what is familiar and easy. In the tenth and eleventh centuries this natural inclination – or lazy-mindedness if I may so express it – reverted, in reaction against monastic culture, to that of the fields and forests, and to simple folly for the sheer fun of it. Thus many elements of agricultural festivals associated with former pagan cultures survived throughout Christendom, and even the liturgy itself became a target for parody and caricature legitimized by the church annually in the ceremonies pertaining to the Feast of the Ass (a distortion of the Balaam sequence in the *Ordo Prophetarum*), the Feast of Fools, the Boy Bishop and Carnival (Shrovetide) (see p. 44 above). Yet however much these rebellious explosions of natural man may have contributed during the twelfth and thirteenth centuries to the repertoire of comic ideas – 'routines' as professional comedians would call them – especially in the realm of knockabout farce, it is to be doubted whether they could ever have contributed much to the development of the more intellectual and serious notion of comic narrative with its emphasis upon story-line, a balanced structure and appropriate characterization. At least Dante's justification of his choice of the word 'comedy' to describe his philosophical epic poem makes no concession to such junketings. For him the word 'comedy' is appropriate because his story begins in adversity (*Infernus*), and 'in the end it is happy, pleasing and to be desired, being *Paradisus*'. And his words and images, moreover, are signs (allegory) chosen to lead readers of the poem towards an understanding of the shape of ultimate reality.[10]

It was thus in this twin-headed condition – sublime, reconciliatory and romantic narrative viewed from one standpoint, or rebellious, corrective and grotesque incident viewed from another – that notions of comedy, and what that word described, reached Chaucer, Lydgate and the anonymous authors of the French *mystères*, the English cycles, and the contemporary moralities and saint plays. In short, by the start of the fifteenth century – whether in France, Flanders, Germany or England – it had become possible, from an artist's view-

[10] See Nevill Coghill, 'The Basis of Shakespearean Comedy', in G. Rostrevor Hamilton (ed.), *Essays and Studies* (London, 1950).

point, not only to choose between 'high' or romantic comedy and 'low' or farcical comedy, but to opt to bring the one into conjunction with the other in the service of romance or play: by then the 'signs', in the neo-Platonist sense of the word, were beginning to rival the 'ideas' and to assume a life of their own; and a much more modern interpretation of the distinction between 'the sublime' and 'the profane' was beginning to emerge in consequence, the former directed to provoking a contemplative delight, the latter to the more vulgar and simpler pleasures of merriment and laughter.

Thus in drama, as in sculpture and painting, the calm, reflective statements of the romanesque era came steadily to be replaced by more forceful, demonstrative and individualistic forms of expression, emotional, theatrical and often deliberately shocking. This shift of emphasis and technique is visible all over Europe in the gargoyles, corbels and roof-bosses of gothic churches, in the fanciful marginalia of illuminated manuscripts, in wood-carvings on pew-ends and choir-stalls; it is also strikingly apparent in the proliferation of comic ideas incorporated into sermons, romances, fabliaux and plays to sharpen and define their moralistic purpose.[11] In England this spirit informs Langland's *Piers Plowman*, Chaucer's *Miller's Tale* and *Franklyn's Tale*; it informs *The Castle of Perseverance* (*c*. 1408); and it is the very life-blood of Lydgate's *Mumming at Hertford*.

The *Mumming at Hertford* (Trin. Coll, Camb. MS R.3.20) is a light-hearted entertainment devised for the young Henry VI, about 1425, to celebrate New Year's Eve in the Banquet Hall at Hertford Castle:[12] it is also the first complete, surviving English text of a wholly secular entertainment.

The poet-presenter introduces a group of six actors; they are described as 'hynes, here stonding oon by oon' (l. 25), i.e. as humble working-men. They have come to complain to the King 'Upon the mescheef of gret adversytee' in which they find themselves. So we know immediately where we are: we are about to witness a comedy. Quickly we learn why these 'sweynes' who look 'ful froward of ther chere' are now so wretched: they all have the misfortune to be married to shrews, and beg the King to restore them right of mastery in their own homes. The comedy arises from this inversion of normality, the so-called fair and gentle sex having turned into viragos

---

[11] See M. D. Anderson, *Drama and Imagery in English Medieval Churches* (Cambridge, 1963); G. R. Owst, *Literature and Pulpit in Medieval England* (Cambridge, 1933); and Irena Janicka, *The Comic Elements in the English Mystery Plays against the Cultural Background, particularly Art* (Poznan, 1962).

[12] For the complete text, with critical introduction, see G. Wickham (ed.), *English Moral Interludes*.

rougher than proverbial Turks and Amazons, while the visibly tough, bearded breadwinners are subjected to every kind of physical indignity and mental cruelty.

Lydgate then advances us to the second movement of his 'play', a meeting with these shrewish wives. One of them speaks for all six. She starts by citing Chaucer's wife of Bath, challenges the very idea of mastery belonging to men as of right, and goes on to substitute customary usage as justification for their own claims to mastery. And so, in their turn, they ask the King to give judgement for them.

The third movement of the comedy – the reconciliatory one – is advanced through a spokesman for the King himself, probably a herald. 'The question raised', he says, 'is so important and of such universal application that it would be most imprudent to deliver a snap judgement. Time is needed to sift all the evidence in order to arrive at the right answer.' Judgement is thus postponed for a year: in the meantime wives will not be denied what they claim to be their customary rights; but single men are warned to weigh up the likely price of getting married while they are still free to do so. Thus the comedy ends on a jocular note appropriate to the festive occasion. The King, we should note, was still a bachelor.

Here, then, the formula for the construction of comedy, as a type of literary narrative, is faithfully followed and then transferred bodily to the stage. There it is reinforced with the comic realism of everyday life, each married couple depicted being vividly re-created with details particular to their way of life, yet all of them exaggerated and so inverted as to produce grotesque effects that are comic in themselves. Pictorially this is especially so of the butcher 'stoute and bolde / That killéd hath bulles and boores olde,' who 'for al his brode knyff' and 'his bely rounded lyche an oake' is nevertheless routed by his even tougher wife.

In English literature it is not until the end of the century, when we reach Henry Medwall's *Fulgens and Lucres* (1497), that we will again find this same command of romantic comedy both in overall shape and in particular incident. That this is due to loss and destruction of scripts rather than to lack of them is virtually certain, since these intervening decades mark the advent and rapid numerical growth of professional acting companies – the 'players of enterludes' – in so many noble households; and such companies could not have satisfied their masters if they lacked a suitable repertoire of interludes to play.[13] Some clues at least to the likely nature and quality of these missing scripts can be gauged from study of the *farces, soties* and *entremets* which proliferated rapidly during the same period in France and in

[13] See G. Wickham, *English Moral Interludes*, pp. v–xvi.

the Low Countries, many of which have survived (see p. 49 above).
What these reveal, above all else, is the extension of comic method to
pillory in words and deeds the professional and commerical classes in
society – doctors, merchants, lawyers and civil servants – as well as
the habitual targets of marital and extramarital relationships, disobe-
dient children and disrespectful servants.[14]

In England the Wycliffite preacher John Ballard and Henry Medwall show themselves to be of the same mind when the former asks:

> When Adam delved and Eve span,
> Who was then the gentleman?

– and when the latter makes his Lucres decide to marry the man
whose claim to merit lay in his own achievements rather than in
inherited wealth and titles. However, even if we lack the rich treasury
of scripts that has survived in France, the same tendencies can still be
charted with ease in the treatment accorded to biblical and homiletic
narrative in the miracle cycles, moralities and saint plays. None of
these can be regarded as comedies in point of structure; but all of them
contain passages, even whole scenes, of sustained comic incident and
characterization where an armoury of comic moods and methods is
deployed to define and demonstrate the doctrinal points at issue.
Lack of space in a short essay limits illustration to selective example
here; it must suffice therefore to take a brief look at the most famous
medieval group of comic figures, Lucifer and his *diablerie*, and one or
two other specific uses of comic treatment of character and situation
in religious plays.[15]

In all four surviving English cycles Lucifer owes his Fall to pride and
vanity. Once he has fallen, it is dramatically necessary for him to be
regarded as a figure of pity and ridicule; it is also theatrically necessary for the audience to see this change clearly reflected in his costume and person. He is thus made to retain the outline of his former
angelic shape, including his wings, but all the details have become
grotesque parodies of the original image: feet are translated into
cloven hooves, hands into vultures' claws, the smooth gilded skin
into tangled fur, the teeth into fangs, the gorgeous wings garnished
with peacock feathers collected from the castle keep into a tattered
assortment of goose and hen feathers gleaned from the byre and the
midden. The former archangel has become a gross parody of his
earlier self, at once pathetic and awesome, but also comic. The anti-
thesis in this juxtaposition of images is thus complete, and Christ's

---

[14] See Maxwell, op. cit. pp. 123–34.
[15] Irena Janicka, op. cit., provides some particularly apt illustrations of the
way in which the visual arts parallel literary treatment of devils and vice-
versa. See also Clifford Davidson, *Drama and Art* (Kalamazoo, 1977).

antagonist in the latter half of the cycles has accordingly been reduced to a figure of ridicule before battle is ever joined.

In the Temptation of Eve two more techniques – disguise and analogy – are drawn upon by the York and Chester playwrights to the same end. Satan thus appears in Paradise having changed his costume. Equipped with a woman's face-mask, a pair of false breasts, gloves and a snakeskin to hide his hooves, he assumes a falsetto voice when addressing Eve. By these means he is placed squarely before the audience as an equivocator, a fraud and a cheat. We are expected to laugh, but also to learn.

In the later scenes of the Temptation of Christ and the Harrowing of Hell greater stress is laid upon the language than the costume, especially by the Wakefield playwright. In these scenes the dramatist is particularly concerned with establishing the ignorance and stupidity of all the devils resident in Hell-Castle. They fail to recognize Christ for who He is and, squabbling among themselves, are outwitted by superior intelligence and verbal dexterity. The Chester playwright refines this technique by using cynicism to undercut the boasts of Lucifer in the Temptation: indeed, he never loses control of the malign dimension in his Lucifer. In the Harrowing of Hell the Townley dramatist goes further still, developing the comedy on two levels simultaneously – the romantic and the grotesque – by coupling the idea of Christ as bridegroom to the soul in the lyrical treatment of his principal theme with a diabolic burlesque of parliamentary procedures in Hell itself. Both treatments are as striking and innovative as they are funny for the audience: rude mirth in both instances is brilliantly married to amused delight. The former forecasts Marlowe's self-pitying Mephistopheles, and the latter Falstaff's ribald parody of a royal audience at the Boar's Head tavern in Eastcheap.

Other techniques warrant at least a passing glance: the use of comedy to prepare or stimulate spectators to receive a mystical statement, and direct application of low-life comic realism to scripture. The most familiar example of comic anticipation is in the Wakefield *Secunda Pastorum* where the farcical tale of the stolen sheep concealed in the crib directly parallels the inexplicable mystery of Christ's Nativity that follows immediately upon it. This technique was also to be used by Shakespeare in *1 and 2 Henry IV* where both Prince Hal and the audience are instructed in the qualities required of kingship and the responsibilities attendant upon it by the juxtaposition of tavern (hellish) and palace (heavenly) scenes. Fine examples of low-life realism are offered in the *Ludus Coventriae* by the young man in 'The Woman Taken in Adultery' who flees from his mistress's bed in such haste as to have to leave the stage while still attempting to dress, and by the Wakefield Master in the plays of the 'Scourging' and 'Crucifixion' where the warders and soldiers in charge of the proceedings are depicted as devoid of all pity and treat Christ as a mere object, regarding both activities as forms of sport; the children's game of blindman's-buff and the adult entertainments of bear- and bull-baiting (with gambling attached) provided the models in daily life for the use made of these images in both plays.

The sport of bear-baiting also provides the anonymous author of *Mankind* (c. 1465) with an image to introduce the Vice 'Mischief', and his companions Nought, Nowadays and New-Guise.[16] The whole of *The Castle of Perseverance* is structured on the model of a particular form of tournament, the *Pas D'Armes*, or storming by challengers of a defended gate or castle. Indeed, time and again in the morality and saint plays, popular games provide the authors with a formula that they can develop through the Vices as baited traps to ensnare humankind. Thus each and every Vice, or Deadly Sin, notwithstanding the abstract idea that he or she personifies, comes to be endowed with a realistic identity through the localized settings in which they operate, and the particular way in which, by comic contrasts, they promote their own fraudulent ends. For instance, as 'Mankind' capitulates to the Vices and decides to abandon work and churchgoing in favour of dicing, drinking and wenching in the tavern, the steady deterioration in his character is faithfully reflected by the playwright in his speech. The contrast between true virtue and viciousness is thus exhibited theatrically by incongruity of action and language. When, therefore, we reach the Interludes of John Skelton, John Heywood, William Rastell, John Redford and Nicholas Udall early in the sixteenth century, the foundations had already been laid of a solid tradition of comic modes and methods. It is thus my submission that the debt sixteenth-century English playmakers owed to their much closer familiarity with the rediscovered comedies of Terence and Plautus served to extend and refine comic possibilities in drama rather than initiate them. In other words they became heir to *two* traditions, one Roman, the other Gothic-English, and could draw on both as they pleased. It would take another fifty years or more for this situation to be formally recognized and made explicit by a major dramatist and critic: yet this is precisely what Ben Jonson is saying in the Prologue to *Everyman Out of His Humour*:

> I see not then, but we should enjoy the same licence, or free power, to illustrate and heighten our invention as they did [i.e. the Greek and Latin playwrights]; and not be tied to those strict and regular forms which the niceness of a few (who are nothing but form) would thrust upon us.

[16] See G. Wickham (ed.), *English Moral Interludes*, pp. 1–9.

I maintain, therefore, that from the start of the sixteenth century onwards English playmakers became possessed of a choice – a choice that became steadily clearer as the century advanced – between two distinct types of comedy: the one classical and corrective in its purpose, the other Christian, romantic and reconciliatory. Jonson was to prefer the former, Shakespeare the latter; though neither of them was to adopt so narrow an approach to his work as to exclude essays in the other option.

The start of the sixteenth century produced in John Skelton and John Heywood two writers whose surviving work illustrates the use of both inherited techniques and novel applications of them. It also saw the establishment at court of a professional company of actors led by John English.

Skelton, according to his own claims in *The Garland of Laurel*, wrote three plays, of which only one survives: it is important that one of the missing pair should be that *Achademios* which he describes as 'a comedy'.[17] *Magnificence* (1515) is described on its title page as 'a Goodly Interlude and a Merry' (i.e. 'a moral play but an amusing one'). In its construction at least it conforms to Chaucer's and Lydgate's understanding of comedy: thus the character of the title-role is quickly reduced to a state of suicidal wretchedness, in part by evil counsellors who persuade him to abandon moderation ('Measure') and in part by his own ability to resist 'Despair'; in the nick of time the Cardinal Virtues come to his rescue, and redemption is achieved through a dawning consciousness of his own folly, followed by a determination to use greater discretion in future. It thus ends happily.

This 'comedy' is thus at once classical (in being firmly harnessed to Dame Fortune and her wheel) and corrective (in impressing the effects of folly upon its audience), and redemptive and reconciliatory (in its treatment of Magnificence himself); or, classical in form and Christian in spirit. Yet it departs from classical precedent and follows the example of the cycles both in its shape which is tragicomic and reconciliatory rather than farcical and punitive, and also in failing to concern itself exclusively with characters 'in povert plounged lowe': the protagonist is the spirit of kingship incarnate, and his antagonists are all courtiers. Most of these courtiers are, of course, counterfeits: vices whose clothes, manners and language conceal both their vulgar origins and their malign intentions. The play thus most nearly resembles that 'mongrel tragi-comedy' so much disliked by Sir Philip Sidney.

Abstractions, however, as these Vices may be – Counterfeit Countenance, Crafty Conveyance, Cloaked Collusion and the other

[17] *The Complete Poems of John Skelton, Laureate*, ed. Philip Henderson (London, 1931).

'seemers' who, like the Chester Lucifer tempting Eve, deploy every known form of disguise to cheat their employer and master – they are also satirical portraits (however generalized) of the cynical tribe of new-rich Tudor civil servants on the make: each is equipped with a verse metre of his own, an original technical device through which Skelton both achieves variety and individualizes these characters. This technique was bold and effective enough to hold the stage for the rest of the century: assumed names, borrowed clothes, feigned voices and racy language combining to contrast the outer with the inner man and to bring about an endless sequence of deceptions followed by unmaskings. A century later this method still had enough life left in it to supply Ben Jonson with the central device for the construction of *Volpone* and *The Alchemist*, and Shakespeare with a convenient instrument for the discomfiting of Falstaff.

If Skelton used abstract personifications, it was not because he knew no better. In *The Garland of Laurel* he included

> Horace also with his new poetry [i.e. *The Art of Poetry*],
> Master Terence, that famous comicar,
> With Plautus, that wrote full many a comedy . . .

among his own predecessors, while Medwall's *Fulgens and Lucres* offered him precedent for the direct portrayal of living men and women. What we have to recognize is that the shift of emphasis within a moral interlude – more especially in a 'merry', or satirical, one – from theological to social and political issues which occurs in the early Tudor period created special dangers for both playwrights and actors: dangers that could best be deflected by oblique rather than direct methods of characterization. No one, therefore, who hoped to discuss kingship or government of the commonwealth on the stage, particularly at court, could afford to jettison abstract virtues and vices as vehicles for such debate since the very anonymity of such characters provided the playmaker with just that shield of ambiguity that he needed to protect himself and his players.[18]

John Bale, some twenty years after the production of *Magnificence*, would still opt for the retention of abstract persons both in *Three Lawes*

---

[18] Even this protective device was not a guarantee of immunity. At Gray's Inn a play by John Rowe, sergeant-at-law, was presented at Christmas 1526, when Wolsey's unpopularity was at its height: although the play, not unlike *Magnificence* in its general drift, had been written much earlier, Wolsey was convinced that it was a satire directed principally at him. Rowe himself and Thomas Hoyle, one of the leading players, were both committed to prison for a short while: see Sidney Anglo, *Spectacle and Pageantry and Early Tudor Policy* (Oxford, 1969). On Skelton's relations with Wolsey, see William O. Harris, *Skelton's Magnificence and the Cardinal Virtue Tradition* (North Carolina, 1965), esp. pp. 3–45.

and in *Kyng Johan*, as would Sir David Lyndsay in *Ane Satire of the Three Estates* and the anonymous author of *Respublica* (1553). In Elizabethan England the device would, on occasion, still be retained; but, much more importantly, it would be transmuted by Chapman and others to form the basis of 'humours' comedy where variety of incident and situation serves to illuminate a dominant characteristic like 'hypocrisy' or 'irritability' from as many angles as possible.

The point at issue is that the retention of abstract personifications in Tudor drama was a matter of choice: for much of the century the device served (as much on grounds of common prudence as of aesthetic principle) positively to help playmakers in their efforts to exhibit the discrepancies between outward semblance and actuality in the conduct of affairs of state, an incongruity best suited to stage treatment in terms of satiric comedy. Comic incident and other comic techniques besides this one thus continue to be interpolated into serious plays of the Tudor era along lines familiar to audiences and similar to those developed during the fifteenth century both in religious plays and in secular entertainments. In other words the outward form remains stubbornly tragicomic rather than comic.

One very important aspect of this question in Henry VIII's England was the swelling tide of anticlericalism that burst its banks when Cardinal Wolsey was appointed Papal Legate. Even Skelton threw discretion to the winds and wrote satire of unprecedented ferocity, pillorying the opulence of Hampton Court and York House together with the vanity of their builder-owner who dared, notwithstanding 'his base progeny / And his greasy genealogy', to outface his sovereign. The portrait becomes vivid through the accuracy of its detail and the simplicity of the vocabulary:

> No man dare come to the speech
> Of this gentle Jack-breech,
> Of what estate he be
> of spiritual dignity . . .

> 'My lord is not at leisure!
> Sir, we must tarry a stound,
> Till better leisure be found!
> And, sir, ye must dance attendance,
> And take patient sufferance
> For my lorde's Grace
> Hath now no time nor space
> To speak with you as yet!'
> (*Why Come Ye Not to Court?* ll. 616–39)

The realistic detail is again paramount, and the use of direct speech to convey it is itself indicative of the direction in which comedy was moving.

Wolsey was outraged and clapped Skelton into prison (see fn. 18, p. 57). Somehow the rift healed, as Skelton felt able to dedicate his *Replycacion* (1527) to the cardinal. However, this outburst and others like it made it far easier for playmakers to point their satire at the clergy at large and to direct audiences' attention to their flagrant forgetfulness of their vows, their constant concern with money and possessions, and their ruthless gulling of their superstitious flocks. It was John Heywood who, in English drama, first seized upon this new opportunity for comic invention. Here there was no longer any need for the distancing effects of abstract personification in characterization or use of the historical past. Avoiding kings and courts, Heywood sets his plays in town or country parishes and then peoples them with humbler folk: the priests, doctors, merchants, and the husbands and wives, familiar to us in French farce. Daily life, the weather, food, confidence tricks and tricksters, the inversion of norms, double meanings and witty conversational games provide him with his subject matter. Heywood's comedy is almost wholly corrective, and often flavoured with the niceties of the lawcourts: it is grounded in the discrepancies between outward appearances and inner man, between words and deeds, as was the case with Skelton's courtly Vices; but it possesses another dimension, the discrepancies between man's physical desires and social opportunities, coupled with his wish to control his environment and his inability to do so.

Thus Heywood's disreputable Pedlar in *The Foure PP* outwits the three professional men who are his social and intellectual superiors; John John is not only cuckolded by the parish priest in *John, Tyb and Sir John* but is made the instrument of his own discomfiture by his wanton wife; and in *The Play of the Weather* Jupiter is dethroned and humanized, to arbitrate between the conflicting desires of a merchant, a huntsman, a gamekeeper, a water-miller, a wind-miller, a lady and a laundress. Neither the gamekeeper nor the laundress is above criticizing his or her employer:

Small is our profit [says the former] and great is our blame.
Alas! For our wages, what be we the near?
What is forty shillings, or five mark, a year?

Charged with envy by the lady, the laundress retorts tartly:

It is not thy beauty that I disdain,
But thine idle life that thou has rehearsed,
Which any good woman's heart would have pierced.
For I perceive in dancing and singing,

In eating and drinking and thine apparelling,
Is all the joy, wherein thy heart is set.
But nought of all this doth thine own labour get;
For, had'st thou nothing but thine own travail,
Thou mightest go as naked as my nail.[19]

Heywood can thus mix satire with humour, and play the moralist predominantly as he does in *Witty and Witless* and *The Play of Love*; but he is at his best when he assumes the role of empirical humanist, and matches correction with tolerance and a gentle mixture of cynicism and faith. By constantly pitting authority, whether derived from rank or books, against experience, he signposts a road towards *Love's Labour's Lost* and *A Midsummer Night's Dream*, where the way of the world is to be read in women's eyes, in men's manners, and in the phases of the moon.

With the Reformation, drama in England reverted sharply towards moralist techniques in the service of propaganda and polemic. This did not inhibit invention – indeed, it encouraged satire of an outrageously outspoken kind – but it frosted the gentler forms of comic release: these appear to have died with Sir Thomas More or to have sought sanctuary in schools and universities disguised as agents of education within Greek and Latin texts.[20] Satire, however, eventually outreached itself, as it has a habit of doing when given its head: governments whose interests it aspired to serve took fright and legislated against it both on the stage and in print.[21] When calmer times returned, it was itself the major casualty: into the vacuum thus created the gentler forms of comedy emerged cautiously from their academic hiding places, led by a bevy of dons, no longer by churchmen. Nicholas Udall, Thomas Ingelend, George Edwards, Mr

[19] *The Dramatic Writings of John Heywood*, ed. John S. Farmer (1905, reprint, Guildford, 1966).
[20] Aristophanes' *Pax* was performed at Trinity College, Cambridge, in 1546 when a stir was created by the flying machine for Scarabaeus devised by Dr John Dee. On the performance of Latin and Greek plays during the Tudor era, see F. S. Boas, *University Drama in the Tudor Age* (Oxford, 1914); T. H. Vail Motter, *The School Drama in England* (London, 1929); and L. B. Campbell, *Scenes and Machines on the English Stage during the Renaissance* (Cambridge, 1923).
[21] See G. Wickham, *Early English Stages* (London, II (Pt 1), pp. 54–149. The leading English anti-Catholic satirist was John Bale, a sometime Carmelite friar converted while at Cambridge, who thereafter served Thomas Cromwell and Archbishop Cranmer and wrote many plays until he was forced to flee the country after Cromwell's execution. From him playmakers learned to equate the Pope with Antichrist, priests with devils and Protestant reformers with the prophets, saints and martyrs. It was a technique that Roman Catholics could easily reverse and apply to a Protestant sovereign and his ministers. Parliament felt sufficiently concerned about this issue to take legislative action against it in 1543.

Stevenson and Francis Merbury are the names we have to reckon with. All of them genuflect to classical precedent; but was this any more genuine than Skelton's graceful obeisance?

Martin Bucer, Regius Professor of Divinity at Cambridge and author of the first serious treatise on dramatic theory in England, stated in his *De Honestis Ludis* (presented to Edward VI in 1551) that the principal purpose of acting 'comedies and tragedies' was to 'provide their public with wholesome entertainment which is not without value in increasing piety'. He goes on to say that 'it is more important to modify the poetic style than to subtract anything from the duty of edifying the audience'. As if that were not enough, he adds:

> So that Christ's people . . . may profit from religious comedies and tragedies, men will have to be appointed to the task of preventing the performance of any comedy or tragedy which they have not seen beforehand and decided should be acted.

In this discourse Bucer shows himself to be aware not only of Aristotle's *Poetics*, but also of 'that wit, that charm and grace of language . . . in the plays of Aristophanes, Terence and Plautus', yet he advises the young king in his conclusion that:

> those to whom God has granted it to excel in these matters should choose to employ their gift to his glory rather than to hinder the good desires of others by untimely criticisms, and that they should prefer moreover to present comedies and tragedies in which knowledge of eternal life is manifestly clear (even if some literary niceties are lacking), rather than plays in which both spirit and character are defiled by impious and disgusting interchanges of buffoonery, even if some pleasure is given by refinements of wit and language.[22]

Either Bucer's advice was taken seriously, or his views were shared by his academic contemporaries and successors.

With the appearance of *Gammer Gurton's Needle* (1553), Lydgate's and Heywood's homely world of village japes and jealousies reappears on the stage, but it has now been thrust into a firmly latinized plot structure; Udall's *Ralph Roister Doister* (1552) unquestionably reveals more respect for Plautine example than any previous English comedy, and could fairly be described as an anglicized *Miles gloriosus*; but in all the rest – *Jack Juggler, Damon and Pithias, Horestes, Misogonus, New Custom*, and so on – the homiletic strain, however jocularly treated, predominates, and the authors constantly have recourse

---

[22] Bucer's *De Honestis Ludis*, written in Latin, formed part of his *De Regno Christi*: an English translation of the former is printed in Appendix C of my own *Early English Stages*, II (Pt 1), pp. 329–31.

to comic techniques lifted from Bale, Heywood and the cycles, thus preserving and revitalizing the traditional English predilection for tragicomedy. Francis Merbury in *The Marriage Between Wit and Wisdom* (*c.* 1576) was prepared to lift large chunks out of no less than four earlier plays – *Gammer Gurton*, Preston's *Cambises*, Redford's *Wit and Science* and *Misogonus* – and unashamedly amalgamate them into a single Interlude. It plays well and is very funny, but one suspects that the homiletic frame into which Merbury fitted the pieces was the least important of his concerns.

By the 1570s, therefore, there are grounds for thinking that the acting companies – particulary their leaders – were beginning to set a higher premium on a play's capacity to entertain than on the ethical or social messages that its author hoped to figure in theatrical images, and that authors who sought to earn a living from selling plays to professional companies were ready to cooperate. As a result English comedy escaped the fate that was overtaking *commedia erudita* in Italy at this time, and the banning of all professional acting that occurred in France.[23]

An important question in this context is that of copyright. Dramatists in Elizabethan England surrendered control over their scripts to the acting company once they had been paid for them, unless of course they were writing for choirboys or students. As it happens, most of the comedies that have reached us from the Marian and early Elizabethan periods are of the latter kind. To this extent, therefore, they cannot be regarded as representative of the mainstream of public taste: the building of the Theater (1576), the Curtain (1577) and the playhouse at Newington Butts at much the same time gives us some idea of how this was shaping, since it was the actors, not the playwrights, who raised the necessary capital and thus dictated what was presented on their stages. Yet the year 1576 also saw the establishment of the first Private Playhouse, built by Richard Farrant for choirboy actors and subsequently managed by William Hunis and John Lyly before its untimely closure in 1584. The battle to decide the future of English comedy that was to be fought out between actors, playwrights and public over the next fifty years had thus already been joined.[24]

[23] An Edict of the Parlement of Paris banned all religious plays in the capital in 1548: provincial cities followed suit, piecemeal, over the next fifteen years. Secular plays, provided they were licensed and not regarded as seditious, continued to be tolerated; but, lacking regular patrons, playhouses and capital support, they survived on a far more precarious basis than in the earlier half of the century.

[24] This essay forms the basis of a chapter on 'The Genesis of English Comedy' in Vol. III of my *Early English Stages*, to be published in 1979 by Routledge and Kegan Paul and by Columbia University Press.

3

Comedy in Italy

FELICITY FIRTH

IN THE fifth century BC Epicharmus of Syracuse, writing on Italian soil the earliest recorded comic pieces, made up a play about the currently fashionable philosophy of Heraclitus. All is flux, Heraclitus is said to have said, life is a continual becoming, nobody is the same man today as he was yesterday. In Epicharmus' play, a debtor refuses to pay his debts. 'Why should I pay,' he asks, 'since yesterday when I contracted the debt I was one man, and today I am another?' His creditor sets about him with a stick. When taken to court and accused of violent assault, the creditor's defence is that he too has become another man since yesterday; it is yesterday's man who should be sent to prison. This ancient joke is remarkable in that it contains in a prophetic germ two themes, neither of them intrinsically humorous, which were destined in a later age to become inextricably linked with the whole Italian comic tradition: one, the preoccupation with the concept of identity; and two, the insistence upon wit or intellectual virtue as the ultimate human value. Here in embryo is the astute reply dear to Boccaccio. Here is identity as a source of fun; 'let's pretend to be somebody else' is, after all, the impulse at the heart of most Renaissance erudite comedy. Here is Arlecchino scoring off the learned Doctor from Bologna. Here is Goldoni's pragmatism, and here, too, is the philosophical question of the nature of identity from which springs the whole dark comedy of Pirandello.

Intellectualism in one form or another stamps the Italian comedy. The vernacular erudite drama of the sixteenth century was a far more living and complex thing than is often supposed, but it was created in a spirit of emulation and calculation which inhibited its development to an extent we can only guess at. However, this very intellectualism did make a vital contribution, here, at the birth of the modern genre. Renaissance man was in every sphere obsessed with his search for ideal forms; it was the age of recipes and recommendations for perfection: in town planning, architecture, education, domestic mores, courtly manners, statecraft, and in art and literature as well. Comedy to a literal formula seems a contradiction in spiritual terms, and yet it is to this search by European and predominantly Italian scholars for an ideal comic idiom that the tradition of modern literary comedy owes its being.

The history of the formulation of the recipe is a long one in which theory and experiment alternate. Perhaps it begins with Petrarch, who is supposed to have written at least one Latin comedy and perhaps more in about 1330, which he destroyed years later on rereading his efforts in the light of his study of Terence. Throughout the fifteenth century humanists wrote Latin plays as an academic pastime drawing on various traditions for their inspiration, on medieval popular and religious themes, on novellistic sources and on classical models, with results that were diverting if heterogeneous. But towards the end of the century Plautus and Terence were tightening their grip. They were becoming widely known. In 1433 Donatus' fourth-century commentary on Terence had been rediscovered, and in most cases it accompanied the editions of Terence that were printed from 1471 onwards. Plautus had made his big impact in 1428 with the unearthing by Nicholas Cusanus of those twelve of his twenty comedies which had remained unknown during the dark ages. Plautus and Terence were used generally by those learning to converse in Latin, and during the last thirty years of the century there were many performances of the old Roman plays given by scholars, courtiers and even by church groups. Performances of translations were put on as well, at the court of Ferrara, for instance, where the theatre became an instrument for furthering political prestige. A revival of the theatre went hand in hand with the passionate cult of definitions, so that while German, French and Italian scholars with latinized names were writing learned commentaries on Terence and analyses of the nature of comedy in general, Italian courtiers and amateur players were performing their own original vernacular plays, based on the old models and emerging as approximate illustrations for the work of the theorists.

In the second half of the century the commentators developed a new approach, for now they had Aristotle to hand, and a living theatre of their own to give immediacy to their subject. (Aristotle's *Poetics* only became well known in Italy after Robortello and Maggi brought out their commentaries in 1548 and 1550; Horace's *Ars poetica* they had always had.) The Renaissance critics, however, did not refer to their own contemporary theatre; they were in search of timeless laws; their task was to establish the ideal purpose and principles of comedy, and their concern was with, for instance, the question of invention versus imitation, the relation between rhetoric and poetry, the definition of the ridiculous, and the function in comedy of plot, character, sentiment and diction. In broad terms the Terentian commentators of the first half of the century seem to have done the spadework for the great prescriptive essays of Robortello, Castelvetro and Scaliger which achieved European renown during the second half. Questions of comic function, form and style had mostly been settled already and in detail; it only remained for the later critics to adopt and adapt an Aristotelian approach to a well-examined subject. What chiefly matters in all this is that rigid rules were laid down, the freedom of the medieval theatre was lost, and comediography became a science.

The structural rules are familiar, and the codifiers seem to echo each other over most matters. Fit subjects for comedy are 'low, trifling matters', 'disturbances', 'actions that occur in the ordinary life of citizens'. Characters and plots must be fictitious, but verisimilitude must be the guiding principle in their creation. Characters must be consistent. Plots may be simple or complex but must follow a strict routine of engagement, complication and resolution within five acts. Certain time-honoured devices – Aristotle's peripeteia (reversal of fortune) and agnition (discovery) – may bring about the final happy outcome. The recommended time limit for the action is sometimes twelve hours, sometimes twenty-four, but unity of place is insisted on. Diction, whether the play is in prose or verse, must be colloquial. The theorists agreed, too, in their insistence on that unconvincing notion, the moral and didactic purpose of comedy. The question of the possibility of a comic catharsis was in particular explored by these followers of Aristotle, in their dedicated pursuit of comic parallels to concepts born of tragedy.

But for all their sophistication the academic theoreticians still had the sense and simplicity to consider the risible to be the distinguishing mark of comedy. Castelvetro and Maggi examine the phenomenon of laughter at length; Scaliger, the most liberal of them all, finds in it the touchstone of all comedy. His contribution lay largely in his questioning of the necessity for slavish imitation of Terence. 'There was not just one manner of comedy,' he maintained, 'for so long as comedies won laughter they needed nothing else.'

Space has been given to these law-givers because, however much one may find their approach contrary to the spirit of comic and poetic invention, their achievement was the definition of a genre. From the sixteenth century onwards a comic dramatist in Europe knew what he was doing, whether striving for classical perfection by adherence to the norm, or striking off on his own to prove its invalidity.

The Renaissance vernacular comedies are built in practice roughly upon the Terentian model. They are also endlessly imitative and repetitive; they are too long; they are more or less devoid of psychological interest or emotional depth, they are complicated on the surface and hollow at the core. They provide us with a puzzle. In the nineteenth century they were dismissed as arid, unoriginal and cold. Yet their vast numbers can only persuade us that people must have enjoyed them. It strikes us now that the nineteenth-century reader would of course be the last person to enjoy one of these comedies. The sixteenth-century Italian theatre draws its spirit from Boccaccio. Its worldliness is not fortuitous; it is a proclamation of faith in the fun to be had on 'this side', in the possibilities of a finite world where man himself is the ultimate measure. The trickster-protagonist of this theatre plays with his humanity, his identity, his wits and his instincts, untroubled by intimations of immortality or by any further self-awareness than that of knowing himself to be a fine fellow.

The liberating breeze of humanistic philosophy blows through these plays and occasionally unites with the afflatus of an individual genius to produce a masterpiece. Certainly something more was needed than the ancient formula, even when infused with the modern spirit. The relative failure of Ariosto is perhaps typical of what happened when court poets wrote comedy to prescription for the prestige of princes. His plays are good, amusing, readable even now, but, as his prologues show, he was inhibited by fear of comparison with his ancient models, and nowhere in his comedies do we find the brilliance inexhaustibly let loose in the *Orlando furioso*. He has the distinction of having written the first noteworthy comedy in the vernacular, *La Cassaria* (*The Comedy of the Chest*, 1508), and his other plays, *I Suppositi* (*The Counterfeits*, 1509, translated by George Gascoigne in 1572 as *The Supposes*), *Il Negromante* (*The Necromancer*, 1520), *La Lena* (1529) and *La Scolastica* (*The Academic Comedy*, unfinished), serve as excellent examples of the genre they represent.

The typical comedies of the period were not brilliant. The student in search of a masterpiece of the time can only consider pieces which differ in some essential way from the 'typical' output of Ariosto, Bibbiena, Aretino, Caro, Cecchi, Della Porta, and others. Three plays stand out and none of them is representative of the mainstream. *La Mandragola* (*The Mandrake*, 1518) by Niccolò Machiavelli has brilliance, certainly, structured as it is upon the rare principles of necessity, economy and purpose. A quite different quality lifts the anonymous *La Venexiana* (*The Venetian Comedy*, rediscovered in 1928, original date uncertain) out of its century, the near-naturalism of its honest, sensual love scenes. *Il Candelaio* (1582) by Giordano Bruno is an unwieldy giant of a play which soars above its peers in yet other respects, in its vigour and vehemence, and in its fierce mixture of unremitting obscenity and clowning on the one hand and of disdainful detachment and self-mockery on the other.

La Mandragola must undoubtedly have its place in this chapter, and to balance the picture we should do well to place beside it a play chosen for contrasting and complementary features. Pietro Aretino's *La Cortigiana* (*The Comedy of the Court*, 1525) is as sprawling as *La Mandragola* is streamlined, and will serve to give us some idea of the scope of the Italian erudite comedy in its heyday.

Machiavelli's *Mandrake* surely transcends its genre by reason of its ambiguity and its depth, qualities absent almost by definition from other comedies of the time. To the reader accustomed to the shifting focuses of modern drama, one feature of Renaissance comedy in general stands out: the singleness of its perspective. There is, usually, only one layer of meaning to perceive: the top layer. The necessity for consistency of character is one of the most significant tenets of sixteenth-century comic theory. When Bruno's pedant Manfurio, in *Il Candelaio*, is robbed, he shrieks out in Latin. In a modern play he would be unmasked by the experience and show another self. But as it is we laugh not at any contradiction within his personality but only at the extremism of his pedantry. When hypocrisy itself is depicted in the Renaissance theatre, it is transparent, excessive and instantly recognizable. The singleness of perspective, moreover, can be said to extend to the temporal dimension. The critic Nino Borsellino has pointed out that Renaissance comedy depicts a situation rather than a condition, a merely momentary subversion of the natural order. And perhaps this momentary quality is of the essence of comedy, the loss of it accounting for the blurring of genres wherever it occurs, whether in Molière, in Chekhov or in the theatre today.

While it fulfils all the formal requirements of classical comedy, *La Mandragola* has been characterized as tragedy and as satire; one critic speaks of it as a work weighed down with religious sadness; it is a commonplace to call it cynical, and to see in it the dramatic expression of the philosophy behind *The Prince*. It is a play that differs from other works of its time in that the reader's understanding of it depends upon his own view of life. It is ambiguous, too, in that it is multi-layered, and herein lies its depth. In this instance we are not looking simply at the surface of life. The characters let us glimpse into their deeper, hidden, more uncertain selves. This plot is no 'momentary subversion', nor are the characters defined solely by their function within it. The power of the play lies in its demonstration of the capacity of the human psyche, which we see performing gymnastic feats of persuasion and adaptation, of circumvention and self-deception. It is not only a comedy of manners about the depravity of contemporary Florence; what we recognize in its dark vision are durable truths about humanity itself.

The story is based on a *beffa*, a clever practical joke, partly drawn in this instance from Boccaccio's story of Catella and Ricciardo Minutolo (*Decameron*, III. 6). The *beffa* is a basic pattern which lies at the core of the Italian humorous tradition, originating in stories and plays well before Boccaccio's time and still flourishing today in the popular media, very much its timeless self, for example, in the plays of Eduardo and Peppino de Filippo. Studies have been made of the *beffa*, about whether and why it makes us laugh, about whether and in what way it is cruel, and about the essential difference between those stories where the emphasis is on the *beffatore*, the joker, and those where it is on the *beffato*, the dupe. There is also a whole category of Renaissance stories, and plays too, in which the *beffatore* becomes the *beffato*, which follow the classic pattern of deception followed by disaster, followed in turn by a greater deception, which serves as a 'remedy'. However, whereas in these plays the *beffa* is often an end in itself, executed gratuitously because the gull is stupid and is there to be tricked, in Machiavelli's play it is an action which arises of necessity from a given network of relationships.

Callimaco is a spirited and resourceful young man in love with Lucrezia, the conscientious wife of Nicia, a doctor of laws who is coarse-grained by nature, complacent and self-absorbed. Nicia has sweated to achieve his education, is rich, has a beautiful wife, and now all he wants is a son. His clever friend Ligurio, with no money and no professional status, is riled by Nicia's unworthiness and stupidity. Nothing is going to stop Callimaco, who has come all the way from Paris to conquer Lucrezia. Ligurio is delighted to sell his services in any scheme which will make a bigger fool of Nicia. Maliciously he brings his superior intelligence to the famous plot, whereby Lucrezia is to take a potion, believing it to be a distillation of mandragora, a fertility drug with the unfortunate reputed side-effect of poisoning the first man who sleeps with the taker. The plan is for Callimaco, disguised as a vagrant, to be dragged in off the streets to suffer the effects of the poison, and he is tucked up in bed with Lucrezia by the solicitous and unknowing husband himself. Lucrezia has been persuaded to submit to all this by Frate Timoteo, a jobbing casuist with a smooth and saintly exterior, whose motives are venal, though there is a marked suggestion too that he derives vicarious fleshly pleasure from such adventures, as he does from the confidences of his penitents.

The motives in this play are never arbitrary, although the so-called corruption of Lucrezia is a puzzle to some. Callimaco has one night in which to reveal all to her: his love, the plot, her own sensuality, the possibilities of an affair with him, and indeed in one night she is won over. Suspect perhaps is the fact that she expresses her 'conversion' to him the next morning in terms which come almost verbatim from Boccaccio, but Machiavelli may have lifted them because he found them convincing. They are certainly delivered with a firm and rational determination – according to Callimaco who reports them. Might he have touched the story up a little? The play raises questions to the end.

Pietro Aretino's *La Cortigiana* (*The Comedy of the Court*, 1525), again, formally fulfils the classical requirements (if we allow it its double plot), but this is a heterogeneous, episodic and untidy play, consisting of 106 scenes and a busy shifting cast which seems even more populous than its actual twenty-four. It is a vindication of the defence of the vitality of the Renaissance literary theatre on the grounds that it is a *speculum vitae*, and indeed Aretino's observation of the life of his times is spontaneous and effervescent. This technique of presenting his subject as a series of swift, unrelated sketches has been described as 'documentary', but the word does not suggest the high colour of his work.

We are given a vivid, highly spiced picture of popular life. A whole scene is devoted to an account of the disgusting conditions in which servants were expected to eat. We see the peremptory procedures of the street police; Alvigia, the pious witch-cum-procuress, gives us a practical inventory of the tools of her trade, and a convincing glimpse of her own practical attitude towards it. Another character describes lyrically the warmth and cheer, the sounds and smells, of a tavern. We are presented with a gallery of Roman citizens, priests and ped-lars, rogues, servants, courtiers and policemen who rush about, chase each other, meet and separate at a rate which suggests that this very speed was an essential feature of the comedy. Occasionally there is leisure for a reasoned conversation between disenchanted courtiers on the theme of the greed and corruption prevalent at the papal court.

Again, the *beffa* lies at the heart of the play, this time a series of *beffe* played by clever people in response to the vertiginous attraction exercised upon them by the stupidity of their gulls. The equation of wit with virtue is part of the ethic of the Italian comedy from Boccac-cio's day to our own. Even Pirandello, in a light moment, could write a play like *Liolà*, which shows the extent to which this view of a certain kind of cleverness has penetrated Italian tradition. It has been pointed out that whereas the Anglo-Saxons look back for an archetype of virtue to King Arthur, dupe and Christian, the ancient hero of Magna Graecia has always been Odysseus of many wiles. His legacy is handed down to us through the intriguing servants of Roman com-edy, through characters in the Renaissance as diverse as Ligurio in *La*

Mandragola and the ebullient Rosso of *La Cortigiana*, through Arlecchino and Brighella – first in the *commedia dell'arte* and later in Goldoni
and Gozzi – through the tricksters of the various dialect theatres
down to the Pulcinella-like figures made famous by the de Filippo
brothers in Naples in this century.

The two chief victims of the gratuitous *beffe* in *La Cortigiana* are the
vain courtier Parabolano, who is tricked into bed with a baker's wife
whom he takes to be the noble and remotely adored Livia, and Maco,
the simpleton from Siena. Maco is a trusting provincial whose aspirations to become a courtier make him easy game for the painter Andrea
and his friends, who almost boil him alive as they recast him in the
'mould' of a courtier.

Various other tricks are used to keep the action moving and all have
this in common: that in every case the notion of identity is used as a
plaything. The first *beffa* occurs in Act I and will serve as well as
another to illustrate the features of the device. Parabolano the fop
gives his servant Rosso two tasks: he is to buy some lampreys and
deliver them to Messer Maco of Siena, and he is to take Parabolano's
coat home for him while he goes for a stroll. Now it is not in the nature
of the Italian *beffatore* to stand in the street with another man's coat
and money and not to see in these objects potential instruments for a
deception. Simple robbery does not tempt him; the *beffa* requires art.
Rosso dons the silk coat and swaggers up to a fishseller from Florence,
declaring himself to be the Pope's own household caterer. He orders
ten lampreys, offers the man papal patronage and tells him he will be
paid by the sacristan at St Peter's. In the sacristan's ear he whispers
that the fishseller is half-mad and his wife possessed of ten devils.
The astonished vendor is seized by the priests and tied to a pillar to be
thrashed, while Rosso makes off with both the lampreys (five of
which he keeps) and the money for their purchase. At the end of the
play, when all is sorted out and *beffatori* and *beffati* are reconciled,
Parabolano's words seem to sum up the code which lies behind the
trick:

> *Fisherman*. And what about me? Am I going to get my lamprey
>   money back?
> *Parabolano*. You'll have to forgive Rosso, won't you, Fisherman,
>   seeing as you've been such a feeble little Florentine as to let
>   yourself be tricked by him?

This is in no sense a Romantic Christian reconcilement, nor yet a
parody of such a thing. Nor is there any classical idea of correction or
retribution in this tradition where 'good' and 'bad' are replaced by
'quickwitted' and 'dull'.

A word about Fortune before we leave the Renaissance theatre. As love is the noble name given to the prosaic and acquisitive sensuality which gives positive motivation to its characters, so Fortune is the name they give to whatever negative circumstances stand in their way. The goddess Fortuna has to rear her head in every godless age, as a powerful external force antagonistic to man, fabricated in the absence of evil to provide him with a worthy adversary, whose defeat will prove to him his own resourcefulness and *virtù*. Theatrically she is a success; she replaces the villain. An earlier theatre embodied the powers of darkness in the figure of a devil; a later, or at any rate a more evolved, one will depict the flawed personality, but it is a feature of this theatre of the surface to attribute all reverses to adverse chance. Not that the amoralism of the age of Aretino and Machiavelli was in any sense ingenuous; but the accepted response to what other ages call 'evil', to abuse and corruption for example, was not a moral or emotional indignation, but an intellectual response which emerged as ridicule, irony or satire. In dramatic terms the corrupt man is Fortune's agent, and is only of interest to the Italian Renaissance hero insofar as he aids or obstructs him in the achievement of his practical ends.

Ultimately belief in Fortune is responsible for the redeeming spirit of this theatre, the spirit of resilience and optimism which accompanies the refusal to look beneath the surface. One phrase, with variations, seems to echo right across the century: 'pensiamo al rimedio', 'let us think of a remedy'. That a 'remedy' is always there for the finding, that Fortune can always be outwitted, or indeed exploited as an ally, is the philosophy of every schemer and determined lover from Volpino and Fulcio, the cunning servants in Ariosto's first play *La Cassaria* with their frequent expostulations to the goddess, to the valet Panurgo in Della Porta's *La Fantesca* (*The Servant-Girl*, 1592), whose words to his master Essandro in Act I, Scene 5, might have been taken from almost any play of the century:

> Master, remember that to despair will bring about the ruination of your hopes; and that to have recourse to tears rather than to remedies is the mark of a mean-spirited man who does not truly wish to see the fulfilment of his desires. . . . One must look Fortune boldly in the face. A good heart in misfortune is misfortune halved.

It is ironical to reflect that the age which devoted so much energy, scholarship, money and time to the definition and creation of a literary 'premeditated' comedy gave birth spontaneously to an illegitimate artisan comedy which was ultimately to usurp its sister's title. When people refer to the *commedia* or to the Italian comedy they are usually referring to the *commedia dell'arte*, the comedy of the trade.

This theatre, first heard of round about the middle of the sixteenth century, was the creation of the actors, and in its incalculable influence was to constitute Italy's greatest contribution to the European comic tradition. Its origins have been much discussed. Some historians claim it to be directly linked with the Atellan *fabulae* of the third century BC, basing their claim upon the use of masks and of improvisation, and on the physical resemblance seen between certain type characters. Maccus, for example, white-robed, humped and hook-nosed, is held to be the direct ancestor of Pulcinella. Nobody claims an unrecorded and uninterrupted continuance of the Roman mime throughout the dark ages, however, and the facts of the emergence of the *commedia* remain a mystery. Its most obvious spiritual forebears are to be seen in the tumblers, minstrels and charlatans of the medieval carnival tradition. The *commedia* can be considered the very purest kind of theatre. Its basic material requirements are bare boards in the corner of any public square, masks, and a few traditional garments: the rest lies in the actors' skill.

There was a great deal of cross-fertilization during the second half of the sixteenth century between the premeditated erudite comedy and the improvised comedy, with the result that, while the private amateur theatre of the courts and academies grew less rigid and rarefied, the theatre of the professionals became acquainted with a vast fund of plots, devices, styles and conventions which it could transform with its own particular alchemy and reproduce infused with life and colour for the popular stage. Princes started by hiring professional actors for elaborate clowning where it was required or for spectacular acrobatic feats. Later they often employed whole companies, and these were frequently in demand by visiting ambassadors, requesting the loan of their services at foreign courts. The two traditions borrowed from each other extensively, but throughout they retained their differences. The erudite comedy was always dignified, avoided farce, did not wear masks and worked from a fully scripted text. The *commedia* was distinguished by the following features: its professional status; the use, within certain limits, of improvisation; the special function of the mask, or *maschera*, a word used to denote both the literal facial mask and the complex stock character it represented; the use of certain devices or *lazzi*; and lastly by its probably indefinable quintessential spirit.

It is fundamental to an understanding of the *comici dell'arte* to realize that they lived by their art, and that to do this they had to win the attention and the attendance of a wide audience. The bugbear to be avoided at all costs was any moment of boredom on the part of the audience, and to this end there had to be plenty to see: monsters, animals, fireworks, gods, acrobatics, magic, *beffe* of the most physical and farcical variety, mock fights with flour and soot as well as with cudgels and blunderbusses, madness and death both feigned and 'real', every conceivable variation on the theme of disguise, explicit obscenity, feats of eating, any trick of the trade that provided novelty. Where, in the seventeenth century, troupes had a stable theatre to act in, they developed complex stage machinery and the spectacular element could be exploited even further.

The basic framework for the *commedia* play was the scenario or *canovaccio*. There are still a thousand of these businesslike documents extant; they give the main outline of the action and contain instructions for exits and entrances, movements, recommended comic business and the content of speeches. A *maestro* or *corago* would run through the scenario with his troupe before a production, suggesting innovations and ensuring coordination of interpretation. The outline was then pinned up behind the scenes for reference. At the same time each actor had his *zibaldone* or commonplace book, containing stock speeches, jokes, songs, tirades, tricks and *lazzi* which he would know by heart and draw on as they were required. Within this system he was trained also to improvise. The *commedia improvvisa* in fact demanded a high degree of skill and a very disciplined approach from its actors. Andrea Perrucci, writing his treatise on the art of acting in both types of theatre, in 1699, stresses that in the improvised comedy it was not possible for an actor to walk straight into a part without preparation or instruction. And special techniques were required of the actors even when improvising. The lovers, for example, were portrayed as straight characters with the same dignified unmasked faces as in the literary drama. The actors who played them had to be well read, well spoken and competent to yearn and plead off the cuff with Tuscan eloquence. An ability to parody Petrarch, so much admired by the erudite audiences in their playwrights, was now required of every Flavio, Lelio and Isabella.

Highly specialized, too, was the art of acting in a mask. Unlike its counterpart in ancient Greece or in China and Japan, the *commedia* mask did not have a fixed expression, and the uncovered mouth allowed the actor a certain flexibility. But whatever emotion the face could not convey was conveyed by the body, and the Italian players, in France especially, developed mime to a fine art. Gherardi in his *Théâtre italien* (1694) gives a description of his friend Tiberio Fiorilli, the famous Scaramouche, keeping an audience laughing for a quarter of an hour with a wordless mime of fright.

But perhaps the skill above all others which distinguishes the *commedia* from other forms of theatrical expression is the ability required of the actor to assume a whole personality as he dons his mask. The masked comedy drew a great deal of its strength from the principle of familiarity, from the immediate recognition by the audience of the figure of Arlecchino, Tartaglia or Pantalone, regardless of the identity of the player. In effect, the appeal was similar to that exercised by Charlie Chaplin, the Marx Brothers, or the modern comic with his own television series. It is the pleasure of knowing and not knowing, of watching a predictable figure with familiar, even loved, idiosyncrasies, in an unpredictable or fantastic situation. It was probably this speciality of the *commedia* clown which was responsible for his life-span of 300 years, and for the spread of his fame over the whole of Western Europe. Hundreds of actors put on his persona as they put on his costume and won for him the kind of devotion that is accorded, through different channels, to a popular comedian today.

The *maschera*-persona was not a static finite phenomenon nor a simple one. K. M. Lea in her basic study *Italian Popular Comedy* stresses its composite and evolutionary nature:

> As a mask represents a collection of individuals, so the idea of a mask emerges from a study of individual presentations. The mask of Pantalone is the abstract of the behaviour of innumerable Pantalones: anything that a Pantalone did or said is a potential, anything that he continued to do is an actual, formative influence towards the development of the mask. . . . We only want to know what Pantalone did on a certain occasion in order to enrich our idea of what he might do in the future.

It follows, she continues, that the quality of evidence is for once less important than the quantity, and unfortunately the brief glimpse at the masks that we can afford ourselves in this chapter is bound to be inadequate. Gone now, are the parasite and the procuress of erudite comedy; gone too are the clerics. The heavy father has become Pantalone, the Venetian merchant, and the cunning servant is replaced by the *zanni* figure, who gradually evolves in two directions and becomes distinguished as two characters: as Arlecchino the clowning credulous servant, and as Brighella his crafty colleague. Akin to Arlecchino is the Neapolitan Pulcinella with his nutcracker profile, baggy white costume and sugarloaf hat. The pedant has turned into the Doctor from Bologna, known as Baloardo or Balanzone, who is also the forebear of the famous stammering blue-spectacled Tartaglia. The *miles gloriosus* becomes the swaggering Capitan Spavento, now credited with Spanish origins. All except Pantalone had a number of alternative names. Arlecchino was basically the same character as Truffaldino and as Pedrolino (who became Pierrot in France); Brighella resembles Scapino at home, and Scapin and Mascarille in France. Scaramuccia emigrated early to France where he became the inimitable Scaramouche.

There is only space to look at one of these figures in any kind of detail. It is a temptation to choose the relatively coherent image of Pantalone, authoritarian, avaricious, often unbecomingly amorous, the symbol in his time of the gap between the generations. But to give a brief indication of the complex way a mask evolved we shall do better to take a look at Arlecchino. He begins his recorded history at the end of the sixteenth century as a ragged porter from Bergamo (his conjectured origins go back to the clown-devils of the early Middle Ages); he was refined and sophisticated during the heyday of the Italian players in France in the seventeenth century by the famous Harlequin Dominique (Domenico Biancolelli): here his motley patches became the regular pattern of brightly coloured diamonds that we know; he was lent pathos by Thomassin (Tommaso Vicentini) and poetic fantasy by Carlin (Carlo Bertinazzi). While he gained subtlety and grace in France in the eighteenth century in the paintings of Watteau and in the plays of Marivaux, he remained his old self in Italy where he was given a final burst of creative energy by the actor-manager Sacchi, who played the Truffaldino role, in traditionally farcical fashion, in the plays of Carlo Gozzi. Harlequin probably owes his longer survival in France to the romanticizing process. His melancholy air still hangs about him in paintings by Cézanne, Picasso, Georges Barbier and others, and in his traditional present-day role in mime and ballet.

The original Arlecchino was not romantic. He is first mentioned by name in 1584, by which time he has distinguished himself from Brighella; Brighella directs the plot, organizes the escapes, the assignations, the marriages and disguises, while Arlecchino gets it all wrong, muddles the messages, has everyone constantly on the brink of disaster. He compensates for his foolishness by a kind of acrobatic wit; he walks on his hands and on stilts, he can fall from great heights or produce a hump without padding. Gradually the clown takes over from the devil and the beggarly porter, but for all his simplicity, he retains something of his diabolical origin. He is ugly with a black half-mask, hairy cheeks and bushy eyebrows; he has a snub nose, tiny eye-holes and a carbuncle on his forehead. He is a tremendous impersonator and will appear in disguise as anything from an emperor to an astronaut. He sometimes suffers a sex change, is astonished to find himself a bride, or a goddess, or a mother surrounded by dozens of baby Harlequins. He is the most enigmatic of the masks, stupid and cunning, clumsy and graceful, sensual and innocent, quickly grieved and quickly comforted, a child and, according to some, the reincarnation of Mercury himself.

The *lazzi* could be verbal jokes, set pieces of business, set pieces of comic dialogue, or a mixture of the three. Riccoboni in his *Histoire du théâtre italien* (1727) calls them 'inutilités', useless because they did not further the plot. The word comes from the Tuscan *lacci*, 'laces' or 'links' (in fact interruptions) in the action. There are *lazzi* of fear, of mixed grief and joy, of fainting, of hiding, of sleepwalking, of servant tricking master, and so on, many of which are recorded in the still extant commonplace books; many of them depend for their humour on crudity, many more on play upon words.

The technique of the *commedia* players was to take a Roman plot, for instance – seven of the Locatelli collection of scenarios are adaptations of Latin comedies – pep it up with *lazzi* and tirades, rename the characters Pantalone and Coviello, and put it on the stage. With the theme of Plautus' *Menaechmi* they went to town, so that in the early scenarios we find twins everywhere; twin Pantaloons, twin captains, twin servants to twin masters, in one case sextuplets. From the Romans they learnt the importance of a well-constructed plot, and in turn they brought new life to the erudite material. A big change in balance was partly caused by the introduction of women to play the female parts. The most famous of these, Isabella Andreini, largely created the tender role of the inamorata; the cheeky servant girl, often called Colombina, was the female counterpart to the zany. The *commedia* audiences expected proposals, love scenes and lovers' quarrels now to take place on stage. Another change is that all the characters lose social status: duels become beatings and comic speeches become silly jokes; but as buffoonery and parody take over, life is infused into the old devices, and at first dignity is well lost. The possibilities of disguise take wing when Truffaldino appears as a parrot. Other borrowed devices – girls masquerading as boys, lovers hidden in chests, feigned death, old men in love, clowns turned princes, the simple processes of cuckolding and feasting – not always successful in a literary context, revive to find their true element in farce.

In the end it was probably excessive reliance upon farce which brought about the demise of the *commedia* in Italy. The admirable purity of this unpretentious genre is succinctly expressed by K. M. Lea:

> We do not care about Pantalone and his mistress, we do not mind if Pulcinella and Colombina quarrel for ever; nor do we ask for probability in the ways they obtain or cheat each other; all that we want is to see them doing it again.

The drawback of the pleasure is that it brings diminishing returns. As the *commedia* continued into the eighteenth century, more *lazzi* and *burle* (something between a practical joke and a subplot) were introduced; there were longer musical interludes; obscenity was running riot; eventually most of the material appears to have been extraneous to any kind of plot. Imaginative resources were running low. Carlo Goldoni, in his introduction to the Pasquali edition of his works (1750), gives his own view of the degeneration of the improvised theatre, and while he condemns the use of masks and of improvisation anyway as being not conducive to verisimilitude, he attributes its impoverishment ultimately to its increasing reliance upon facile farcical effects in the struggle to win back its flagging audience.

It is difficult to say what sort of a service or disservice was done to the *comici dell'arte* by Goldoni. In a sense he prolonged their life by incorporating them into his plays, as Regnard and Marivaux did in France by rather different means, and yet by stripping them of their masks and making them learn their lines, by civilizing them and endowing them with bourgeois characteristics, it could be said that he extinguished their essential spark. Pantalone grows serious again; he acquires a kind of patriarchal dignity as, the embodiment of worldly common sense, he advises his children against all forms of impulsiveness and excess. Colombina has become Mirandolina with a household to run and servants of her own to see to. The comedies are played in theatres and for the most part are set in living rooms; the comics have in effect been dragged indoors and domesticated.

Venice, where Goldoni wrote, though formally an aristocracy, had its own instinct for democracy. The governing councils of nobles were subject to their own laws; sumptuary laws forbade ostentation, and, masked by the beaked domino, the servant was free to mix with his master in the gambling house, the theatre or the café. Consequently the egalitarian fever which seized European intellectuals in the eighteenth century found in Venice a society already immunized. So it cannot be said that Goldoni's motives in creating his bourgeois theatre were political, in the way that Steele's were, or Diderot's. His motive was simply to please; he wrote plays to fill the theatres and had a tradesman's instinct for knowing what people would like, for while abandoning the techniques of the *commedia* he was careful not to lose its audience. He needed no theories of comedy, merely seeking to bring about 'il dilettevole solletico all'uman cuore' ('the delightful tickle at the human heart'). Indeed in his 1750 preface he writes, 'I think that rather than the precepts of Horace or Aristotle, the Laws of the People are to be scrupulously observed.'

He deliberately set about a programme of theatrical reform. While he disliked Molière's emphasis on a central protagonist, his search was for a comedy which, like Molière's, should stem from character. His artistic manifesto is the play *Il teatro comico* (*The Comic Theatre*, 1750) which heralded the renowned season of the sixteen new comedies, all written and produced in under a year. In this play he makes a plea for naturalism, for 'true and recognizable characters', and for social criticism, not only for its moral value but on the grounds that it makes for good entertainment.

His secret was to foresee that it would delightfully tickle the heart of his emerging bourgeois public to recognize themselves – prejudice, materialism, social aspirations and all. He flattered their mercantile spirit, filled his plays with images of the dignity of honest trade and the fatuity of patrician idleness. Typical is his portrayal of Menego Cainello, the gondolier in *La putta onorata* (*The Honest Girl*, 1748) who declares with pride 'We serve, it's true, but ours is a noble service and does not dirty our hands.' It is a complimentary portrait on a small canvas, full of topicality and detail. The geographical position of Venice, her architecture, her values, her language, even her economic condition make themselves felt in these plays. We are in an enclosed pacific world where half of every day is devoted to pleasure, where no one's business is private, and where a man's property is the measure of his worth.

Goldoni confined himself to the surface of life, but to paint the surface with accuracy, warmth and humanity is to understand what lies beneath it. Goldoni's triumph is his reproduction of the domestic atmosphere. The daring of his realistic effects is astonishing; we have everything from a traffic jam of gondolas on stage to the performance of the most menial domestic tasks, but the real genius of this playwright lies in his ability to convey minutely the surface repercussions of clashes between the sexes, between the generations, between the strata of society, all observed within the context of the family setting. Personal tensions, money problems, social expectations and disappointments, these are his themes, and all of them illumined by his 'inexhaustible hilarity', to quote the critic Momigliano, that quality of sunny geniality which suffuses this finite world where the laws make sense and conformism is the ticket of entry.

Goldoni wrote more than 250 plays altogether. Among the best known are *Il servitore di due padroni* (*The Servant of Two Masters*, 1745), *La bottega del caffé* (*The Coffee Shop*, 1750), *La locandiera* (*The Mistress of the Inn*, 1753), *I rusteghi* (*The Boors*, 1760), *La casa nova* (*The New House*, 1761) and *Il ventaglio* (*The Fan*, 1764). Outstanding for their portrayal of local atmosphere are: *La putta onorata*, *Le baruffe chiozzotte* (*The Squabbles at Chioggia*, 1762) and *Il campiello* (*The Little Square*, 1756); and for humorous treatment of the aristocracy: *La famiglia dell' antiquario* (*The Antiquary's family*, 1749) and the *Villeggiatura* (*Country Holiday*) trilogy, 1761. For sheer lunacy one might choose *L'impresario delle Smirne* (*The Impresario from Smyrna*, 1760); and for poignancy, the last play he wrote before, finally defeated in his quarrel with Gozzi, he left to spend the rest of his years in France: *Una delle ultime sere di carnovale* (*One of the Last Evenings of Carnival*, 1762).

La casa nova is a typical comedy of the triumph of bourgeois values. Anzoletto, bullied by his social-climbing bride Cecilia, has moved into a magnificent apartment which he cannot afford. The whole havoc of house-moving is brought on to the stage; builders and decorators go about their business maddeningly slowly; a massive four-poster bed is assembled before us and taken down again. Motives are petty and emotions unheroic. The curiosity of the neighbours as, through windows, they watch the new people's furniture being carried in; the youthful condescension of Cecilia when she calls on them; the friction that arises between Cecilia and her unwanted sister-in-law; the compulsion of the parvenus to overspend: Goldoni shows that life is made up of such things. His delight in his craft is most evident, however, in the dénouement, when disaster is only averted by the intervention of Anzoletto's plain-speaking grocer uncle, who finally pays the bills and takes the couple, temporarily, into his own house.

Count Carlo Gozzi made a final bid to revive the old *commedia*. Famous for his quarrel with Goldoni, whose works he found trivial and coarse, and whom he virtually drove into exile in 1762, his positive contribution to the comic tradition is slight. His plays are fantastic magical fairy-tales. He purposely chose childish themes, in the first place to prove a malicious point in his polemic – that any nonsensical rubbish could fill a theatre. They are defiantly ill made, infused with mockery of others, but supremely of himself and of his chosen genre. As a foil to his exotic adventures of princesses and magicians he brings on the familiar *commedia* clowns, complete with Venetian dialect and full of topical quips. These scenes are the best; they exploit the perennial joke of the Yankee at the court of King Arthur or of the Cockney in the streets of Old Pompeii.

Gozzi was a rabid reactionary. His *L'augellino belverde* (*The Beautiful Little Green Bird*, 1765) is an attack on illuminism. Any hint of egalitarianism was anathema to him, yet he saw the popular *commedia* as the legacy of a glorious past, and his traditionalism was his avowed reason for preserving it. The years he spent writing for the Sacchi troupe were his happiest, and his account of them in his memoirs provides a lively insight into the theatrical mores of the time. But his use of the *comici* is too topical and satirical. Unfortunately all that lives on of Gozzi are his plots, and these are not his own. They were drawn from old sources, the *Thousand and One Nights* and the *Pentameron* of Basile. The *Love of Three Oranges* (1761) and *Turandot* (1762) survive as ballet and opera, but the plays themselves are now rarely performed.

Italy can be said to have made four major contributions to the comic tradition: in the formulation of its laws for all Europe in the sixteenth century; in the spontaneous generation of the *commedia dell'arte*; in the early 'slice of life' naturalism of Goldoni, and finally in the total reversal of comic values implied by the ambiguities of Pirandello. The nineteenth century added little. As the bourgeois element grew stronger, the purely comic vein was dissipated. It was the age of the *pièce à thèse* and of social realism, the most 'serious' century so far in Italy's history; the Risorgimento was no laughing matter. Ibsen enjoyed a vogue in Italy and had many imitators.

And so it remains for Pirandello to open up again the possibilities of comedy. Once the eternal certainties had been swept away by Darwin, Marx, Freud, Einstein and the most disillusioning war of all time, Pirandello was to be responsible for the conception and propagation of a new theatre of reflection and uncertainty. Laughter provoked by art would never be the same again, would always be counterbalanced by a sense of menace. Notions of identity, masquerade and deception may still have comic possibilities, but they are now never free from philosophical implications, and the pretended occurrences on the stage evoke a real event in the auditorium – the posing of such questions as: Am I the man I was yesterday? Am I the sum of my past actions? Or am I only present in the constantly changing roles I play for other people, and in the series of distorted impressions they receive of me? Is there any truth in what I am?

Humour for Pirandello is the 'sense of the contradiction of things'. He placed the principle of ambiguity and its accompanying hollow laughter so firmly on the stage that the principle of verifiable truth was thereafter more or less relegated to the realm of the commercial 'well-made' comedy, film or television piece. His influence, much of it indirect, is felt by many modern playwrights. He was after all the man who expounded fully and repeatedly in the theatres of Rome, Berlin and Paris the idea echoed many years after his death by Harold Pinter:

> There are no hard distinctions between what is real and what is unreal, nor between what is true and what is false. The thing is not necessarily either true or false; it can be both true and false.[1]

It is one of countless echoes of an old theme, for there have been relativists in every age. Modern physics, says Bertrand Russell, is on the side of Heraclitus. So, indeed, is the modern theatre. It would be too neat to make out that the theatre has come full circle since the time of Epicharmus' existentialist litigant; better perhaps to conclude with the sober suggestion that there is nothing new under the comic sun.

[1] Programme note to *The Room* and *The Dumb Waiter*, quoted by J. R. Taylor, *Anger and After* (Harmondsworth, 1963), p. 300.

4

Comedy in Spain
and the Spanish *comedia*

J. C. J. METFORD

TWO CHARACTERISTICS distinguish the tradition of comedy in Spain: popular appeal and freedom from restraint. Except for a classically minded minority, purity of form has never been the first consideration of generations of Spanish dramatists. Their intent was to please their public by giving them what they liked, not what misinterpreted Aristotelian precepts prescribed. The Spanish view of literature is that, if it is to reflect life, it cannot be compartmentalized into sacred or secular, high or low, tragic or comic, but that it must reveal the interpenetration of opposites. Thus the generic and most frequently used word for 'play' is *comedia*, a dramatic form in which tragedy may be mixed with comedy, characters may range from noble to base, and in which there is no limitation of subject matter. The fate of kings and the amours of servants; the beatification of saints and the exploits of bandits; bloodthirsty vengeance and elaborate fooling are not separated into easily defined genres but combined and synthesized. The result to the purist might be what Lope de Vega, the supreme practitioner of the art, described as a Minotaur, half of one kind and half of another, Terence mixed with Seneca, but it gave pleasure to the patrons of the theatre. As he pointed out, it was they who provided the dramatist's daily bread and thus made the rules which the writer ignored at his peril.

Although textual evidence for the Middle Ages is either lacking or fragmentary, it is evident from peninsular ecclesiastical and municipal records that popular taste in drama was much the same then as it was when Lope de Vega wrote. Acrobatic, musical and Thespian skills derived from *mimi* and *histriones* were perpetuated by *juglares* (jongleurs) and *bufones* (clowns) who traversed the regions reconquered from the Moors. From the eleventh century onwards, particularly in Catalonia, 'farces' – intrusive humorous episodes – provided the comic seasoning for Easter and Christmas liturgical plays in Latin and in the vernacular. Boy bishops (*obispillos*) presided over Twelfth Night horseplay and burlesque ceremonial. A carnival-like procession escorted the Host in the Corpus Christi parade. There was no sense of impropriety in the use of the comic to relieve, or more probably heighten through contrast, the religious significance of an occasion. That this was a fashion which persisted well beyond the medieval period is demonstrated by the introduction of comedy into peripatetic performances on carts of the religious *autos* (moralities) of the sixteenth century. An example is the *Aucto de los desposorios de Joseph* (*Joseph's Marriage*) in which a *bobo* (simpleton) not only provides the laughter but motivates much of the action.

By the mid-fifteenth century popular drama was in vogue in castle halls, providing entertainment during banquets and similar festivities. There is some doubt as to the exact nature of the *momos* which were performed on these special occasions but they certainly involved disguising, mumming and the presentation of playlets with comic ingredients. In time these developed into more elaborate compositions with simple plots and a variety of characters. Such were the *églogas* (eclogues) which Juan del Encina wrote in the early sixteenth century for the household of the Duke of Alba. Their setting is bucolic, their arguments uncomplicated, turning on such motives as the rivalry of a courtier and a shepherd for the hand of a skittish shepherdess. They exemplify the convention which had by then been established of amusing the aristocracy with the antics of boorish rustic characters speaking in dialect. Similar methods were used by Encina's contemporaries Lucas Fernández, one of whose farces provides an early example of the use of the braggart soldier, and the Lisbon goldsmith Gil Vicente, who wrote plays in Portuguese and Castilian for the amusement of the court. The scatological language used by some of his fools and rustics indicates the lack of squeamishness among the royalty of his day – an attitude favourable to the development of low comedy even in exalted places.

The influence of the classical ideals of the Italian Renaissance may be seen in some of the works of these early dramatists and is apparent in the writings of the first theoretician of the *comedia*, Bartolomé de Torres Naharro. Influenced in his practice by his mentor, Terence, he wrote most, if not all, of his plays for Spanish communities in Rome and Naples. These are works of satirical and moral intent in which, in comic situations, Torres castigates with Erasmus-like caricature braggart soldiers, parasites and brawling servants. In the Prologue to his *Propalladia* (1517) – 'the first things of Pallas' as he called his collected works – he speculated on the nature of comedy. For the most part his opinions were conventional, derived as was usual in his day from Donatus, Horace and Cicero. He distinguished comedy from tragedy in that the latter shows heroic struggle against adversity, whereas the former is 'an ingenious arrangement of notable incidents, ending happily, and in dialogue', but he recognized that differentiation between genres was not the Spanish practice. He classified dramas into *comedias a noticia*, plays based on everyday manners observed in the world around us, and *comedias a fantasía*, works which are products of the imagination, but which nevertheless appear to be true to life.

Torres Naharro was writing for a critical and well-read audience. Lope de Rueda, a few decades later, operated in Spain and performed his plays not only for noble households but also for the populace gathered in town squares. Born in Seville, and a goldsmith by trade, he became Spain's first recorded actor-manager, assembling a troupe and writing plays for them. As well as performing on his own account, he hired his services to municipalities and ecclesiastical bodies. His comic speciality was the *paso*, a short incident revolving around stereotyped characters – foolish peasants who are easily conned by quack doctors or students; old men deceived by young wives; and sextons with a propensity for bad Latin tags, drink and amorous adventures. He had the gift of creating instant comedy out of the simplest of situations. An argument between husband and wife about the price they will charge for olives not planted; an impecunious student pretending to be ill to avoid paying for a dinner and then being found out; two servants explaining to their master why they have not been at work. Such incidents provide fine opportunities for clever actors to amuse and delight the spectators before the *paso* ends with a cudgelling all round, which was the conventional way of clearing the stage at this period.

Looking back on similar performances that he witnessed in his youth, Cervantes commented on the primitive nature of the stage which these actor-managers would set up in public places – four benches set out in a square, with five or six boards laid across them, making a platform a few feet from the ground, an old blanket drawn aside by two cords forming what was called a tiring room, behind which were the musicians, who sang ancient ballads without a guitar. These inconveniences were remedied by the development of fixed public theatres from the 1560s onwards. They began with the hiring for a number of performances of *corrales*, yards surrounded by blocks of houses. Later these sites became permanent, with a fixed stage and a gallery, thus permitting the presentation of more elaborate plays. Four-act comedies in which the influence of Plautus and Italian sources were evident became popular, and there was no shortage of playwrights to provide them.

These improvements in the physical conditions of producing plays, coupled with incessant demand for entertainment on the part of audiences grown accustomed to assembling at fixed locations, led to the creation of a dramatic form, the *comedia nueva* (new play) which dominated the stage for more than 200 years. Basically, it was the traditional *comedia* of the later sixteenth century refined and improved. Reduction of the classical five acts to four and then to three made the development of the plot more logical and subject to fewer interruptions: exposition in the first act; complication in the second; and resolution in the third. Movement was swift, the average play taking about two hours to perform.

This rapidity of presentation was assisted by the variety of verse forms employed. The basic metre was the native eight-syllable ballad measure, the *romance*, with assonance in alternate lines, ideal for narrative and normal dialogue and easily learned by actors who would not find it difficult to adlib if their memories failed them. For special effects there were verse forms of Renaissance Italianate derivation. Soliloquies were often expressed in sonnets; the alternating eleven and seven lines of the *silva* provided rhythmic delicacy; and the stately *octava real* could be used for grave matters and to slow down the tempo. With such varied musicality at his disposal, the dramatist could make the total effect of his play similar to the impact of a symphony on a modern concert audience.

Essentially this new type of *comedia* was 'romantic'. Its exponents, while paying lip-service to the supposed superiority of plays written according to the classical canons of good taste, would defend themselves on the grounds that they were writing not for the small band of intellectuals but for the *vulgo*, the common man. He would not judge a play in accordance with its strict observance of the unities, but from the point of view of entertainment. 'The drama's laws, the drama's patrons give.' Therefore the seventeenth-century Spanish dramatist, like his predecessors, claimed that, although he knew the rules of art, he would lose money if he did not give the public what they wanted; that is, a good story, swiftly and competently told, whether or not the action was spread over days or years or moved from one place (or even from one country) to another. Perhaps this outright defiance of the classical rules was Spain's principal contribution at that time to the liberation of European comedy from strict adherence to prescribed principles – a liberty which was not fully exploited in France until the Romantic period.

Cervantes, a classicist by temperament, although more liberal in practice, caused the priest in *Don Quixote* to castigate both those who wrote and those who took pleasure in such plays:

> According to Tully, plays should be the mirror of human life, example of behaviour and image of truth, but those which are performed nowadays are mirrors of absurdities, examples of fool-ish actions and images of lewd behaviour. For what greater ab-surdity can there be . . . than for a child to come on in swaddling clothes in the first scene in the first act and in the second already a full-grown bearded man? And what greater foolishness than to depict for us a valiant old man and a cowardly young one, a speech-making servant and a counsellor page, a beggarly king and a scullery-maid princess? And what can I say of their obser-vance of the time in which the actions they present can or could take place . . . ?   (Part I, ch. xlviii)

In fact, although the unities of place and time and the conventions of decorum were not always observed, it would be difficult to find plays as absurd as those Cervantes describes. Moreover, the audience enjoying *comedias* in Madrid and in the provincial capitals was by no means the common herd. Even a superficial reading of almost any *comedia* will show that the average Spanish theatregoer, like his Elizabethan and Jacobean counterpart, was capable of the quick appreciation of classical references, historical allusions, puns and quite complicated euphuistic language. Spanish audiences were not ignorant and many of them, particularly priests and religious, who were allowed to sit in a reserved section of the theatre, knew all about the classical rules. What they sought was not refinement but enter-tainment. This accounts for the other 'romantic' characteristic of the new *comedia*, the disregard – as in the past – of the distinction between genres. Tragedy and comedy are not separated but intermingled. Few of these *comedias* qualify as outright tragedies, and almost none as tragedies in the classical sense. Many have tragic themes and tragic elements, but in all of them there is a strong comic element, whether of the darker or the lighter variety. In fact, the word 'tragicomedy' is frequently used to describe such mixed plays.

To act these *comedias*, there were established a number of profes-sional companies to perform in the theatres of Madrid, Seville, Valen-cia and Barcelona and to go on tour to other centres where the municipalities would either sponsor their appearances or employ them direct. Whether the composition of these companies was determined by the plays which were written for them, or whether the personnel of the companies influenced the construction of the plays – probably a mixture of both factors – they were both remarkably uniform in structure. The leader of the company was the *autor*, originally the author who wrote plays and gathered actors to perform them. As the demand for *comedias* grew, he bought plays from the *poeta*, the dramatist, often a man of literary interests, who wrote for money rather than for fame. Thus the *autor* developed into the actor-manager, who contracted actors and might well play a part himself, usually the *barba*, the bearded one, that is, the king or the father, or some similar grave personage. Mothers are difficult characters to handle in comedy and were for this reason mostly avoided. If one were required, or a stern duenna were necessary, the actor-manager's wife would usually play the part.

The principals of the company were two kinds of actors – necessary on account of the inherent 'romantic' characteristic of the *comedia*, the mingling of high and low life. These were the *galán*, the handsome young gallant, playing the courtier, lover or similar hero's part, and his valet or servant. Their female counterparts were the *dama*, the lady courted by the gallant, and her maid. If subplots were required – and most *comedias* had them – these roles were increased by the addition of an extra *galán* and another *dama*, often with their servants. These arrangements were conducive to stock characterization, but it is a tribute to the skill of the best Spanish dramatists that, even within these limitations, they could produce variations which prevented their characters from appearing stylized.

Gallant and lady provided plot and subplot, and the most complicated intrigues which were essential to Spanish comedy. Spanish dramatists, for all their disregard of the unities, nevertheless strictly observed the principle of decorum. These 'high' characters would suffer the pangs of unrequited love, could be noble or villainous in their actions, could express themselves wittily, but would never be diminished in status by becoming the principal source of laughter, even if their actions were quietly ridiculed. The contrary was the role of the servant and, where required, of the maid. Either singly or together, they provoked laughter by aping their betters, commenting earthily on their superiors' highflown sentiments, or behaving contrary to the code of honour.

The servant was usually played by the actor who was often the most renowned member of the company, the *gracioso*, or funny man. One of them, 'Juan Rana', the pseudonym of Cosme Pérez, became so famous that a number of interludes[1] were written specially for him, and his comic skill made his name proverbial. As a character, the *gracioso* inherited the traditional role of the *bobo*, the fool of the older pastoral plays, but he was also much influenced by the clown of the *commedia dell'arte*. (Italian companies were popular in Spain.) For him

---

[1] See pp. 95–6 below.

the dramatist wrote good lines and devised many comic situations, yet he must also have indulged in antics of his own which have not been recorded but which may be inferred from the condemnatory writings of the moralists who wished to suppress the *comedia*.

The playwright who brought the *comedia* form to perfection and bestrode his generation 'like a colossus' was Lope de Vega. Born in 1562, a child prodigy who was reputed to compose verses even before he could write, he was educated at a Jesuit college and then, most probably, at Spain's foremost university, Alcalá de Henares. By the time he was twenty, he had already established a reputation as a poet and was one of the members of a close-knit coterie of Madrid writers and wits. His love of the theatre brought him into contact with a married actress, Elena Osorio, the one great love out of the many in his life. When she abandoned him for a wealthy admirer, he castigated her and her family in some libellous verses which resulted in a harsh sentence of eight years' banishment from Madrid.

From the point of view of his art, this was probably the best thing that could have happened to him. It brought him into contact with a vigorous school of dramatists in Valencia, where he was encouraged to write plays. When he moved to Toledo he found scope for his literary talents. His experiences of life and love served him well as secretary to the Duke of Sessa whose amorous epistles he composed. When at last he was able to return to Madrid, he did so as the natural leader of one school of writers and the declared enemy of a rival group. Their mutual antipathies and satires on each other's works are to be found embedded in many of the *comedias* of the age. These references, now intelligible only to literary scholars, must have caused many knowing nods of the head and appreciative laughter on the part of Madrid playgoers who were well aware of the literary quarrels in the capital.

Although Lope de Vega found time to write innumerable other works, both prose and verse, his main concern for the rest of his life was the theatre. His disciple and early biographer, Montalbán, attributed 1800 plays to him: he himself, at the end of his life, spoke of 1500. Modern research is prepared to grant him at least 350–400. In addition to this, Lope de Vega found time not only for two wives in succession but also a number of mistresses, including a ten-year affair with an actress, Micaela de Luján. Perhaps the tender sentiments that lovers in his plays express in such eloquent verse are reflections of skills which he himself must have possessed for the winning of hearts.

Lope de Vega's success as a dramatist is attributable to his workmanlike handling of the *comedia*. His facility in versification, the clarity of his style and the deftness with which he developed the action meant that the plays were easily apprehended by the average boisterous Madrid audience which, like its modern counterpart, was inclined to be as much preoccupied with its private concerns as with what was taking place on stage. Lope de Vega utilized the neat division of the *comedia* into three acts to establish a conventional development of the plot, much as the modern writer of detective stories plans out his chapters, so that his devotees would know almost to the line where exposition, complication and resolution would occur. Their pleasure was derived from the dramatist's neat contrivances to sustain their interest by means of intricate interweaving of plot and subplot, surprise happenings and disappointments leading to the final union of true lovers.

In a humorous verse address to a learned literary academy in Madrid in 1609, in which he defended himself for writing plays that did not conform to the classical rules of art, Lope de Vega gave it as his opinion, tested in practice, that dramatic genres should not be kept separate: comedy should be mingled with tragedy because 'such variety gives such great delight'. He knew from experience that audiences liked to be moved to tears and then to find relief in laughter. This is the formula he applied successfully to most of his plays which have stood the test of time. A tragic event, like the rape of the bride from the village of Fuenteovejuna, is made bearable by the mock-heroic behaviour of some of the rustics. Instead of meting out violent death – the conventional end for would-be adulterous wives – the husband in *El castigo del díscreto* (*The Prudent Man's Justice*), discovering that his wife has allowed her intended lover a nocturnal assignation, disguises himself as the gallant and gives the lady a sound thrashing. This arouses laughter similar to that provoked by the ending of one of the *Decameron's* peasant tales. This play is in notable contrast to those that turn on the strict application of the code of honour. If compared with another of Lope de Vega's plays with almost the same title, *El castigo sin venganza* (*Justice Without Revenge*), it reveals how comedy could be used to show up the absurdities of the code and point the way to more sensible behaviour. In the latter the Duke of Ferrara, discovering his wife's love for his bastard Federico, binds her, covers her with a cloth and leaves her in a darkened room. He tells his son to kill the traitor whom he will find there and Federico, always obedient to the father whom he loves, unwittingly murders the duchess. In contrast, the prudent man avenged himself in a way which was contrary to the code of honour but consonant with justice and good sense.

Many of Lope de Vega's plays depend on the mingling of tragic and comic episodes, the prescription which best suited his audience; but he also wrote true comedies in the modern sense: plays in which the emphasis is on character and situation, plays into which sorrow or pathos may intrude but which are intentionally serene in their outcome. Federico, the hero of *El halcón de Federico* (*Frederick's Falcon*), the plot of which is based on a story in the *Decameron*, is the pattern of true love who is prepared to sacrifice everything for his lady. In this case, she is rich and prefers another nearer her social rank. Federico, to hide his poverty, retires to the country where, in due course, the lady, now a widow with a young son, becomes his neighbour. The boy falls ill and says that nothing will cure him but Federico's falcon which he has admired from afar. To humour her son, the lady sends Federico a message to say that she will dine with him, and he, having nothing on which to feast her, serves up the falcon, his one precious possession. To the English mind this may seem either ludicrous or pathetic. In the Spanish way of thinking, Federico has behaved like a true hidalgo in honouring a guest at whatever cost, a constant lover who will not fail his lady. His fidelity is rewarded because the widow, recognizing his virtue, marries him. Inevitably the *gracioso*, Federico's servant, is present at each crucial moment to add his earthy comments and in this way make acceptably real a story which might otherwise have bordered on the farcical.

Lope de Vega's genius as a writer of comedies is best shown in plays which were not derived from novelistic sources but were largely of his own invention and were about people of his own day. Most of these works have as their heroes men of *capa y espada* (cloak and sword), that is gentlemen of lesser nobility who frequented Madrid and had plenty of time and opportunity for amorous intrigues. These plays usually turn on the need to outwit the vigilance of a parent or guardian in order to win the affections of a beautiful girl who, according to the custom of the day, was kept in purdah-like seclusion, allowed out only for mass or a visit to her confessor. The cerberus in *El acero de Madrid* (*Madrid's Iron Tonic*) is the unbending duenna Doña Teodora, whose charge, Belisa, is in love with a young gallant, Lisardo. To be with her, he employs two stratagems. At a hint from him, Belisa pretends to be ill. Lisardo and his *gracioso* servant, Beltrán, appear in her house as doctor and assistant and prescribe long walks and draughts of 'iron' water from a chalybeate spring. He then persuades his friend Riselo to pretend to pay court to the duenna and thus divert her attention from the lovers. There are the usual complications when Riselo's lady becomes jealous of his attentions to Doña Teodora, but these are resolved to the satisfaction of the lovers and the contentment of the audience.

A society ruled by strict conventions provides a suitable milieu for the writer of comedies. In tragedy the hero is driven to his fate because the unwritten laws of society demand it. In comedy these rules are ingeniously circumvented to the benefit of the hero, although society is satisfied in the end when hero and heroine are united in marriage.

This distinction may be illustrated by *La moza de cántaro* (*The Kitchen Maid*). Doña María is a much-courted beauty, but one of her suitors is driven to strike her father, a terrible affront to his honour which, in obedience to the code of honour, can only be assuaged with blood. As there is no son to undertake this duty, Doña María behaves unusually for a woman, but in a manner which would win approval from the honour-conscious audience: she kills her suitor. Up to this point Lope de Vega was writing a play which could be expected to turn into a revenge tragedy, although the protagonist in this case was, unexpectedly, a woman. Conventionally, Doña María would herself be killed by one of the suitor's relations, in accordance with the inexorable code of honour. Instead the play turns into a comedy. While her family try to obtain pardon for her crime, Doña María, in disguise, flees from Madrid, and works as a kitchen maid who carries the water from the well in a pitcher (hence the *cántaro* of the title). Don Juan falls in love with her. Despite the apparent difference in rank, he decides to defy convention and marry her, but, naturally, the law of hierarchy is not broken because, as the audience knows, Doña María is really Don Juan's social equal.

That nothing but the strict observance of rank and degree is conducive to happiness is demonstrated in another comedy, *El perro del hortelano*, the title a proverb: 'The gardener's dog can't eat the produce, but won't let anyone else do so.' In this case the dog in the manger is Diana, Countess of Belfor, courted by the Marquis Ricardo, but in love with her secretary Teodoro, whom she cannot marry because he is beneath her station. Nevertheless, she will not let Teodoro marry one of her ladies, Marcela. Overcome by passion, she demeans herself by asking Teodoro's advice in the supposedly hypothetical case of a lady in love with a lowly person. Seeing his opportunity, Teodoro lets it be known that he is really the son of Count Ludovico, held captive in Malta by the Turks. There is thus apparently no obstacle to marriage. Diana's punishment is that Teodoro's story is false. She has to suffer because she has allowed her passion to overcome her obligation to society. Similarly, in *La villana de Getafe* (*The Country Maid from Getafe*), Don Félix is suitably punished for seducing Inés, a humble girl, and then abandoning her. He is led to believe that Inés has inherited considerable wealth and hastens to marry her, only to discover the trick that has been played on him. Her honour is saved, but Don Félix is disgraced by the unequal match.

These bare summaries, while showing his skill in creating plots, do scant justice to Lope de Vega's gift for characterization and character development. One example of these qualities must suffice. *La dama boba* (*The Stupid Lady*) is a character study which shows how love can transform even the mentally backward. In this play there are two sisters unequally endowed by nature. Nise is clever, attractive and full of social graces; Finea is deformed, wrapped up in herself, and a half-wit. Nise has no difficulty in attracting suitors but, when the family introduces a prospective husband to Finea, he flees after hearing her stupid conversation and seeing her ungainly attempts to dance. To compensate for her inferiority, Finea's uncle wills her a fortune. Laurencio hears of it and, as he cynically explains to his *gracioso* valet, is prepared to marry anyone provided she is rich. His wooing gradually transforms Finea into a witty and accomplished lady. This change is cleverly brought about in the action of the play so that the metamorphosis does not strain the credulity of the audience.

Equal to Lope de Vega in skilful manipulation of the *comedia* formula, although not so prolific – some 400 plays claimed by him, but barely 80 extant – was Gabriel Téllez, a monk who wrote under the pseudonym of Tirso de Molina. He was composing plays at least as early as 1612 when he lived in Toledo at the house of the Mercedarian order to which he belonged. His most active period of association with the theatre was from 1621 to 1625 when he frequented academies and literary circles in Madrid. For reasons possibly political, the Junta de Reformación (Reform Commission) of the Council of Castile chose to make an example of him on the grounds that he wrote 'profane plays' (although many members of religious orders did so unhindered). His order promoted him but sent him for safety to distant Trujillo, near the Portuguese border, where he continued to write and publish plays, wisely using a 'nephew' as real or fictitious cover and thus creating problems of attribution for the modern literary scholar.

Tirso de Molina's particular strength lay in his power of invention. Using a restrictive formula – main plot, lady and gallant; subplot, *gracioso* and lady's maid; or the pairs doubled – he contrived a variety of situations which he cleverly worked into a unified whole. The theme in his comedies was love tested and proved by *celos*, a word which means much more than 'jealousy' in that it calls up a gamut of a lover's emotions, from fear of losing his lady to the desire to kill any male who dares so much as to look at her. Without *celos*, said Tirso de Molina, love could not exist. Many of his plays which can be classified as comedies are skilful variations on this theme. This, he explained, was the main reason why he rejected the unity of time. 'What chance', he asked, 'has a gallant to conceive jealousy, proclaim despair, console himself with hope, and display the other emotions and fluctuations of feeling without which love is of no esteem', if the dramatist has no more than a day at his disposal for the action?

Tirso de Molina's skill in handling a complicated plot may be observed in *La villana de Vallecas* (*The Country Maid from Vallecas*). The play opens in Valencia where an army captain, Don Gabriel de Herrera, using the pseudonym of Don Pedro de Mendoza, seduces, under promise of marriage, Doña Violante and makes off towards Madrid. At an inn on the way he encounters – curious coincidence – a real Don Pedro de Mendoza who is going to the capital to marry Doña Serafina, a bride who has been chosen for him. Accidentally, the captain's servant mixes up the luggage; and the feigned Don Pedro finds himself in possession of jewels, money and letters of introduction. He presents himself as the bridegroom to the discomfiture of the real Don Pedro who is driven out of his fiancée's house as a usurper. Meanwhile Doña Violante, disguised as a countrymaid, arrives in Madrid, where Serafina's brother falls in love with her. The real Don Pedro, to his astonishment, lands in prison on a charge of seduction, but Violante's discovery that he is not the man who has deceived her leads to the dénouement in which Doña Violante is made an honest woman through marriage to Don Gabriel, and the injured Don Pedro obtains his intended bride.

From this bare summary it would seem that no audience could follow the twists and turns of such a complicated plot, yet in its exposition Tirso de Molina handles his materials so deftly that a theatregoer would not be in the least confounded. Clever dialogue, witty description and musical versification keep the action moving swiftly to a satisfying conclusion.

It is difficult to select from the works of the many contemporaries of Lope de Vega and Tirso de Molina representative comedies which depart significantly from the formula these two masters managed so deftly. Most are competent, many are outstanding, but all can be said to be variations on an accepted pattern. There is, however, one dramatist who is different in many ways from the rest. Juan Ruiz de Alarcón y Mendoza was an outsider who came to Madrid from Mexico and found considerable difficulties in gaining acceptance in the literary circles of the capital. His American accent set him apart, and his physical deformities proved unattractive. In themselves these drawbacks might have gone unnoticed had Alarcón not been conscious of his undoubted talents as a writer and displayed them in a way that provoked the jealousy of his fellows. They revenged themselves by satirizing him in biting verse lampoons and overt references to him in their plays. He was resented as an intruder when he settled in Madrid in 1615, and was not missed when he gave up writing and accepted a government post in 1625.

His dramatic career was therefore short, and the plays he wrote do not exceed two dozen. This may explain why they are more carefully constructed and have greater individuality than any others from the enormous number written at the time. Moreover, Alarcón stands out from his contemporaries because, although accepting the conventional formula of the *comedia*, he used it intentionally to a moral end. His comedies are all implied criticisms of the vices of society, particularly of those of its members who subscribe to ideals of nobility and honour, and yet act in a way which belies their beliefs. His most famous play, imitated by Corneille in *Le Menteur*, is *La verdad sospechosa*, an attack on slanderers and liars. García returns home from the university an inveterate liar and, through his actions, becomes involved in a number of situations, amusing in themselves, but each revealing the depths to which a man can sink if he does not live up to his ideals. García's mistake is his belief that lineage, not deeds, confers honour. In somewhat revolutionary fashion, considering the hierarchical beliefs of the age, his father tells him that if he does not behave nobly then he ceases to be noble, and that a man of low birth may attain nobility through his actions.

The other great dramatist of the period was Pedro Calderón de la Barca, whose most significant plays were of tragic or religious intent. He nevertheless wrote a number of comedies which soon became known abroad and which were translated and adapted for the English Restoration stage. The best-known of these works is *Casa con dos puertas mala es de guardar*. From internal references to gardens, statues, fountains, the king and his courtiers, it would appear to have been written early in 1629 for the amusement of Philip IV's French queen, Isabel de Borbón, during her residence in the Palace of Aranjuez. The success of the play depended on the exploitation of the resources of the stage, a recess at the back, which could simulate an inner room, flanked by two exits through which actors could appear and disappear with split-second timing. This is the scene of the main action, the house in which Laura lives and which has two doors, as required by the play's proverb title: 'It is difficult to watch over a house with two doors.'

As comedy, the play depends on establishing risky situations where social conventions come near to being broken but are not actually contravened. Representatives of morality are Félix, who keeps his sister Marcela in seclusion so that his honour shall not be besmirched by gossip that he is trying to marry her off to his friend Lisardo, who comes to visit him, and Fabio, Laura's father, who has to prevent any scandal occurring in his house. As is usual in so many *comedias*, a woman, like Eve, is the catalyst. Marcela, veiled, has already encountered Lisardo at a nearby convent and, to encourage his obvious interest, momentarily lifts her veil when she sees him again in the street. She then arranges for them to meet at Laura's house. Félix, too, is brought to the house. He has been in love with Laura, deserted her for Nise, then realized that it is Laura whom he has loved all the time. To win him back Laura contrives, through the agency of her maid, to induce Félix to visit her. The lovers are thus together under the same roof but the men must not know of each other's presence, nor must the father discover them. Calderón's skill as a manipulator is shown by the way in which he almost allows the lovers to be caught but gets them offstage in the nick of time. He also exploits Lisardo's presence to establish the conventional motive of jealousy, so that Félix thinks Laura has another lover in her room. Most of the action takes place in the dark, which adds to the comedy, when characters hide unaware of each other. As Spanish plays were performed in the afternoon, this called for fine acting and the suspension of disbelief – something a seventeenth-century audience was quite prepared to accept.

From these necessarily abbreviated accounts of some of the more significant Spanish *comedias*, it would seem that Dryden was right when he censured Spanish dramatists for cumbering themselves with too much plot. It is certain that action takes precedence, and that the notable Spanish contribution lies in the invention of intrigues and complicated situations. Characterization is stylized, and individual characteristics emerge in the course of the action. Nevertheless the whole was subservient to the unifying force of a typically Spanish conception of the true nature of comedy, which may be summarized along the following lines.

In a strictly hierarchical society, subscribing to high ideas of honour, dignity and personal conduct, comedy arose in one of two ways. Comedy was possible where reality fell short of expectation, or it could arise through attempts to circumvent the strict codes imposed by society's view of what it should be like, even if the ideals were not always attainable. Nevertheless there was a limit to the licence that could be permitted in a play. The code could be challenged seemingly successfully, right up to the last moment, but in the end it must be seen to prevail. Lovers, whatever their previous behaviour, must eventually conform by being married off; villains must be unmasked and then made to acknowledge their misdeeds; individuals who insist on their individuality must in the end submit to the norm. The ultimate reason for this is that human society is the microcosm of the divine order and its laws the expression of the laws of God. There may be aberrations in human behaviour – and those who err make the best protagonists for comedy – but in the end God's justice prevails.

In this sense *El burlador de Sevilla* (*The Trickster of Seville*), attributed to Tirso de Molina, written about 1630 and the *comedia* with the most lasting influence on European literature, may be considered a comedy. It is probably based on two folk legends: the statue which accepts an invitation to dinner; and the tale of a priapic gallant of Seville who was irresistible to women. In this play, Don Juan Tenorio, the gallant, is in many ways an attractive young man, brave, lighthearted and witty. His weakness arises from his low estimation of women. 'Woman is made of glass: if tested too hard she will soon break', says the Spanish proverb. Don Juan's pleasure is to outwit women, not primarily for sexual satisfaction, but for the thrill of tricking them into submission. Each of his victims is caught because of a weakness in her character – Doña Ana because she has arranged for her lover to visit her by night; Aminta, the peasant, because she is dazzled by Don Juan's wealth; Tisbea, the fisher-girl, because she refuses, out of pride, a lover of her own station. Audiences are fascinated by success and undoubtedly follow the succession of Don Juan's conquests with secret, if grudging admiration. Then the ideal prevails: God is not mocked, as Don Juan's servant warns him after each seduction. Ultimately, evil deeds will be punished. 'You give me so much extended credit' (*Tan largo me lo fiáis*, the title of an earlier version of *El burlador de Sevilla*), says Don Juan. For a young man, death is far off, and in any case last-minute confession will obviate punishment. Unfortunately for Don Juan, he is not given this opportunity. The statue of Doña Ana's father, the memorial to the man he killed in escaping from her chamber, which he has invited to dine, drags him down to hell before he has time to repent. This is not a tragic end. The play is a comedy, because the protagonist's challenge to the divine order is ignoble. He is not a good man striving against inexorable fate. Although villainy appears to succeed for a time, it is defeated in the end, and order, both social and divine, is re-established.

Seventeenth-century Spanish audiences demanded more for their late-afternoon entertainment in the theatre than a three-act *comedia* of a few hours' duration. This gave rise to the elaboration of an earlier and somewhat simpler comic form, the *entremés*, a word probably derived from *inter missum*, 'something put between', and, in this case, a short interlude intercalated between the acts of a *comedia*. Almost every dramatist of note attempted this form. Cervantes, in his youth, had seen Lope de Rueda present his *pasos*, and continued the tradition in his excellent *entremeses* (which are far more entertaining than his serious plays). A good example of his skill is *El juez de los divorcios* (*The Divorce Judge*), in which various couples present their complaints and tell of their dislike of their partners but are refused alleviation because 'the worst agreement is better than the best divorce'.

The acknowledged master of the *entremés* in the first half of the century was Luis Quiñones de Benavente, who was said to have written hundreds of these interludes. Many of these are topical, with local references which are now difficult to interpret, so that much of their wit is lost, but their humour and the comic force of their simple plots can still give pleasure. Although many stock characters are introduced, there is also a wide range of types from the low life of Madrid, and the works are in many cases picaresque novels in miniature. There is much covert bawdy dialogue and many surprisingly daring plots like that of *Los mariones* (*The Gay Boys*) in which two effeminate young men behave like women and are courted by their ladies who act the part of male lovers.

Slightly younger than Quiñones de Benavente, and much in vogue in the latter part of the century, was Agustín Moreto, who used the *entremés* to ridicule types like the *valiente*, the 'tough', who is not as ferocious as he seems. He had a notable talent for developing complicated intrigues which provoked slapstick conclusions. A good example is *Los órganos y el reloj* (*The Organs and the Clock*), which derives its title from the indecision in an impoverished small town about purchasing either an organ or a clock as well as appointing a barber and a sacristan. Two students pretend to be barber and organ builder, and their abandoned sweethearts (disguised) apply for the post of sacristan. Moreto's skill lies in his ability to present plots like this within the brief confines imposed by the short time allowed for the playing of an *entremés*.

The change of dynasty from Habsburg to Bourbon at the beginning of the eighteenth century led to a cultural division between those who adhered to the traditions of the previous age and those who wished to follow the more fashionable precepts of French neoclassicism. As far as the stage was concerned, this meant the continued popular vogue of the old Spanish *comedia*, refurbished to meet the taste of the day, but leaving the genre essentially unchanged in style and content. The public enjoyed music, spectacle and transformation scenes which involved the use of elaborate stage machinery. Among the most persistently popular plays were those of Antonio de Zamora, whose involved comedy *El hechizado por fuerza* (*The Forcibly Bewitched*) was immortalized in a painting by Goya, now in the National Gallery, London.

The most lively contributions to the popular theatre came from the pen of Ramón de la Cruz. He perfected the *sainete* (titbit), a one-act comic piece, somewhat longer than the *entremés* (a genre which was suppressed as 'scandalous' in 1780 by the Council of Castile). These playlets were intended as a *bonne bouche* to conclude a performance after a longer play. Characters were chosen from the more colourful types of the lower orders, plots were complicated, the intent satirical and the whole salted with wit.

Neoclassical dramatists wrote for an intellectual minority and devoted themselves mainly to tragedy. Their purpose was to make Spanish literature respected abroad by emulating foreign writers in their respect for the rules of art. When they ventured into comedy, they did so with a view to instruct as well as to entertain. Leandro Fernández de Moratín (1760–1828) defined comedy as the representation 'in dialogue of an event which happens in one place within a few hours involving certain persons, through which, and through the opportune expression of manners and characters, the vices and common errors of society are made to look ridiculous and truth and virtue are thereby commended'. He followed these principles in his plays which were intended not only for instruction but also as examples of the way in which comedies should be written if they were to impress foreigners who subscribed to Gallic principles of good taste. A short work, first performed in the *Teatro del Príncipe* in Madrid in 1792, *La comedia nueva* (*The New Play*), ridiculed writers' mutual admiration societies and the absurdities of the drama of the day which were praised by the imaginary author's friends. Moratín puts into the mouth of the 'rational' character, Don Pedro, his own views regarding the need for theatrical reform: writers should obey the rules and, if they refuse, should be compelled to do so by an enlightened government. He sent a copy of his play to the king's minister, the Count of Floridablanca (a man of 'taste', as may be deduced from Goya's portrait of him), and with it a petition that a committee for the reform of the theatre should be established. Unfortunately the count appointed as chairman a general who knew a great deal about the art of war but little about the art of the theatre. His remedy was to draw up a list of 'unsuitable' plays and ban them.

Legislation, Moratín realized, could not correct public taste: example, he hoped, would help to improve it. This was the main purpose of his original comedies which exalt the power of reason and the need for humanity in social relationships. They were intended to show that obedience to the rules is no obstacle to theatrical competence. This is evident from the mastery which Moratín displays in *El sí de las niñas* (*Young Girls Consent*, 1806), a play which attacked the restrictive way in which women were brought up at home and in convents, causing them to conceal their feelings, to lie and to deceive. They say 'yes' in obedience to parental commands when their inclinations are otherwise. This is the invidious situation of Paquita, who leaves her convent to be married to a middle-aged gentleman, Don Diego, chosen for her by her overbearing mother. Paquita is in love with Carlos, Don Diego's handsome nephew. The young lovers are driven to deceit and finally to despair, but are united through the humanity of Don Diego who behaves as a man of feeling and renounces his claim to the bride.

Since Moratín's day there has been no lack of well-written and highly entertaining comedies, but few have more than local interest. In a society that was inward-looking, much concerned with personal problems and wary of expressing too explicitly political or religious concepts which were not universally acceptable, the comic dramatist's scope was restricted in the nineteenth century and after to reproving, without appearing too revolutionary, the foibles and follies of his largely middle-class audience. Technical perfection and the ability to amuse therefore replaced ideological leadership as the dramatist's objective. Manuel Bretón de los Herreros was the most successful of these writers over many decades, his popularity due in no small measure to his verbal dexterity and his ability to present the picturesque types beloved by his audience. In *A Madrid me vuelvo* (*I'm Going Back to Madrid*) a gentleman, disillusioned by the noise, discomforts and deceits of the capital city, seeks relief in the countryside, only to find that it is equally discordant and full of intrigue. This play displays the conventional cynicism which was acceptable to the audience. To go further and make a radical attack on social institutions would have ruined the author. *La escuela del matrimonio* (*The School of Matrimony*, 1852) well illustrates these limitations. Ostensibly it deals with the problems of incompatibility in marriage, exemplified by the discords in the lives of three couples who are sufficiently 'modern' in outlook to contemplate divorce. They are saved from this socially unacceptable course by the wise counsel of a woman who represents traditional standards and admonishes them: 'Divorce is a poor remedy and the scandal – worse!' Spanish society had scarcely changed since Cervantes's day!

To enumerate nineteenth-century writers of comedies equal in ability and output to Bretón de los Herreros would be to produce a catalogue of talented authors famous in their day but equally stigmatized as mainly of historical interest. Manuel Tamayo y Baus, whose main claim to be remembered is that he anticipated the plot of Leoncavallo's *I Pagliacci*, is typical. In *Lo positivo* (*Positivism*, 1862) he showed considerable dramatic skill in humorously contrasting belief in human values with the bourgeois creed of 'no sentiment in business', but had not the courage or the inclination to condemn, except possibly by implication, the economic order which created that creed. In the same way, the prolific José Echegaray, who won a Nobel Prize for Literature in 1904, possessed considerable comic and satirical talent, even if he held that 'the sublime in art is in tears, grief and death'; but few read his comedies now.

The advent of the cinema in the twentieth century did not diminish the popularity of the theatre in the large cities of Spain. Until the 1930s, in Madrid, except during Holy Week and periods of national mourning, on almost any evening at least eight theatres would be presenting plays. The same was true, though perhaps the number was not so large, for the provincial capitals. Such was the demand for new works and so frequent the change of programme that hundreds of plays were written in the early decades of the century. If success-fully produced, they had an assured market outside the theatre in the form of inexpensive paper editions which circulated widely, particu-larly in towns that lacked theatres.

That no more than a small number of enduring masterpieces emerged from so much dramatic activity is attributable to the nature of the audience, which continued to be respectable urban middle class. Standards were set by the well-dressed matrons and their charges who frequented matinées (in Madrid, early evening perfor-mances, for this was considered the correct time for ladies of good family to be abroad). They applauded plays that were amusing, not too demanding intellectually, and portraying characters and situa-tions within the range of their own experience. There could be com-plications, tears and sighs, when fortune was temporarily against the hero or heroine, but all was expected to turn out well in the end, proving the platitude (frequently expressed by one of the characters) that life in a hierarchical, God-fearing society, in which everyone, especially servants, knew their place, was the best form of existence. This reassurance was especially necessary in times of civil commo-tion and social unrest which so frequently beset twentieth-century Spain.

One versatile dramatist, Jacinto Benavente, contrived both to meet the demands of such an audience and, at the same time, to rise above mediocrity, achieving international recognition through the award of a Nobel Prize for Literature in 1922. Technically competent, good theatre and demonstrating a gift for characterization, his 172 plays, most of them (although with tragic elements) ultimately comedies, are marred by his reluctance to do more than chide petty vices while attempting to correct manners. By nature Benavente was a tradi-tionalist who, after experiencing in his early years the difficulties which face the writer of 'serious' plays, decided to work within the restrictions imposed by the society which he had once attempted to reform. A good example of his abilities and his limitations is *Los intereses creados* (*Vested Interests*, 1907) in which conventional *commedia dell'arte* characters are used to expose hypocrisy and corruption and to prove the redeeming quality of true love.

Benavente, like other dramatists of his day, wrote the words for a peculiarly Spanish vehicle for comedy, the *género chico* (minor genre), that is, one-act farces, partly sung. These were for the most part set in Madrid, the characters popular types as seen through the eyes of sentimental, middle-class local patriotism, and the themes their complicated love affairs, practical jokes and lighthearted quarrels. Two brothers, Serafín and Joaquín Álvarez Quintero, changed the setting to Andalusia, diminished the musical content, emphasized the dialogue and became masters of the genre in a revised form. They brought colour, wit and gaiety to the stage and created comedies set in a folkloric world of women in *mantillas* and men with guitars which foreigners imagine to be typically Spanish. For some critics, their contemporary Carlos Arniches was their superior in that, although utilizing the comic conventions of the *género chico*, he revealed the sadness and hopelessness of the picaresque existence of the poor people of Madrid.

Understandably, the serious writers of the 'Generation of '98' (so called because of their preoccupation with the rehabilitation of Spain after the loss of Cuba) were alienated from a theatrical public which demanded to be entertained rather than instructed. Their appeal was to an intellectual minority which could best be reached through the essay, poetry and the novel. Thus Miguel de Unamuno, who, when a young man, wrote an essay to demonstrate that the best way to reach the people was through a revival of the popular techniques of Spanish Golden Age drama, managed to get eight of the eleven plays which he wrote performed, but with scant acclaim. Even when he attempted farce as a means to inculcate a serious message (*La Princesa doña Lambra* and *La difunta* (*The Deceased*), both 1909), he was too cerebral for the audience he wished to impress. They and their successors preferred sentimental comedies as written by Martínez Sierra.

When writers of real talent and public concern turned to the theatre, even if it meant scant reward either in terms of money or public recognition, they were more inclined to tragedy than to comedy, or favoured symbolic or poetic drama. Many of the great literary names of the twenties and thirties therefore do not appear in this survey. Two dictatorships, civil war, repression, censorship and enforced or self-imposed exile have deprived Spain of much literature, including comedies which might have brought delight as well as salutary instruction. Thus playgoers in Spain of taste and intellect have been obliged until recently to content themselves, in respect of new or experimental comedy, with reading (if they could obtain them) works written abroad, like the French translations of the

Beckett-like plays of Fernando Arrabal. Meanwhile, insignificant although entertaining comedies by Alfonso Paso dominated the commercial theatre. Nevertheless it must be acknowledged that Miguel Mihura, a writer for the humorous periodical *La Codorniz* (*The Quail*), has shown that he can do for the Spanish stage what Ionesco has done for the European theatre, although his idiosyncratic combination of wit and absurdity is perhaps something only Spaniards can fully appreciate. He demonstrated that, even under a dictatorship, comedy can be the means whereby the little man can mock authority, and the intellectual can discreetly protest against a society hemmed in by conventions.

Within the last years, following the demise of General Franco and the attempted liberalization of Spanish institutions, there are prospects of a revitalization of the Spanish theatre. The old public is disappearing or has disappeared. A new generation, anxious to experience in Spain significant plays similar to those they have read about or seen abroad, will provide the new audience. There is no lack of dramatic talent to cater for this new enthusiasm.

5

Comedy in France

W. D. HOWARTH

IF THERE is one characteristic that distinguishes post-Renaissance French comedy from that of other European countries, it might be defined as a recurrent search for aesthetic purity. Not only did French classical dramaturgy eschew any mixing of the genres, so that scenes of comic relief in tragedy, such as Shakespeare creates with his porter and his gravediggers, would have been quite unthinkable in the French tradition; but even within comedy itself the seventeenth-century practitioners inherited from their Renaissance predecessors a keen regard for the distinction between comedy and farce. Comedy, if it was to be acceptable to critics and cultured playgoers, must deal in a refined way with a refined subject matter; while the grosser, coarser kind of comic material was to be banished to the sub-literary genre of farce. This characteristic notion of a hierarchy of genres and styles has been a dominant feature of the French attitude towards dramatic writing from the sixteenth through to the twentieth century; and if a similar attitude has also from time to time found favour in other countries, this has been during periods (such as the eighteenth century) when French influence has prevailed abroad. As might be expected, practice has not always corresponded to theory, even in France, and the history of French comedy shows a frequent revitalizing of the literary form by inspiration from foreign, or popular, sources; but such borrowings have nearly always been controlled by an overriding respect for formal and tonal unity.

'A portrait of the manners and conversation of men and women of good breeding': this definition of comedy by Pierre Corneille is important not only for what it includes but also for what it leaves out; and that his exclusion of what we should call genuinely 'comic' material was no accident is shown in the same passage, written in 1660, in which he looks back on his first play. *Mélite* (1629) has the sort of conventional plot in which one can see the influence of the Italian pastoral tradition: two lovers are separated by the trick of a jealous rival, and on the discovery of his trickery they are enabled to marry. One detailed development of the plot shows Éraste, overwhelmed by the (false) news of the death of Tircis and Mélite, of which he believes he is the cause, going temporarily out of his mind. Thinking he is in Hades, he greets his friends as mythological characters, and keeps up a sustained flight of fancy for 150 lines. To the modern reader this imaginative episode, with its extravagant fantasy, constitutes the most obviously comic element of the play; yet it was precisely this extravagance that caused the older Corneille to deplore it, as a youthful concession to popular taste inconsistent with a more sober and restrained view of the nature of comedy. The half-dozen plays Corneille wrote in keeping with this doctrine between 1629 and 1635 were largely responsible for establishing the formula of literary comedy that was to remain in favour for so long; though his own most celebrated comedy *Le Menteur* (*The Liar*, 1642) was to incorporate into this formula a much more imaginative kind of comic writing, derived in this instance from a Spanish model. The hero is a seventeenth-century antecedent of our own Billy Liar: a compulsive mythomaniac for whom the truth is never interesting enough, and whose flights of fancy constantly land him in trouble. While his counterpart in Alarcón's original is finally punished for his failing, Corneille's dénouement lacks this moral element. Dorante is presented in a sympathetic light, and as we laugh at the discomfiture of his bewildered valet or at the mortification of his outraged father, we connive at his peccadilloes in the interests of pure entertainment.

But the influence of the Spanish *comedia*, while producing some pleasing examples of comedy based on fantasy and burlesque, was limited; and the inspiration that revitalized French comic drama came from the popular farce tradition despised by the purists. For both the native French farce, surviving from the Middle Ages, and the *commedia dell'arte*, more recently acclimatized in France by a succession of Italian troupes, were to be exploited and developed by Molière the playwright, to cater for the needs of Molière the comic actor. French farce was no more than a simple sketch focusing on the caricatural presentation of recognizable types, in the manner of a modern TV comedy series; plot was rudimentary, and what mattered were characters and relationships – especially the conjugal relationship in a domestic situation. In the fifteenth-century *Le Cuvier* (*The Washtub*), for instance, a henpecked husband is forced to write out and sign a long list of duties imposed on him by his shrewish wife: rise at dawn, light the fire, wash the dishes, make the bed . . .; when she overbalances and falls into the washtub, he is able to claim that rescuing her does not figure on the list, and he agrees to pull her out only after negotiating a (no doubt temporary) alleviation of his domestic burden. Italian farce, by contrast, dealt with the fortunes of young lovers, aided by a resourceful servant to overcome the traditional obstacle (a father's disapproval, a favoured rival): the action was quick and lively, and interest derived from the complications of a relatively intricate plot.

At the beginning of his career Molière borrowed freely from both of these farce traditions; but at a certain moment we can see Mascarille, the scheming, extrovert italianate valet whom he had created in his early plays, being replaced by the more passive, reflective Sganarelle whose origins are in the French farce, and who was to inspire the most characteristic creations of the mature Molière. Only once did the playwright return to the Italian manner, and the late play *Les Fourberies de Scapin* (*Scapin's Tricks*, 1671), though stigmatized by Molière's contemporary Boileau as a regrettable concession to popular taste, is a fine example of the fully developed *commedia*-style comedy, combining lively, amusing dialogue with vigorous physical action in a fast-moving plot controlled by Scapin's fertile genius.

Characters like Mascarille or Scapin may be said to symbolize the comic dramatist himself: they manipulate the other characters like a puppeteer with his marionettes. But this is two-dimensional theatre: Scapin, Mascarille and the stock Italian types who surround them are 'flat' characters, as Corneille's Dorante had been; they lack that extra dimension of truth to life with which Molière was able to endow his Sganarelle type and its later derivatives. There is abundant contemporary evidence of the way in which the Sganarelle figure brought out the comic actor's gifts:

> Never was anything seen so diverting as the posturings of Sganarelle behind his wife's back. His facial movements and gestures give such a convincing representation of jealousy that even without speaking he would be recognized as the most jealous of men. . . . One would need the brush of Poussin, Le Brun or Mignard in order to do justice to his admirable antics. You never heard such a simpleton, nor saw such a foolish face; and one doesn't know whether to admire the author more for the way he has written the play, or the way he acts it.

This was no mere literary comedy, but comic drama depending on the complete integration of the spoken word with all the ancillary arts of mime, gesture and movement; and when the same Sganarelle figure, from his rudimentary beginnings in a one-act sketch, developed into the central comic character of five-act verse plays, French classical comedy was given a new and quite distinctive form. The landmark in this respect is *L'École des femmes* (*A School for Wives*, 1662); and the critical debate this play aroused enables us to assess Molière's true relationship to the popular farce tradition. The plot is conventional, combining material from an Italian and a Spanish source; but what interests the spectator is less the twists and turns of the plot, or the outrageously contrived ending, than the way in which the central character of Arnolphe is presented, as the source from which much of the plot, and most of the comic effect, derive. This is surely what we mean by 'comedy of character': the mainspring of the comedy is no longer the dramatist's arbitrary whim, as he manipulates a group of pasteboard puppets, but the actions and reactions of a convincing psychological type, placed in a certain situation which forces him to reveal the absurdity of his dominant obsession. In Arnolphe's case, this is his fear of being made a cuckold. He has reached middle age without marrying, but has selected as his prospective wife a young girl whom he has brought up in seclusion so that she shall be too naïve and ignorant to deceive him. While he is away from home Agnès meets, and falls in love with, the young Horace; and in a series of soliloquies by Arnolphe, and scenes between him and Agnès, we are shown the progress of his outraged sense of possession and wounded pride, and the development of his jealousy as he realizes he now loves the girl too much to let her go. When he finally goes down on his knees and pleads with her, offering in unambiguous terms to share her with Horace, this is not pathetic (as such a plea might be in a different context) but richly comic: Arnolphe has forfeited our sympathy by his selfish, tyrannical behaviour, and we know Molière himself played the scene in an exaggerated, farcical style, 'with ridiculous sighs and rolling his eyes in an extravagant manner'. This did not suit the purists, however, who saw in the play an unsatisfactory mixture of two separate styles. Molière must make up his mind, says their spokesman Lysidas in *La Critique de l'École des femmes* (*A School for Wives Criticized*, 1663), the brilliant conversation piece in which the author defends his play against current attacks: either *L'École des femmes* was a farce – in which case Arnolphe should not have been shown with those lifelike and sympathetic traits that go towards making him a rounded character – or else it was a comedy 'according to the rules' – in which case the central character should not be portrayed in such a ridiculous light. Certain aspects of the play, in other words, were too 'comic' to deserve a place in a 'comedy'. Molière's reply, expressed by the enlightened character who represents his views, is simple but far-reaching: there is no reason, Dorante says, why a character should not be a sympathetic representative of ordinary men and women in some respects, and a figure of fun in others. With this basic formula, at an early stage in his career, Molière consciously inaugurates the fusion of the refined literary comedy then in vogue with the aesthetic principle of popular farce: that is to say, the arousing of laughter by caricatural exaggeration of selected traits of human behaviour.[1] Some contemporaries dismissed him scornfully as 'the finest farce-player in France' – but, seen in its proper light, such an appellation is a tribute to the distinctive element by which this gifted playwright, desirous of exploiting his own talents as an actor, succeeded in revitalizing a literary form which was in danger of becoming characterless and insipid.

While the knockabout antics and other elements of visual spectacle that we normally consider typical of farcical comedy are not entirely absent from L'École des femmes, they are confined to scenes with servants and are unimportant in the overall composition of the play; and the same could be said of most of Molière's major comedies. If we analyse the other kinds of comic material present in such a play, we can distinguish various sorts of verbal comedy: scenes of patterned dialogue, which make us laugh by means of repetition and contrast; inventive rhymes, and ingenious use of the verse form, whose comic effect depends on surprise; and passages parodying the heroic style of tragedy, which amuse us by their incongruity in a domestic context. Some of these features, it is true, are independent of characterization, and show the virtuosity of an author exploiting all the possibilities that literary comedy offered; but there is no doubt that the most distinctive comic element is that deriving from Arnolphe's character, as every step he takes turns to his disadvantage, and he passes from complacent self-confidence to bewildered frustration. This process, so characteristic of Molière's mature plays, illustrates a form of intellectual comedy in which the mechanism of popular farce can still be seen, but in which it is translated from a visual, physical medium into something more cerebral. Molière has taken over two variants of the basic formula of farce. More commonly, the action depends on the interplay between a gullible, naïve character with a dominant obsession (the Sganarelle type) and a scheming knave who exploits that obsession (a development of the earlier Mascarille): this pattern is common to Tartuffe (1669), Le Bourgeois Gentilhomme (The Would-be Nobleman, 1670), Les Femmes savantes (The Learned Ladies, 1672) and Le Malade imaginaire (The Imaginary Invalid, 1673). Sometimes, however – this is notably the case with L'École des femmes and Le Misanthrope (1666) – the trickster is absent, and the central figure, the object of our laughter (these characters were invariably played by Molière himself), brings about his own downfall. This he does by his egoism and complacency, and by an unreasoning reliance on doc-

[1] See Introduction to Molière, L'École des femmes and La Critique de l'École des femmes, ed. W. D. Howarth (Oxford, 1963).

trinaire theory rather than empirical practice. With Arnolphe, everything is subordinated to his obsession with cuckoldry, and the elaborate precautions he has taken to guard against conjugal misfortune:
he is the deceived husband of the farces, transformed into a
respected, worthy citizen whose one *idée fixe* makes him a figure of
fun. And, like the rest of Molière's heroes, he provides an admirable
illustration of Bergson's theory of laughter: such characters are comic
because of the rigidity of their outlook on life, the mechanical inflexibility of their behavioural responses. Monsieur Jourdain, the
'would-be nobleman', who is quite happy to wear a new coat, made
with its pattern upside-down, once his tailor has persuaded him that
this is the latest fashion among the gentry, is another excellent
example of this comic rigidity: everything he says or does is determined by the way he thinks the nobility behave. Another example is
Argan, the hypochondriac hero of *Le Malade imaginaire*, who carries
his obsession with ill-health and medicaments to such lengths that he
anxiously asks how many grains of salt he should take with his boiled
egg. These are caricatural portraits, it is true, and sufficient imagination has gone into their creation to make them ready targets for our
laughter; but the reality they caricature is never so remote that they
become mere creatures of fantasy.

The critical problem posed by Molière's formula for comedy based
on character – how far can the playwright go in presenting a
'rounded', sympathetic figure and still make him the mainspring of
the play's comic effect? – is seen at its most acute in the case of *Le
Misanthrope*. Here, the comic pattern of the character whose practice
contradicts his doctrinaire theorizing is so intellectualized and refined
that its affinities with the mechanism of farce are often overlooked.
Alceste, the idealist who denounces all hypocrites and flatterers, is
only too keen to have his own superior merits recognized, and only
too ready to make compromises with his ideal of sincerity in the case
of his love for the coquette Célimène. However, the issue is blurred by
the fact that Alceste delivers telling criticisms of the society in which
he lives – which does seem to be largely composed of fops and frauds;
while matters have been further confused by critics who see in the
Alceste–Célimène relationship a 'confessional' account of Molière's
own marital misfortunes. When we laugh at Alceste it may well be, to
use a contemporary's felicitous phrase, with 'the laughter of the
mind'; but that should not obscure the family likeness between this
opinionated, irascible character, living in an unreal fantasy world
where he is right and everyone else wrong, and the Sganarelle-figure
as he appears in Molière's other comedies. There can be little doubt
that a production that brings out this family likeness will be nearer to
the spirit in which the play was originally conceived than the

nineteenth-century interpretation which saw Alceste as the noble victim of a heartless and hypocritical society.

A comparison of *Le Misanthrope* with Wycherley's adaptation of it in *The Plain Dealer* (1676) not only serves to emphasize the streamlining and refinement that French comedy had undergone at Molière's hands – in that the English playwright finds it necessary to fill out the latter's plot, to add subplots, and to introduce a much greater variety of comic tone – but also underlines at the same time the continuing, fundamental link between Alceste and the farcical Sganarelle. Whereas Wycherley's Manly, though equally extreme in his condemnation of hypocrisy and insincerity, is given some retrospective justification by the treachery of Olivia and Vernish, and is finally allowed to find compensation in the devoted love of Fidelia, the relationship between Alceste and Célimène is characterized by a real ambiguity. It is impossible to be sure of the true nature of Célimène's feelings and of the degree of sincerity which underlies her declared affection for Alceste, and consequently impossible to dogmatize about the latter's moral justification for his jealous behaviour; but what is certain is that, whatever his justification, Alceste constantly makes himself ridiculous by his vanity, pomposity and readiness to take offence. In other words, in *Le Misanthrope* character remains the mainspring of the comic action, whereas in Wycherley's play we are much more concerned with the working-out of a complicated plot, whose outcome hardly at all depends on the character of the Plain Dealer.[2]

Not that Molière himself was unskilled at plot-comedy: as we have seen, *Les Fourberies de Scapin* marks a brilliant late return to this genre. And it would be wrong in any case to present Molière as the author of a single, exclusive type of comedy. If his five-act verse comedies like *L'École des femmes*, *Le Misanthrope*, *Tartuffe* and *Les Femmes savantes* were to enjoy – and still do enjoy – a special prestige, these plays form only a small proportion of the thirty-odd that he wrote. Others, written to a similar formula, are in prose; Molière also wrote, for court performance, a number of 'comedy-ballets' to the music of Lully and others, in which literary comedy was enhanced by the added delights of sung dialogue, choreography and spectacular visual effects; nor should one overlook the importance in his drama of satire directed against pedants and professionals of all kinds: his portraits of affected poets and pedantic doctors must have scored more than one telling hit against the ornaments of the profession and the idols of the salons.

But more and more, in the century following his death, the variety and virtuosity of Molière's comedy were lost sight of, and his name

---

[2] A similar remark could be made about the way in which Wycherley treated the basic material of *L'École des femmes*, in incorporating it into *The Country Wife* (1675).

became almost exclusively associated with the formula that had produced *Le Misanthrope* and *Tartuffe*. This is well illustrated by the fate of
his *Dom Juan*, which when it had appeared in 1665 had been at once a
remarkable attempt to acclimatize into the France of Louis XIV the
freer and more turbulent Spanish *comedia* of a generation earlier, and
a virtuoso display of Molière's own range of comic writing. Public
outcry by the devout cut short the play's run, and it was never revived
in Molière's lifetime; but it had been a box-office success, and after his
death Thomas Corneille was commissioned to present it in a more
acceptable form. This he did by removing, or toning down, the most
provocative elements – and by turning the play into verse, thus not
only making it 'respectable' but giving it an additional literary cachet.
And it was in this emasculated form that *Dom Juan*, recognized today
as one of Molière's undoubted masterpieces, which, for all the problems of interpretation posed by its casual – or hasty – composition,
nevertheless possesses the real stamp of genius, was to be known to
the public for no less than 170 years.

A culture so timid towards the outstanding plays of the past was
inevitably unadventurous with regard to new productions by
contemporary dramatists. The thirty or forty years following
Molière's death in 1673 did, it is true, produce talented playwrights
who were able to stand on their own feet, and who made a distinctive
contribution to French comic drama within the framework established by Molière. Florent Carton Dancourt, in *Le Chevalier à la mode*
(*The Man About Town*, 1687) and other comedies of manners, satirized
the social climbing of an increasingly mercenary bourgeois society;
Alain-René Lesage's *Turcaret* (1709) contains a much more biting
satire of various kinds of financier, and offers a very cynical view of
the society in which they operated; while Jean-François Regnard, in
plays like *Le Légataire universel* (*The Universal Legatee*, 1708), created a
lighthearted type of comedy largely dependent on verbal inventive-
ness and a sense of the inconsequential. But writers of lesser talent
were to find themselves more and more inhibited by the example, and
the reputation, of Molière – a state of affairs encouraged by the
conservatism of the Comédie-Française (founded in 1680 by a royal
decree amalgamating existing troupes). At the 'House of Molière', as
this theatre was soon familiarly called, everything favoured derivative, second-hand versions of his five-act comedy based on character:
But once the inspiration had gone from these plays – and it was not
long before playwrights were complaining that Molière had 'taken all
the interesting characters' – this became a very trite formula: plots and
episodes repeat each other, and comic invention gives way to senten-
tious moralizing. The one original development within the kind of
comedy favoured by the Comédie-Française was the *comédie lar-*

moyante or 'tearful comedy' pioneered by Nivelle de La Chaussée. La Chaussée's own disposition is said to have been passably cynical, but he recognized what his contemporaries wanted: a pretext for that public display of feeling that would enable them to prove their superior sensibility, and hence their moral worth. In his first plays La Chaussée retained a certain comedy of manners, as well as the traditional valet roles; but by the time of *Mélanide* (1741) and *La Gouvernante* (*The Governess*, 1747) the 'tearful' formula is fully developed. Truly comic writing has gone by the board; and if the definition 'a portrait of the manners and conversation of men and women of good breeding' does still fit such plays, the prime purpose of this framework of contemporary manners is now to show virtue undeservedly subjected to a series of trials. The spectator's tears flow in sympathy as the heroine submits passively to her misfortunes; appropriate moral platitudes underline the lesson to be drawn from the situation; and when the happy ending arrives the audience has enjoyed a thoroughly improving experience. La Chaussée was not without his critics, whose good taste led them to deplore such facile excess; though Voltaire, who called the new genre 'a kind of tragedy fit for chambermaids', himself contributed in no small way to the vogue for sentimental comedy, and was to follow La Chaussée in dramatizing Richardson's novel *Pamela* in this manner.

Though the intrinsic merit of such plays is slight enough to the modern reader, they have – like their English counterparts, the sentimental comedies of Steele and others – a certain historical importance in that their serious tone and moral emphasis prefigure the domestic drama of the next generation, whose greater attention to realistic setting in turn looks forward to nineteenth-century social comedy. The attitude towards comedy which, accepting Terence as its patron, rejected the extravagance of imaginative comic writing in the name of sober truth to nature may seem to have found little obvious expression in the mainstream of modern European drama; but the evolution of this kind of comedy, which purports to offer a faithful portrait of reality – an evolution that can be traced from Corneille, through La Chaussée, via Diderot and some of his contemporaries, to Dumas *fils*, Augier and Sardou a hundred years later – has left a not unimportant mark on French dramatic literature. Moreover, the end-term of this evolution – a comedy of manners with a strong social relevance – has affinities with, even if it cannot be proved to have influenced, the later masterpieces of Ibsen, Chekhov and Shaw. The best eighteenth-century French play inspired by this concept of domestic drama (indeed, the only one to have remained in the repertory until the twentieth century) is *Le Philosophe sans le savoir* (*The Unconscious Philosopher*, 1765) by Michel-Jean Sedaine. Diderot had argued, in the theoretical treatise attached to *Le Fils naturel* (*The Natural Son*, 1757), that both tragedy and comedy, as they had evolved in France, were outmoded, and that the meaningful drama of the future would belong to an intermediate genre of 'serious' plays capable of portraying in a responsible way the occupations and interests of ordinary people; Sedaine follows Diderot's precept, and his portrait of a merchant's household successfully illustrates the latter's recommendation that plot should derive from 'conditions' (that is, professional and social environment) rather than from the excessively abstract 'characters' of classical comedy. Sedaine's play denotes at one and the same time a return towards traditional comedy when compared with La Chaussée and Diderot (if only in the caricatural figure of a snobbish aunt, through whom the aristocratic prejudice against trade is satirized), and an advance in the direction of didactic comedy, in that it presents a humanitarian plea, very much of its time, against the barbarous custom of duelling.

Although, as a result of the conservatism of actors, critics and public, the most typical comedies produced at the Comédie-Française in the eighteenth century did not venture far from the formula established by Molière, the two outstanding comic dramatists of the century both derived their strength from alien traditions. The first of these, Pierre Carlet de Chamblain de Marivaux, made his name at the rival theatre, the Comédie-Italienne, and throughout his career was to have only moderate success at the Comédie-Française; indeed, his pre-eminence among the playwrights of this period between the classical and Romantic eras was not recognized until the twentieth century. Marivaux's most characteristic plays are a remarkable example of that 'streamlining', or search for purity of form, that has left its mark on French comic drama at various periods. He does not portray 'characters' in the accepted sense (his typical protagonists are the conventional young lovers from the Italian comedy, possessing few distinctive attributes and varying little from play to play); he seems not to have been interested in plot for plot's sake; and he showed equally little interest in the realistic portrayal of the contemporary scene. In fact, his comedy represents a throwback to the earlier dramatic tradition of the pastoral, whose stylized shepherds and shepherdesses, inhabitants of an Arcadia that never was, had ample leisure to analyse the progress of their amorous relationships. And whereas in his early plays the plot, like that of the typical pastoral, does involve a threat from a jealous rival, as in *Arlequin poli par l'amour* (*Arlequin Polished by Love*, 1720), or possibly a change of partners, as in *La Double Inconstance* (*The Double Inconstancy*, 1723), it was not long before the characteristic Marivaux plot was purged of even such distractions, in order to focus exclusively on the relationship between

one pair of lovers. External obstacles – a jealous rival, parental opposition – are replaced by a subtler form of internal, psychological barrier:
pride, timidity, the desire to remain independent, more rarely – as in
Les Fausses Confidences (*Misleading Secrets*, 1737) – class prejudice; and
Marivaux's peculiar genius enabled him repeatedly to create variations on this apparently restricted theme of developing emotional
awareness on the part of two young lovers. His young couple are
brought together, and their conversation quite literally constitutes the
action. Each wishes to attract the other, but neither wishes to be
caught; they fall in love; they become aware of their feelings; they
resist; they yield – a delicate series of stages that a conventional
comedy plot either ignores or takes for granted.

This is another kind of comedy in which the belly-laugh is
nonexistent, and in which our laughter – or our smile – acknowledges
a more muted comic effect. Occasionally Marivaux's servants, in a
cruder counterpoint to the refined behaviour of their masters, will
provoke a broader laugh, but essentially his is a type of comic drama
that calls for intellectual cooperation on the part of an audience
attuned to nuances of subtle conversational exchanges. Scornful contemporaries bestowed on Marivaux's writing the label *marivaudage*,
though the term is nowadays used more appreciatively to denote a
highly personal style which may be mannered and affected, but
which endows this author's dialogue with a truly unique status as the
generator of dramatic action. To take one example: the plot of *Le Jeu de
l'amour et du hasard* (*The Game of Love and Chance*, 1730) has at first sight
more than a little similarity to that of Goldsmith's *She Stoops to Conquer*
(1773), but a comparison of the two plays serves only to emphasize
differences of approach. At the beginning of the French play Silvia,
the heroine, decides to change places with her maid Lisette in order to
observe her suitor Dorante, who is coming to visit her, the more freely
without committing herself; what the audience knows, though Silvia
does not, is that a similar plan has occurred to Dorante, and that he
has changed places with his valet Arlequin. A highly contrived situation, perhaps – but once this contrivance has been set up there are no
further complications, and the action progresses in a series of meetings between the lovers, amusingly parodied in parallel scenes
involving Arlequin and Lisette. The dénouement can be brought
about only by the development of the characters' feelings for one
another: there is no intervention from outside, and it is the gradual
exploration by the lovers of their own, and each other's, feelings
which constitutes the action of the play, as they pass from initial
shame at being attracted by someone they consider to be a servant, to
a frank acknowledgement of their love and (in Dorante's case) a
proposal of marriage in spite of the misalliance he fancies he is

committing. Goldsmith's purpose is quite different, though Marlow too, like Dorante, takes his fiancée for a servant, and is finally brought to propose marriage to her despite disparity of rank. However, this is merely part of a whole series of comic misunderstandings, starting when Marlow and his friend are maliciously given to believe that the Hardcastles' house, to which the former is coming as a suitor, is an inn. The plot depends furthermore on an eccentric quirk of character: the diffident Marlow, so tonguetied in the presence of ladies, is as bold as brass in the presence of innkeepers and maidservants. This is something we are asked to take for granted: there is no subtle development of character, and the repeated misunderstandings are an end in themselves, as a means of arousing laughter, rather than stages marking the progression of a psychological action. The English play, though a good deal more decorous than its predecessors of a hundred years earlier, possesses much greater variety of tone and content than the French: it is amusing, lively and altogether more coarse-grained than Marivaux's delicate manner.

A cruder and more vigorous kind of comic material, such as was hardly ever absent from English comedy from the time of Shakespeare to that of Sheridan, was not unknown on the French stage; however, banished by custom from the Comédie-Française, and becoming increasingly rare at the Comédie-Italienne, it had been relegated to the popular theatres of the fairgrounds. These originally ephemeral theatres had acquired permanent status by the beginning of the eighteenth century, and their *parades*, or short comic sketches, kept alive the tradition of popular farce. Such plays, frequently licentious and obscene, and always possessing a freedom of language and subject matter unknown in the official theatres, attracted wealthy and noble patrons besides those of the lower classes; indeed, later in the century there was quite a cult for the *parade* in the private theatres fashionable among the nobility, and it was by writing *parades* for private performance that Pierre Caron de Beaumarchais made his début as a playwright. Beaumarchais's attitude towards the theatre was very much of his time: he was a sincere supporter of Diderot, and his first full-length plays were exercises in the moralizing genre of domestic drama. As such, they are not unsuccessful – and certainly worth more than Diderot's own plays – but they are entirely lacking in the sparkle and zest that characterize his two great comedies, *Le Barbier de Séville* (*The Barber of Seville*, 1775) and *Le Mariage de Figaro* (*The Marriage of Figaro*, 1784) – plays which Beaumarchais himself always held in lower esteem than his serious dramas, and which owe a big debt to his apprenticeship in the *parades*.

At first sight, *Le Barbier de Séville* might well have been written at any time in the previous 150 years. The main outline of its plot, its characters and its overall comic style are all highly traditional, though at any time it would have stood out as an excellent example of fast-moving plot-comedy depending on a valet's clever scheming. For Figaro, in this first play, is of the same family as Mascarille and Scapin, and all the Crispins and Frontins of eighteenth-century comedy. Count Almaviva and the *ingénue* Rosine are no less traditional as the sympathetic young lovers whose union Figaro brings about, while Bartholo is the conventional jealous guardian, and Bazile, though more sharply individualized, is still a recognizable version of the scholar of the farces, pedantic, grubby and mercenary. *Le Mariage de Figaro* on the other hand, even at first sight, is a much more unusual kind of play. It contains the same traditional elements, but much more as well. There is a genuinely pathetic element in the role of the Countess – for Almaviva has now been married long enough to have tired of his wife, and to be hankering after an affair with Figaro's fiancée Suzanne, so that the Rosine of *Le Mariage* has a strong affinity with the heroines of tearful comedy, as the virtuous wife abandoned by a heartless husband – or rather, she would fit squarely into that tradition if Beaumarchais had not endowed her with sufficient spirit to join forces with Suzanne and outwit her husband, and if she too were not hovering on the brink of a sentimental attachment with the young page Chérubin. The play contains a strong satirical element, strong enough to ensure its banning for several years by the censor: it attacks, through the mouth of Figaro the common man, not only the nobility's abuse of privilege but a whole range of political and social abuses from which France was suffering in the decade leading up to the Revolution: a corrupt and incompetent judiciary, arbitrary imprisonment, unjust taxation, censorship – and, as a further instance of the influence of serious didactic drama, there is also an eloquent plea for the rights of women in a society where they suffered a heavy legal and economic disadvantage. Finally, in this second play Figaro has developed considerably from the stereotyped valet of *Le Barbier*: he is scheming no longer on someone else's behalf but for himself. And when his marriage seems secure, at the end of Act III (after the count's threat to marry him to the elderly Marceline has been foiled by the surprise discovery that she is his mother), there is a novel twist to the plot, as Figaro is misled into thinking that Suzanne is in league with the count to deceive him. At this point Figaro grows into a fully rounded character, and in the structural *tour de force* of a soliloquy lasting nearly fifteen minutes he surveys his past, reflecting on the roles of birth, environment and above all chance, in shaping the life of the man in the street.

Changes of mood, of pace, of comic style, abound throughout this remarkable play, and it would be no exaggeration to say that *Le*

Mariage de Figaro represents a synthesis of all the elements that had characterized earlier French comedy. In addition, two features stand out as typical of Beaumarchais's manner in both *Le Barbier* and *Le Mariage*: features which are forward- rather than backward-looking, and which establish Beaumarchais as the initiator of much that was to typify nineteenth-century comic writing. The first is a kind of dialogue that stands on its own, largely independent of character and of dramatic situation. Such autonomous verbal comedy was not unknown in the work of earlier writers, of course: it is in fact a stylistic feature particularly characteristic of the *parades*, and the comic effect obtained by this means is the most tangible debt of *Le Mariage*, and more especially of *Le Barbier*, to Beaumarchais's early experiments with this genre. Effects achieved range from the sophistication of the epigram to the simplicity of the pun or other forms of verbal play; while some of the most striking passages (Bazile's tirade on calumny (*Barbier*, I. viii), or Figaro's 'god-dam' speech (*Mariage*, III. v)) depend on something very like a poet's careful arrangement of a phrase, by means of assonance, alliteration and similar devices.

But if this is what gives Beaumarchais's dialogue its distinctive flavour, the most important feature of his dramaturgy is his handling of a play's structure in order to create comic effect. Feydeau, one of the nineteenth-century dramatists who owed most to Beaumarchais, once described his method of composing a comedy as follows: 'When I write a play, I pick out from among the characters those who have a good reason to keep out of each other's way – and I make it my business to bring them together as soon as possible.' This formula could well provide the key to Beaumarchais's own method of composition. One scene in *Le Barbier* (III. xi) and a sequence of scenes in *Le Mariage* (I. vii–ix) stand out as having been constructed in just this way, while the more extended development of a similar procedure underlies the whole of the second half of Act II of the latter play, as well as its Act V finale. Such scenes are obviously highly contrived, and could hardly stand up to logical analysis in the name of naturalism; but they are delightfully entertaining by virtue of the surprise and suspense they generate, followed by a pleasurable relief of tension once the crisis is over. What is more, the procedure is so deliberately artificial – and so largely independent of genuine motivation by means of character – as to constitute a distinctive, and original, technique. As the critic Sarcey was to write of the brilliant scene in Act III of *Le Barbier*, in which all the other characters want to get rid of the unfortunate Bazile as soon as he appears: 'From this one scene, as from a wholly original source, developed a new kind of theatre which was to delight French audiences for a century or more.' And not only French theatre audiences, but theatre, cinema and television audiences all over the Western world, as they are entertained by the mechanics of fast-moving, farcical situation-comedy, have reason to be grateful to the author of *Le Barbier de Séville* and *Le Mariage de Figaro*.

When we come to the playwrights of the Romantic generation, in one sense – inasmuch as they were responsible for liberating French drama from the inhibitions of neoclassical theory – they may be seen as having opened up outlets for comic writing that had never existed before. Even Beaumarchais, forward-looking as he was, had kept his serious drama and his comedies rigorously apart; but Victor Hugo categorically rejected such separation of the genres as artificial. The new drama, he wrote in the Preface to *Cromwell* (1827), must embrace the whole of life: 'the ugly with the beautiful, the misshapen next to the graceful, the grotesque side by side with the sublime'. Though the juxtaposition of 'sublime' and 'grotesque' in Hugo's aesthetic cannot be limited to the inclusion of scenes of comic relief in tragedy, Shakespeare's example was nevertheless very important, and Hugo notes with approval not only the witches in *Macbeth* but also the gravediggers in *Hamlet*. In practice, Hugo's own plays illustrate very well this mixing of the genres, while what is surely the outstanding Romantic drama of the century, Edmond Rostand's *Cyrano de Bergerac* (1898), is also fully in line with Hugo's recommendations. Rostand's play is a sentimental Romantic tragedy – that is, it ends unhappily, and the hero's idealism meets with defeat and death – yet it contains a preponderance of comic scenes, and the author manipulates verbal comedy, comedy of situation and comedy of manners with a historical setting, to form a unique mixture of sentiment, lively entertainment and comic effect.

But such plays cannot really be called examples of 'comic drama'; and the spirit of literary Romanticism was no less hostile to true comedy than it was to the exclusive aesthetic of neoclassical tragedy. For all true comedy is based on the acceptance of certain social norms which the Romantic ethos, exalting the individual in his revolt against society, scornfully rejected. Readers and spectators, instead of laughing at the characters of comedy because they refused to follow accepted patterns of behaviour, now tended to see them as brave idealists defeated by a conformist society; and in this context it might almost seem that the test of a genuine Romantic sensibility was whether or not one identified with Molière's Alceste in his noble isolation from a hostile world.

Only one of the major Romantic dramatists was capable of assuming the necessary objectivity to write not just occasional scenes of comedy but plays in which the comic mood is sustained throughout. However, the position of Alfred de Musset as a writer of comedy is highly paradoxical. He was to write, in lines inspired by a performance of *Le Misanthrope*, of Molière's 'virile gaiety, which masks such a profound melancholy that instead of laughing at the play we ought to weep'; and his own early plays reflect his unhappy love affairs with George Sand and other women. Musset's world resembles Marivaux's, with a similar delicacy of psychological analysis quite unlike the cruder posturings of contemporary Romantic heroes; but it also reveals a greater measure of comic invention, for his young lovers are surrounded by genuinely amusing caricatures. Yet in his most distinctive plays, it is a precarious world, shattered by the sudden intrusion of a harsh reality: indeed, in two of Musset's 'comedies', *Les Caprices de Marianne* (*Marianne's Caprice*, 1833) and *On ne badine pas avec l'amour* (*There is no Trifling with Love*, 1834), the *marivaudage* ends not in the lovers' happy union but in a death. There is the same conflict as we have observed in Marivaux between love on the one hand and pride or self-love on the other; but the selfishness of Musset's characters – especially the women in each case – is too strong, and idealized Romantic love is defeated by the realities of human nature. It is doubtful whether such plays can be called comedies at all; in any case, their peculiar bitter-sweet flavour is quite unique – or was to remain unique until Jean Anouilh reproduced a very similar mixture of moods in some of his plays of the 1950s: *La Répétition* (*The Rehearsal*, 1950), for instance, in which a savage dénouement is imposed on an urbane comedy of manners, reflects the same inability on the part of a disillusioned Romantic to sustain through to the end the optimistic, or escapist, mood of comedy. However, in Musset's own case, while disillusionment and cynicism provide the characteristic flavour of these early comedies, later plays show the capacity to adopt a more detached attitude towards his characters, and to preserve the tone of comedy without entirely forfeiting the Romantic idealism typical of the literature of the period. In *Le Chandelier* (*The Decoy*, 1835), *Barberine* (1835) and *Il ne faut jurer de rien* (*You Never Can Tell*, 1836) there is a complete homogeneity between idealistic theme, Romantic mood and happy ending.

Common to both these groups of plays is their unreality of setting and imaginative invention. Musset's name is also associated, however, with a quite different kind of comedy, which looks back towards the eighteenth century as well as anticipating later developments in the nineteenth. This is the 'proverb', originally fashionable in the private theatres of the *ancien régime* as a short sketch, not unlike a charade, whose action illustrated a well-known proverb which the audience were asked to identify. Already before the Revolution certain authors had specialized in this minor genre, using it as a vehicle for portraits of contemporary society; and when Musset took it up in his turn he produced some brilliant little conversation pieces. The charade element has by now disappeared; there is virtually no plot; and the interest resides in the realistic recording of the speech and manners of a cultured society (once more, the echo of Corneille's seventeenth-century definition is unmistakable). Plays like *Un Caprice* (*A Caprice*, 1837) and *Il faut qu'une porte soit ouverte ou fermée* (*A Door Must be either Open or Shut*, 1845) were soon firmly established in the repertory of the Comédie-Française, where they are still among the most popular curtain-raisers; and with Musset's 'proverbs', comedy of manners comes closer than ever before to the unadorned, documentary 'slice of life' which writers of the naturalist school were to demand as the only valid form of drama.

But in this respect Musset was well in advance of his time, for the nineteenth century was the age of the 'well-made play'; and following the example already set by Beaumarchais, Eugène Scribe and his successors exploited a form of situation-comedy in which plots were held together not by theme or character but by ingenious construction. The term 'well-made play' was of course originally used literally, in a complimentary sense, but it was not long before it took on an ironical, pejorative meaning; and by the end of the century the conventions and artifice of the well-made play had become the principal target of the hostile criticism, both of Zola and other naturalist writers in France, and of Shaw in Britain. However, this criticism was chiefly directed against the incongruous use of this extremely artificial manner in the kind of play in which plausibility and truth to life are usually thought desirable – that is to say, in historical drama, and in didactic comedy with a social message – and not so much against what might be called 'theatre for theatre's sake': the sort of *comédie-vaudeville* which aims at nothing more than entertainment, and in which the playwright's selfconscious manipulation of characters and situations often increases, rather than detracts from, the spectator's enjoyment. As Shaw's term 'sardoodledom' indicates, the historical and social dramas of Victorien Sardou were his particular *bête noire*; while the target chosen by Zola was the social comedy of Alexandre Dumas*fils*.

Here, the characters' behaviour, even if it does illustrate the manners of a particular society, is subordinated to the needs of a thesis. Dumas made no bones about the artificial construction of his plots: 'a dénouement', he said, 'should always represent the arithmetical sum of the situations, passions and characters presented during the course of the play'. One result is that our consciousness of the author's 'mathematical' contrivances often stands in the way of a ready acceptance of the thesis; another is that Dumas's characters either remain the prisoners of an excessively artifical plot – this is the case with the hero of *Le Fils naturel* (*The Natural Son*, 1858) – or else, like Olivier de Jalins in *Le Demi-Monde* (*The Fringe of Society*, 1855) with his celebrated speech comparing the *demi-mondaine* to the flawed fruit in a basket of peaches, are too obviously mouthpieces for the author's own over-literary rhetoric.

In *comédie-vaudeville*, however, the 'well-made play' formula comes into its own. The more ingenious misunderstandings a playwright can pack into two hours, the more mechanically and artificially the plot proceeds from one complicated crisis to another, the better. Nor does it matter how preposterous are the assumptions on which all this rests. For instance, a young man's horse, on the morning of his wedding day, eats a lady's flowered hat, and its loss puts her in such a compromising situation that the wedding reception is suspended while the young man, though a complete stranger, embarks on a frantic search for an identical hat, before the lady's husband can discover its loss. This absurd premiss is the basis of the plot of *Un Chapeau de paille d'Italie* (*An Italian Straw Hat*, 1851) by Eugène Labiche, and the spectator accepts it without demur, for it is part of the charm of such comedy that it generates its own crazy logic: a self-contained system of cause and effect which parodies the logic of the real world. Labiche was one of the great masters of this style: it was he, together with Georges Feydeau in plays like *Une Puce à l'oreille* (*A Flea in Her Ear*, 1907) or *Occupe-toi d'Amélie* (*Look After Lulu*, 1908), who succeeded in raising farcical situation-comedy, embodying the mechanical construction of the well-made play, from the level of ephemeral entertainment to that of an art form taken seriously by students of drama, and consecrated by acceptance at the Comédie-Française. In English drama the influence of the kind of comedy created by Labiche has been equally fertile: Pinero's *Magistrate* and Wilde's *Importance of Being Earnest* testify to this influence – to say nothing of the Aldwych farces of Ben Travers, or the situation-comedies that have proliferated not only in the modern theatre but also in the cinema and on the television screen.

Once more, as in the seventeenth century with Molière and in the eighteenth with Beaumarchais, a derivative and rather lifeless literary comedy was revitalized by borrowing from a more vigorous form of popular theatre. But the comedy of Labiche and Feydeau nevertheless still remains unmistakably a literary form; and although a full appreciation of their plays must depend on visual effect in the theatre, it would be wrong to overlook the role of the polished, witty dialogue which produces constant verbal comedy. Indeed, Émile Augier, another Second Empire playwright, writes of Labiche:

> His theatre gains one hundred per cent on being read, not just seen: its burlesque element stands out less clearly, but the comic element comes fully into its own. When you laugh, it is no longer

with the reflex action of a man being tickled by a feather, it is with a whole-hearted kind of laughter in which the intellect too has its part.

A measure of the traditional character of even this kind of comic drama is provided by a comparison with the iconoclastic novelty of Alfred Jarry's *Ubu roi* (*Ubu Rex*). When it was first performed in 1896, this play had no more than a *succès de scandale*; and it was not until well into the twentieth century that it was taken up by the surrealist avant-garde and hailed as an influential precursor of their own ideas. A burlesque parody of *Macbeth*, *Ubu roi* is the work of a dramatist who has rejected traditional ideas of coherent character, intelligible motivation and logical plot construction: it is a challenge not only to the well-made play but to all drama based on these rational concepts. In that it marks the intrusion of the gratuitous and the inconsequential into the field of artistic creation, *Ubu roi* heralds the breakdown of that respect for purity of form and unity of tone that we have seen as characteristic of the French contribution to European drama.

For in France as elsewhere the twentieth century has witnessed the almost complete abandonment of the conventional notion of separate genres, each with its own aesthetic laws, and kept apart by fixed barriers. The run-of-the-mill drama of the commercial theatre has of course hardly reflected this development, and situation-comedy based on traditional formulas, such as those of the bedroom farce or the thriller, shows little sign of losing its appeal with popular audiences. Among plays with more serious literary or theatrical ambitions, the first quarter of the century continued to produce essays in the classical manner: for instance, in the satirical *Knock* (1923) by Jules Romains, the central relationship between trickster and dupe recalls that between Molière's Mascarille and Sganarelle types, while *Le Cocu magnifique* (*The Magnificent Cuckold*, 1920) by Fernand Crommelynck is a vintage character-comedy, with something of *Le Misanthrope's* enigmatic quality. In some of his plays such as *Amphitryon 38* (1929) or *La Folle de Chaillot* (*The Madwoman of Chaillot*, 1945), Jean Giraudoux chose a traditional form of comedy as the vehicle for the humanistic message which characterized all his writing; but it would be impossible not to see Jean Cocteau, who prefaced his version of the Oedipus tragedy, *La Machine infernale* (*The Infernal Machine*, 1934), with 'an opening act of broad farce', and Eugène Ionesco, who called his one-act play *Les Chaises* (*The Chairs*, 1952) a 'tragic farce', as more representative of the creative spirit of the mid-century, reluctant to be confined by predetermined categories. Jean Anouilh did write several 'rose-coloured plays', as he preferred to call them, in the period before and just after the 1939–45 war; but in his later writing Anouilh has marked out for himself an idiosyncratic no-man's land between comedy and tragedy, and he has never again achieved the unambiguously escapist fantasy of his early *Le Bal des voleurs* (*Thieves' Carnival*, 1938).

The years since 1945 have merely accelerated the process begun fifty years earlier with *Ubu roi*; and, each in its own way, nearly every example of the avant-garde drama of the postwar decades defies classification. Into what conventional category could one possibly put Samuel Beckett's masterpiece *En attendant Godot* (*Waiting for Godot*, 1953) – a play which, for all its comic repartee, offers the most searching reflections on the enigma of the human condition? Moreover, one of the most striking features of the postwar theatre is its cosmopolitan character. French playwrights are now far more likely to be influenced by Pirandello or Brecht, Pinter or the Marx Brothers, than by Molière or Marivaux; and the specifically French contribution to European drama – including a tradition of comic writing which remained so distinctive for nearly three centuries – is now merged in a Western culture whose ceaseless search for new modes of expression pays little heed to national boundaries.

6

English comedy

ARNOLD HARE

To WRITE comprehensively in small compass about four centuries of English comedy is not possible. To write for a predominantly English-speaking readership complicates the problem further – Everyman already has his own idiosyncratic notions on the subject, based on a personal repertoire of the plays he happens to have seen and read and enjoyed. Moreover, to speak of 'English' comedy may be thought presumptuous, when a number of its representative writers – Farquhar, Sheridan, Goldsmith, Macklin, O'Keeffe, Boucicault, Wilde, Shaw – were Irish by birth, or had an Irish upbringing; though since (unlike the later O'Casey, for instance) they wrote consciously in an English context, their inclusion in the tradition is obviously legitimate. Nevertheless, with such reservations to be made, what is attempted here can be nothing more than a personal assessment, and as such is as likely to provoke argument as agreement. Since there has never been a critical consensus about the nature and purpose of comedy in England, this should hardly be a cause for surprise.

The divergence of views concerning it can be neatly symbolized in that 1733 engraving by William Hogarth which has come to be known as *The Laughing Audience*. In the pit of a Georgian playhouse a cross-section of the audience, male and female, old and young, is shown revelling (in one case even to the point of tears of laughter) in the unseen comedy being played out on the stage. But to one side is another character, totally unmoved, not even looking directly at the action before him, looking down his long nose and registering disapproval with every line of his superior countenance. Is he a jealous fellow author? A Puritan, a Jeremy Collier of the 1730s? The generally accepted view is that he is intended to represent a critic, and one nineteenth-century commentator is explicit about him:

> By his saturnine cast of face and contracted brow he is evidently a profound critic, and much too wise to laugh. This it is to be so

excellent a judge; this it is which gives a critic that exalted gratification which can never be attained by the illiterate – the supreme power of pointing out faults where others discern nothing but beauties, and preserving a rigid inflexibility of muscle while the sides of the vulgar herd are shaking with laughter.[1]

Leaving aside the question of whether the comment is intended to be taken ironically or at face value, this notion of laughter as being something vulgar or inferior has bedevilled English comedy from the time of Sir Philip Sidney to that recent school of academic critics for whom the ability to gain pleasure from a work seems an immediate cause of suspicion as to its moral or aesthetic purity.

The difficulty arises from the fact that comedy has more than one function. The traditional view, taken by Sidney to defend poetry against its attackers, was that the prime function of comedy is as a corrective – its object to demonstrate deviations from the ideal, and thereby to drive us to avoid or minimize in our own lives similar shortcomings. Comedy, wrote Sidney, 'is an imitation of the common errors of our life, which he representeth in the most ridiculous and scornful sort that may be; so as it is impossible that any beholder can be content to be such an one' (*An Apologie for Poetry*, 1595). But there is another element in comedy which has been less frequently insisted upon in theory, though by their devotion to it in practice it is undeniably understood by audiences and readers – that positive, life-affirming quality of comedy, the manner in which it induces enjoyment and acceptance of the vagaries, the follies, the foibles, the inequities, the eccentricities, the absurdities of humanity, as a result of which we emerge more reconciled to the strains and stresses of life, more ready to come to terms with its inevitable end.

To be fair to Sidney, he is aware of this life-affirming element in comedy. He calls it delight. But because he realizes that delight can come from other sources too, he tends to depreciate the contribution of laughter. 'Delight hath a joy in it, either permanent or present. Laughter hath only a scornful tickling.' And though he then admits that the two may go well together, he insists finally on the pre-eminence of didacticism in comedy.

> I speak to this purpose, that all the end of the comical part be not upon such scornfull matters as stirreth laughter only: but mixt with it, that delightful teaching which is the end of Poesy.

In practice, both functions are proper to comedy, and often they operate in tandem. But they need not do so; they can operate separ-

---

[1] J. Trusler, J. Nicholls and J. Ireland, *The Works of William Hogarth with Descriptions and Explanations* (London, n.d.), p. 49.

ately; and when this happens the critical tendency in England has often been to follow Sidney, to regard the moral corrective, however poorly carried out, as the important purpose, and to denigrate the life enhancement, however powerful, as a cheaper article. This is essentially the attitude that Goldsmith was later to attack in his *Essay on the Theatre; or a Comparison between Laughing and Sentimental Comedy* (1772), and he ended with a warning of the danger of forsaking humour in the theatre.

> It is not easy to recover an art when once lost; and it will be but a just punishment, that when, by our being too fastidious, we have banished humour from the stage, we should ourselves be deprived of the art of laughing.

Fortunately we were not so deprived; but the argument about the two approaches still goes on.

They can be seen dramatically operating side by side in the late sixteenth and early seventeenth centuries in the comedies of Shakespeare and Jonson. When in the 1590s Ben Jonson stepped forth to whip hypocrisy, he saw himself firmly based in the classical corrective tradition of comedy. Not for him fantastic or Arcadian settings and plots, but a cool realistic look at the urban scene he knew so well, and for which he found precedent in both Terence and Plautus. And many of the characters in his first great success *Everyman in his Humour* (1598, revised and anglicized *c*. 1616) have their prototypes in the Roman comedy – Bobadil the braggart soldier, Kitely the jealous husband, Brainworm the ingenious servant (with a dash in him, also, of the tricky Vice of the medieval morality). But it is one of the minor ironies of literary life that the man who saw himself setting classical restraint against the extravagance of romance was in many ways the least restrained of men and writers. Opinionated, arrogant, flailing wildly around with the gusto of the selfrighteous, attempting to pay off his own personal feuds and enmities by public caricature (*Everyman Out of His Humour*, 1599, and the two plays that followed), he bestrode the narrow world of the London theatrical scene like a twitching colossus. He made (indeed he set out to make) enemies public and private; he had at least one murder on his own conscience; and he looked at the greed, corruption and deceit of the society he saw around him and determined, without fear or favour, to lash the whore in the market place.

In the Prologue to *Everyman Out of His Humour*, the presenter, Asper, might well be Jonson himself.

Away!

Who is so patient of this impious world,
That he can check his spirit, or rein his tongue?

Or who hath such a dead unfeeling sense,
That heaven's horrid thunders cannot wake?
To see the earth crack'd with the weight of sin,
Hell gaping under us, and o'er our heads
Black, ravenous ruin, with her sail-stretch'd wings,
Ready to sink us down and cover us.
Who can behold such prodigies as these,
And have his lips seal'd up? Not I: my soul
Was never ground into such oily colours,
To flatter vice, and daub iniquity:
But, with an armed and resolved hand,
I'll strip the ragged follies of the time
Naked as at their birth . . . and with a whip of steel
Print wounding lashes in their iron ribs.
I fear no mood stamp'd in a private brow,
When I am pleased t'unmask a public vice.
I fear no strumpet's drugs, nor ruffian's stab,
Should I detect their hateful luxuries:
No broker's, usurer's, or lawyer's gripe,
Were I disposed to say, they are all corrupt.
I fear no courtier's frown, should I applaud
The easy flexure of his supple hams.
Tut, these are so innate and popular,
That drunken custom would not shame to laugh,
In scorn, at him, that should but dare to tax 'em:
And yet, not one of these, but knows his works,
Knows what damnation is, the devil and hell;
Yet hourly they persist, grow rank in sin,
Puffing their souls away in perjurous air,
To cherish their extortion, pride, or lusts.

The inheritance of the classical comedy as well as the medieval and
Tudor morality play is clear. Yet the man who could write that was not
the man to submit uncritically to the formal demands of tradition.
Later in that same Prologue (the whole an important statement of
Jonson's beliefs) he defends his right to modify classical practice to the
demands of his subject matter, as the Greeks and Romans themselves
had done; and his later practice makes full use of that freedom.

It is perhaps an open question as to how far in some of his plays
Jonson in the pursuit of morality transcends the limits of his own
concept of comedy. The central character of *Volpone* (1607) may for
some seem to be drawn as such a distillation of greed and acquisitive-
ness as perhaps to be – like Sir Giles Overreach in Massinger's *A New
Way to Pay Old Debts* (1633) – beyond the acceptance necessary for the

corrective precept to apply. And certainly that scene (III. vi) in which Corvino, who has used his beautiful wife as a material treasure, and shut her up for himself as a miser gloats over his hidden gold, then turns and drives her into Volpone's bed in the hope of inheriting Volpone's wealth, reveals a depth of depravity monstrous enough to overwhelm the comic spirit. The manner, too, in which the three confidence tricksters of *The Alchemist* (c. 1612) are allowed to avoid any significant retribution cannot be said to demonstrate social or moral justice, though it may well be both realistic, and at the same time an example of cosmic justice, since their victims become so because of their own overweening greed and cupidity. Perhaps Jonson realized the danger he was running into, or mellowed a little with age, for in the Prologue to the revised version of *Everyman in His Humour* (c. 1616) he limited his aim to the pursuit of folly rather than crime, to

> . . . deeds and language, such as men do use,
> And persons, such as comedy would choose,
> When she would show an image of the times,
> And sport with human follies, not with crimes.

Enough (perhaps too much) has been written about the importance of Jonson's theory of humours to his, and later, comedy. He made claims for it himself (see again the Prologue to *Everyman Out of His Humour*). But it is little more than a statement in terms fashionable in his day of a standard element in comedy – the high concentration into one character of a trait or passion observable to a lesser degree, and among much else, in all of us: but made more obvious by the absence of dilution, and by the sharp focusing of a close-up lens. The method was important to Jonson, but not exclusive. Yet it did contribute much to the strikingly memorable quality of many of his characters – Subtle, Face, Sir Epicure Mammon, Sir Politick Would-be, Zeal-of-the-land Busy. And it is the vitality of these and many other characters and their language, and the stereoscopic reality of his portrait of the teeming urban scene, rather than the moral corrective, that has kept Jonson's five great comedies alive.

Since Jonson's world is largely that of the City, it has become a commonplace to point out that the comedies of William Shakespeare are largely set in the country, the midsummer dream of a wood near Athens, the gentle Arcadia of the Forest of Arden, the cloud-cuckoo-land of the sea-coast of Bohemia. But the real difference between them is much more fundamental – it is Shakespeare's almost universal charity, the absorbing interest in his characters that embraces with affection their follies as well as their virtues.

In comedy, as always, Shakespeare was writing for a mixed audience, and in his plotting he took good care to provide both for his fashionable courtiers and his more down-to-earth groundlings. So by and large the Shakespearian approach juxtaposes the so-called 'high' comedy, involving wit, repartee, perhaps some intrigue and usually some romance, among people for the most part young and apparently with all the time in the world to fleet away the golden hours; and characters drawn much more closely from 'low' life (or the real world, depending on the point of view), village rustics, smalltown craftsmen and tradesmen, pedlars, serving men, discharged soldiers, the parson and the schoolmaster, material for his clowns to embroider and exploit with all their practical skill. The two elements are not always kept separate, but periodically brought together by the plot (*Love's Labour's Lost*, c. 1590; *A Midsummer Night's Dream*, c. 1594), their conjunction adding an additional dimension to the comic implication. Much of the 'high' comedy is intellectual and linguistic – puns, quibbles, incongruity of ideas Shakespeare could never resist; the battle of the sexes, aspects of romantic love (*The Merchant of Venice*, c. 1595; *Much Ado About Nothing*, c. 1599; *Twelfth Night*, c. 1600; *As You Like It*, c. 1600) are a staple of the diet of this timeless picnic set within a walled garden into which such tiresome notions as work and responsibility rarely, if ever, intrude. The 'low' comedy, on the other hand, has its feet firmly set in the lower-middle-class world within which Shakespeare had grown up in Stratford, and which he could observe around him in London – the quirks and quiddities, eccentricities and pomposities, pretentiousness and naïvety out of which he built Dogberry and Verges, Bottom and Peter Quince, Holofernes and Sir Nathaniel, Launcelot Gobbo and Christopher Sly.

These are doubtless in the line of development from the cruder caricatures of the late medieval interludes, but they are much more shrewdly and sympathetically observed. What is quite new and characteristic in Shakespearian comedy is the important role given to women. Whatever lip-service may be paid to male superiority, it is the women who in the final analysis control the action, the women to whom the men are subservient. When the women dwindle into matrimony, they do so in their own time and of their own will. Portia, Viola, Rosalind, Beatrice, Maria – these are no dependent ciphers but fully envisaged human beings; they it is who bend the action – and the men – to their own purposes. George Gordon, in a sadly fragmentary but perceptive study,[2] has suggested that Shakespeare may have found this approach a relief from the man-centred world of his history cycles, and have chafed at the limited role the women in those plays could be given; the world of his comedies is 'a world made safe for

[2] G. Gordon, *Shakespearian Comedy and Other Studies* (London, 1944), pp. 26–7 et seq.

women', in which they can flower and be themselves. Certainly they do flourish; and our memories of the comedies can often be recollections of the heroines, and the actresses who played them. Yet even here, of course, is a paradox. For they were written to be played not by women but by boys. It is a mark of Shakespeare's stunning virtuosity that even this apparent limitation can be turned to account, not just in the element of girls-disguised-as-boys, but the additional turn of the screw when, for example, in *As You Like It*, the heroine Rosalind, played by a boy, is then disguised as a boy, yet at one point pretends to be herself for a simulated wooing scene with the lovesick Orlando, and we begin a moving double fugue of both simulated and real emotion (IV. i).

In other ways Shakespeare turned the tradition he inherited to his own characteristic purposes. That Sir John Falstaff has his origin in a complex of the Devil of the miracle play, the Vice of the morality and the Riot of the interlude, with a touch of the Lord of Misrule, the Fool and the Jester thrown in, there can be little doubt. The Prince in *Henry IV* (c. 1597–8) uses the very labels to describe him – 'that villainous abominable misleader of Youth, that old whitebearded Satan', 'that reverend Vice, that grey Iniquity, that father Ruffian, that Vanity in years' (Part 1, II. iv). Yet if we assert that we feel much in the way of moral corrective when watching Falstaff, we deceive ourselves. Much of the former critical agonizing over the rejection of Falstaff springs from this very fact. If we were to regard Falstaff through medieval eyes, that rejection might seem right and appropriate. It is felt to be unfair or unjust precisely because we do in some strange way identify with Falstaff. That huge hill of flesh, that bombard of sack, that bellowing bull-calf of a coward, braggart, hypocrite, confidence trickster, scoundrel, nevertheless – and however incongruously – is a joyful and glorious example of delight in the pleasure of the senses, and as such he catches our imagination. Seen through his magnifying glass we recognize a fragment of ourselves, that if only we dared we should take pleasure in indulging as he does. No, of course, in real life it would not be possible. A society of Falstaffs would disintegrate in the wildest anarchy. But if only . . .

We envy his command of highly imaginative invective; the very gusto with which he revels in his own grotesquerie is endearing:

> Men of all sorts take a pride to gird at mee: the brain of this foolish compounded clay, man, is not able to invent anything that tends to laughter, more than I invent or is invented on mee. I am not onely witty in myselfe, but the cause that wit is in other men.
>
> (Part 2, I. ii)

But he is much more than just a figure of fun. The genuine delight of

his reaction to a kind word from Dol Common, and his sudden
remembrance of age and frailty and the death's head over his shoul-
der:

    Dol. I love thee better than I love e're a scurvy young boy of them
       all.

    Fal. What Stuffe wilt thou have a Kirtle of? I shall receive Money on
       Thursday: thou shalt have a Cappe tomorrow. A merrie Song,
       come: it growes late, we will to Bed. Thou wilt forget me when I
       am gone.

    Dol. Thou wil'st set me a weeping, if thou say'st so.'

(Part 2, II. iv)

– touches a chord in us, too. This subtlety is far removed from the
medieval devil or the Tudor fool. Shakespeare's humanism is wide
enough to see and to embrace the weakness and the folly and the
delight and the swagger and the sheer love of life itself that sets any
abstraction in perspective: 'Can Honour set-to a leg?' And with this
strange ambivalent character Shakespeare has captured the imagina-
tions of audiences and actors, of Giuseppe Verdi and Edward Elgar,
and of the generality of readers, ever since.[3]

    Nor is this all-round vision confined to major characters like Fal-
staff. Take the two justices, Shallow and Silence, in the same play,
sitting in a Gloucestershire garden recalling a long-vanished youth,
Shallow shoring up his cracking self-confidence with a scaffolding of
name-dropping:

    Shal. I was once of Clement's Inne; where I thinke they will talke of
       mad Shallow yet.

    Sil. You were call'd lustie Shallow then, Cousin.

    Shal. I was call'd any thing: and I would have done anything
       indeede too, and roundly too. There was I, and little John Doit
       of Staffordshire, and blacke George Bare, and Francis Pick-
       bone, and Will Squele a Cot-sal-man, you had not foure such
       Swindge-bucklers in all the Innes of Court againe: And I may
       say to you, wee knew where the Bona-Roba's were, and had the
       best of them all at commandement. Then was Jacke Falstaff,
       now Sir John, A Boy, and Page to Thomas Mowbray, Duke of
       Norfolke.

    Sil. This Sir John, Cousin, that comes hither anon about souldiers?

    Shal. The same Sir John, the very same: I saw him breake Scog-
       gan's head at the Court-Gate, when hee was a Crack, not thus
       high: and the very same day did I fight with one Sampson
       Stock-fish, a Fruiterer, behind Greyes-Inne. Oh the mad dayes

---

[3] J. D. Wilson, *The Fortunes of Falstaff* (London, 1943), pursues the Falstaff
enigma pertinaceously and with insight.

> that I have spent! and to see how many of mine olde Acquain-
> tance are dead.
> *Sil.* We shall all follow, Cousin.
> *Shal.* Certaine: 'tis certaine: very sure, very sure: Death is certaine
> to all, all shall dye. How a good Yoke of Bullocks at Stamford
> Fayre?
> *Sil.* Truly Cousin, I was not there.
> *Shal.* Death is certaine. Is old Double of your Towne living yet?
> *Sil.* Dead, Sir.
> *Shal.* Dead? See, see: hee drew a good Bow: and dead? hee shot a
> fine shoote. John of Gaunt loved him well, and betted much
> Money on his head. Dead? hee would have clapt in the Clowt at
> Twelve-score, and carryed you a fore-hand Shaft at foureteene,
> and foureteene and a halfe, that it would have done a man's
> heart good to see. How a score of Ewes now?
> *Sil.* Thereafter as they be: a score of good Ewes may be worth tenne
> pounds.
> *Shal.* And is old Double dead?

We are as aware as Falstaff is of the vanity and embroidering of the
old man's recollections:

> *Fal.* . . . Lord, Lord! How subject wee old men are to this vice of
> Lying? This same starv'd Justice hath done nothing but prate to
> me of the wildenesse of his Youth, and the feates hee hath done
> about Turnball-street, and every third word a Lye. . . . I doe
> remember him at Clements Inne, like a man made after Supper,
> of a Cheese-paring. When hee was naked, hee was, for all the
> world, like a forked Radish, with a Head fantastically carv'd
> upon it with a Knife. . . . Hee was the very Genius of Famine:
> hee came ever in the rereward of the Fashion: and now is this
> Vices Dagger become a Squire, and talkes as familiarly of John
> of Gaunt, as if he had been sworn brother to him.   (Part 2, III. ii)

But Shakespeare makes us aware, too, of the desperate need of both
Shallow and Falstaff for something to give them a little Dutch courage
in a grim situation: 'And is old Double dead?' There are times when
we, too, have a need to have heard – or to have invented – the chimes
at midnight.

So the laughter is double-edged; laughter with, as well as at, a
display of human weakness. And our reaction is less one of condemnation than of understanding.

Occasionally this rounding-out of the stereotype can cause difficulty, as in the case of Shylock, where the touches of humanity given
him have been enough for later actors to try to turn him against the

design of the play into a semi-tragic figure. At other times, it is only a single flash that transforms a stock figure into a human being. In *Love's Labour's Lost* Don Armado, the fantastical Spaniard, is a variant of the braggart soldier (he is frequently labelled Braggart or Broggart in the Folio text). In the final scene (V. ii), when the farcical pageant of the nine worthies is being presented, a dispute breaks out between him and the Clown, and he is challenged to take off his coat and fight:

> *Brag.* Gentlemen and Souldiers pardon me, I will not combat in my shirt.
> *Du.* You may not denie it, Pompey hath made the challenge.
> *Brag.* Sweet bloods, I both may and will.
> *Ber.* What reason have you for't?
> *Brag.* The naked truth of it is, I have no shirt.

And in the burst of laughter which greets the line, suddenly Armado is a stricken fellow human being.

For the most part except for the so-called 'dark' comedies Shakespeare, unlike Jonson, regards his characters with affection, not contempt. For Hazlitt, this represented a weakness.

> The fault, then, of Shakespeare's comic Muse is, in my opinion, that it is too good-natured and magnanimous. It mounts above its quarry. It is 'apprehensive, quick, forgetive, full of nimble, fiery, and delectable shapes': but it does not take the highest pleasure in making human nature look as mean, as ridiculous, and contemptible as possible.[4]

Hazlitt, of course, is writing with the corrective function of comedy in mind; but in terms of that other function of comedy – to reconcile us to the human condition – what was to him a fault will surely by many others be counted a virtue.

After 1660 a new element begins to take precedence in English comedy – the sense of comedy as structure, the artificial patterning of characters and contriving of situations that leads us through a ritual, often sexual, dance of matching and opposing, identity and contrast, symmetry and asymmetry, in which the structure, however artificial, is designed to throw into relief some aspect of human behaviour or relationship. It is not that this element was totally absent before, but that it was subordinate; now it begins to take precedence over both character insight and moral purpose. Of course this does not just happen precisely in 1660. In the 1620s, in the later plays of John Fletcher, for instance – *Rule a Wife and Have a Wife* (1624) and *The Chances* (1625) – one can see the interest moving towards the increas-

---

[4] W. Hazlitt, *Lectures on the English Comic Writers* (London, 1819), Lecture II.

ingly complicated accumulation and juxtaposition of incident, even at the expense of logic and credibility (and it may not be without significance that these were two of the plays regularly revived during the next century). But the closure of the public theatres during the Commonwealth served as a watershed. In the reopened private or court theatres of the Restoration, with their much more socially restricted audiences, intellectual ingenuity, either of structure or language or both, was what was asked for. Samuel Pepys, a devoted playgoer, found *Twelfth Night* 'a silly play' (6/1/1663), *Love in a Tub* 'very merry, but only so by gesture, not wit at all, which methinks is beneath the house' (4/1/1665), and read with disappointment Fletcher's *A Wife for a Month* 'wherein is no great wit or language' (19/12/1662).

Because the men of the late seventeenth- and early eighteenth-century theatre had no scruple about revising and rewriting earlier plays, what they did to them often reveals a great deal about changes in taste and attitudes. *The Enchanted Island* (1667) by Dryden and Davenant is a version of Shakespeare's *The Tempest* (c. 1611). Dryden, in his Preface to the first edition in 1670, writes:

> Sir William Davenant, as he was a man of quick and piercing imagination . . . design'd the Counterpart to *Shakespear*'s Plot, namely that of a Man who had never seen a Woman: that by this means those two Characters of Innocence and Love, might the more illustrate and commend each other. This excellent contrivance he was pleas'd to communicate to me, and to desire my assistance in it. I confess that from the very first moment it so pleas'd me, that I never writ anything with more delight.

But the new symmetrical structure is yet more complex than that. Since Miranda has Ferdinand, the new male innocent Hippolito must have a female counterpart, so Prospero acquires another daughter, Dorinda. Much play is made of the innocence of the two sexes of each other, and of the emotional complications arising from their juxtaposition, jealousy leading to a quarrel between the men which culminates almost in murder. All, of course, ends (or real life begins) in a double wedding. The conscious patterning extends also to the subplot, where Caliban is given a sister Sycorax, so that at the lower level she may add a female element to Caliban's untutored 'natural' reactions. How Prospero could possibly have kept the infant Duke of Mantua separate for so long on the island, so that he could grow to manhood without sight of the others, never troubles anyone. Probability does not enter into it. The pattern is all. And the comedy emerges from the pursuit of what is essentially an intellectual conceit: What if you could confront mature innocents in this way?

The humour is often at the simple level of innuendo, and
the double marriage at the end produces a crop of adolescent
giggles.

> *Prosp.* . . . For you, Miranda, must with Ferdinand
> And you, Dorinda, with Hippolito lye in
> One Bed hereafter.
> *Alonz.* And heaven make those Beds still fruitful in
> Producing Children to bless their Parents
> Youth, and Grandsires age.
> *Mir.* (*to Dor.*) If children come by lying in a Bed, I wonder you
> And I had none between us.
> *Dor.* Sister, it was our fault, we meant like fools
> To look 'em in the fields, and they it seems
> Are only found in Beds.
> *Hip.* I am o'rejoy'd that I shall have Dorinda in a Bed,
> We'll lye all night and day together there,
> And never rise again.
> *Ferd.* (*aside to him*) Hippolito! you yet are ignorant of your great
> Happiness, but there is somewhat which for
> Your own and fair Dorinda's sake I must instruct
> You in.
> *Hip.* Pray teach me quickly how Men and Women in your
> World make love, I shall soon learn
> I warrant you.   (V)

But there is fair comment on human nature, too. When the two sisters
talk together after having been warned against men by Prospero,
Dorinda says:

> *Dor.* Nay, I confess I would see him too. I find it in my Nature,
> because my father has forbidden me.
> *Mir.* Aye, there's it, Sister, if he had said nothing, I had been
> quiet.   (II)

And in the scene which follows, where they see Hippolito for the first
time, as he broods over what these strange creatures women may be,
Dryden implies some pointed comments on female behaviour as he
sees it:

> *Dor.* Oh Sister, there it is, it walks about like one of us.
> *Mir.* Aye, just so, and has legs as we have too.
> *Hip.* It strangely puzzles me: yet 'tis most likely
> Women are somewhat between men and spirits.
> *Dor.* Heark! it talks, sure this is not it my Father meant,

For this is just like one of us: methinks I am not half
So much afraid on't as I was: see, now it turns this way.
Mir. Heaven! What a goodly thing it is?
Dor. I'le go nearer it.
Mir. O no, 'tis dangerous, Sister! I'le go to it.
I would not for the world that you should venture.
My father charged me to secure you from it.
Dor. I warrant you this is a tame man, dear Sister,
He'll not hurt me, I see it by his looks,
Mir. Indeed he will! but go back, and he shall eat me first:
Fye, are you not asham'd to be so much inquisitive?
Dor. You chide me for't, and wou'd give yourself.
Mir. Come back, or I will tell my Father.
Observe how he begins to stare already.
I'le meet the danger first, and then call you.
Dor. Nay, Sister, you shall never vanquish me in kindness.
I'le venture you, no more than you will me.
Prosp. (within) Miranda, Child, where are you!
Mir. Do you not hear my father call? go in.
Dor. 'Twas you he nam'd, not me; I will but say my Prayers,
And follow you immediately.
Mir. Well, Sister, you'll repent it.   *(Exit Miranda.)*
Dor. Though I dye for't, I must have th'other peep.   (II)

The scene is then set for the first meeting of the male and female
innocents.

Setting an innocent at large in the world of the sophisticated is a
convenient device for throwing an ironic light on the way society
behaves. It is an important element of Wycherley's *The Country Wife*
(1675); similarly the sixteen-year-old Lucy in Henry Fielding's *The
Virgin Unmask'd* (1734), for instance, is the pivot around whose
naïvety in meeting her various suitors Fielding is enabled to build a
structure satirizing marriage customs and the attitudes of the profes-
sions the various suitors represent.

Pepys, who saw *The Enchanted Island* eight times between 7
November 1667 and 21 January 1669, 'could not be more pleased in a
comedy' and called it 'the most innocent play that ever I saw'. To
much of the artificial comedy of this period, 'innocent' is the last word
that might fairly be applied. The young Restoration intellectuals
suffered from sex in the head, and though there were undoubtedly
matters to be probed about the relationship between men and
women, over-indulgence soon turned speculation into cliché, and the
long parade of fashionable *poseurs* becomes tedious, the hothouse
world they inhabit increasingly divorced from reality. For the most

part the attitude of the Restoration playwrights is less one of trying
to be corrective about the artificialities of contemporary social
behaviour, than of revelling in them to a degree bordering on
tedium.

Nevertheless the best of the plays survive not because of what they
have to tell us about ourselves, or to warn us against, but, like those of
Vanbrugh and Farquhar, because of their Jonsonian vitality, and the
pleasure we take in the playwrights' shaping craftsmanship. Though
even the best of them can sometimes be defeated by the complexity of
their plotting, as Congreve was in *The Way of the World* (1700) and
Otway in *The Atheist* (1683), Congreve is redeemed by the monstrous
Lady Wishfort and the delectable Millamant, and Otway in *The Soldier's Fortune* (1681) by the virility of his young soldiers on the loose,
and the indefatigable pertinacity of his bawdy old men. And the game
of the sexes can be played in dialogue that is as formally but as
elegantly shaped as an operatic duet. That between Millamant and
Mirabell (IV. v) is well known. Courtine and Sylvia in *The Soldier's
Fortune* are in the same tradition.

Sylv. Take my Word, Sir, you had better give this Business over. I
tell you there's nothing in the World turns my Stomach so much
as the Man, that Man that makes love to me. I never saw one of
your Sex in my Life make love, but he looked so like an Ass all
the while, that I blush'd for him.
Cour. I am afraid your Ladyship then is one of those dangerous
Creatures they call She wits, who are always so mightily taken
with admiring themselves, that nothing else is worth their
notice.
Sylv. Oh! who can be so dull not to be ravish'd with that boisterous
Mien of yours? that ruffling Air in your Gate, that seems to cry
where e're you go, make room, here comes the Captain: That
Face, the which bids defiance to the Weather. Bless us! if I were
a poor Farmer's Wife in the Country now, and you wanted
Quarters, how would it fright me? But as I am young, not very
ugly, and one you never saw before, how lovingly it looks upon
me!
Cour. Who can forbear to sigh, look pale and languish, where
Beauty and Wit unite both their Forces to enslave a Heart so
tractable as mine is? First, for the modish Swim of your Body,
the victorious motion of your Arms and Head, the Toss of your
Fan, the Glancing of the Eyes; bless us! If I were a dainty fine
dressed Coxcomb, with a great Estate, and little or no Wit,
Vanity in abundance, and good for nothing, how would they
melt and soften me? but as I am a scandalous honest Rascal, not

> Fool enough to be your Sport, nor rich enough to be your prey,
> how glotingly they look upon me!
>
> *Sylv.* Alas, alas! what pity 'tis your Honesty should ever do you
> Hurt, or your Wit spoil your Preferment!
>
> *Cour.* Just as much, fair Lady, as that your Beauty should make you
> be envied at, or your Virtue provoke Scandal.
>
> *Sylv.* The more I look, the more I'm in love with you.
>
> *Cour.* The more I look, the more I am out of love with you.
>
> *Sylv.* How my Heart swells when I see you!
>
> *Cour.* How my Stomach rises when I am near you!
>
> *Sylv.* Nay, then let's bargain.
>
> *Cour.* With all my Heart; what?
>
> *Sylv.* Not to fall in love with each other, I assure you, Monsieur
> Captain.
>
> *Cour.* But to hate one another constantly and cordially.   (II. i)

But, of course, they do pair off, and in the sequel, *The Atheist*,
Courtine's disenchantment a couple of years later is a main line of the
plot.

Through the eighteenth century, the shaping skill retains its
importance. The best of Georgian comedy depends on situation
rather than character or language. Characters are often familiar types
with a contemporary twist to them. Sheridan's Mrs Malaprop (*The
Rivals*, 1775), with her mishandling of the English language, derives
from the same mould as Dogberry: Strictland, the jealous husband in
Hoadly's *The Suspicious Husband* (1774), from the school of Ford and
Kitely. But the playwrights deploy great skill in creating incongruous
situations for them; impersonations and mistaken identities abound,
and much is made of the characters' misunderstanding the truth of a
situation, fully comprehended only by the audience – which then
derives an unholy joy from watching the completely logical pattern of
their progress to near-disaster, and the ingenuity with which they
(usually) extricate themselves. Captain Absolute in *The Rivals* visiting
Mrs Malaprop and being made to read out an intercepted letter to
Lydia which he has written in the guise of Ensign Beverley, full of
scurrilous references to the old lady, and all the time teetering on the
edge of discovery (III. iii); Goldsmith's Marlow and Hastings being
gulled into mistaking the house they were making for as an inn, with
all the comic cross-purposes that follow (*She Stoops to Conquer*, 1773);
Fainwell in Susanna Centlivre's *A Bold Stroke for a Wife* (1718) going
through a series of disguises and stratagems in order to gain the
consent of all four of her reluctant guardians to his marriage to Ann
Lovely and her £30,000; Ranger in *The Suspicious Husband* mistaking
his cousin Clarinda for a whore and her lodgings for a brothel (IV. iv);

the whole sequence of misunderstandings that keep John O'Keeffe's *Wild Oats* (1791) almost permanently on the boil – these are the stuff of Georgian comedy.

This kind of situation-comedy can, of course, in the hands of less competent writers, easily turn into farce, depending for its acceptance on the legerdemain of a group of highly skilled actors (and the eighteenth century had plenty of those). But at its best the situation-comedy is true comedy, and in its zany logic a not over-distorted mirror of contemporary society; a society increasingly dominated by the rising middle class, whose preoccupations and foibles steadily usurp those of the fashionable young things of the Restoration.

There are indeed corrective elements in, for example, Sheridan and Goldsmith; but their lesser contemporaries show all too clearly that this is the weakest area of eighteenth-century comedy. When the Georgians (like the bourgeois in eighteenth-century France) sought for moral purpose, they frequently became sentimental, and Steele's *The Conscious Lovers* (1722), for instance, anticipates La Chaussée's aim of showing virtue under pressure emerging from the trial to point a didactic moral. The enunciation of trite sentiments, and the apparatus of long-lost parents and children that are often associated with the last acts of the poorer plays of this kind, are the barrier to modern enjoyment; and for too long, in a manifestation of guilt by association, they have obscured some of the better plays of the period. Much of the sharpest satire, political, social and sometimes literary, appears in the many afterpieces – farces, burlesques, parodies, musical entertainments – that were a unique eighteenth-century contribution to the theatre, and which, because they do not fit easily into modern playhouse planning and practice, are nowadays largely unknown. But many of them would be worth revival if the opportunity could be contrived. Sheridan's *The Critic* (1779) and Garrick's *The Lying Valet* (1741) have proved themselves in our time. Murphy's *The Citizen* (1761) and *The Apprentice* (1756), Mrs Cowley's *Who's the Dupe?* (1779), and Garrick's *High Life Below Stairs* (1759) and *The Irish Widow* (1772) might well do so too, given the opportunity.

The Widow Brady, the central figure of the latter piece, is a reminder of the frequent use in English comedy of national types, Welsh, Irish and Scots. They had been around, of course, since Fluellen's day, but in the second half of the eighteenth century they proliferate greatly, perhaps as a consequence of the Act of Union and the drift to London of Scots on the make, as well as the ubiquitous presence of Irish actors and writers.[5] Many of them are simple stereotypes; but a handful are more than that. Sir Pertinax MacSycophant in Macklin's

[5] J. O. Bartley, *Teague, Shenkin and Sawney* (Cork, 1954), is an exhaustive study of the fluctuating fortunes of the stage Welsh, Irish and Scotsman.

The Man of the World (1781), bully, hypocrite, financial and political opportunist, is a monstrous figure in the tradition of Sir Giles Overreach; he proved such strong meat that like the earlier political satire of Fielding he was for many years kept off the stage. Now much of the sting has gone, but his views on expediency and his manipulation of Lord Lumbercourt (II. i), his bribery of the lawyers and his political venality (IV), and perhaps most of all his exposition of the art of social and political hypocrisy (III. i) are a powerful piece of corrective satire. Had the supporting characters been stronger, less ciphers drawn from the store of the sentimental play, this might have been a great comedy.

With the nineteenth century, for a time popular comedy dwindled into the stereotypes (Jolly Jack Tars and Hayseed Harrys) and the sentimentality of the melodrama, until rescued in the latter half of the century by Tom Robertson, who began, in plays like *Society* (1865) and *Caste* (1867), the long haul back from stereotypes to individual characters based recognizably on the foibles of the human being we know and live with, and began also to reintroduce into the theatre, however crudely, a concern with some of the frailties of contemporary social attitudes and behaviour.

Even the more sophisticated comedies of the Victorian theatre could not totally free themselves from the stereotype character and other elements of the tearful comedy of the previous century; but the best of them, plays like Boucicault's *London Assurance* (1841) and Gilbert's *Engaged* (1877), are in the tradition of the Georgian laughing comedy; though in the case of the latter, and still more in Wilde's *The Importance of Being Earnest* (1895) – the full flowering of the style – the characters seem to occupy not the world we live in but a world of their own, a never-never-land which, like that of Labiche, has its own rules and rituals and logic.

In *Engaged*, Cheviot Hill, the central figure, has money by inheritance (which he treats with care) and a propensity to fall in love at every possible opportunity. His friend Belvawney has £1000 per annum from the estate so long as Hill remains unmarried. Then it reverts to his uncle, Symperson. Symperson's daughter Minnie is ready to marry Cheviot; so is her friend Belinda, whom Belvawney wants. There is also a Scotch lassie, Maggie, betrothed to Angus, but bought from him by Cheviot for £2. In Act I, in order to save Belinda from the wrath of Major McGillicuddy (from a marriage with whom she has fled by train to Scotland), Cheviot declares her to be his wife. Under Scottish law this turns out to constitute a legal marriage. So there are the three girls and the consequent problems of inheritance (Symperson and Belvawney) and the question of marriage, all depending on whether the cottage in which Act I takes place is legally in Scotland or England (it is situated just on the border). In the end it emerges that the cottage *is* in England, but the garden, where the declaration took place, in Scotland. So Belinda gets her Cheviot after all.

Obviously such a plot is designed to highlight mercenary rather than emotional motives in marriage (especially in the early part of Act III); and in Act I the Scotch trio holds kailyard sentimentality to ridicule. And yet, in a curious way, the logic of the attitudes is so complete within their own special world that we hardly stop to relate them to ourselves or the society we know. We simply sit back and enjoy the enormity of it all. Cheviot making his cash offer for Maggie is a case in point.

Angus. I love her, sir, a'most as weel as I love mysel'.
Cheviot. Then reflect how you are standing in the way of her prosperity. I am a rich man. I have money, position, and education. I am a much more intellectual and generally agreeable companion for her than you can ever hope to be. I am full of anecdote, and all my anecdotes are in the best possible taste. I will tell you some of them some of these days, and you can judge for yourself. Maggie, if she married me, would live in a nice house in a good square. She would have wine – occasionally. She would be kept beautifully clean. Now if you really love this girl as well as you love yourself, are you doing wisely or kindly in standing in the way of her getting all these good things? As to compensation – why, I've had heavy expenses of late – but if – yes, if thirty shillings . . .

Angus indignantly turns down the offer, and Cheviot raises it to £2, again to be refused; but at that point Maggie intervenes.

Maggie. Angus, dear, I'm varra proud o' sae staunch and true a love; it's like your ain true self, an' I can say nae more for it than that. But dinna act wi'out prudence and forethought, dear. In these hard times twa pound is twa pound, and I'm nae sure that ye're acting richtly in refusing sae large a sum. I love you varra dearly – ye ken that right weel – an' if ye'll be troubled wi' sic a poor little mousie I'll mak' ye a true an' loving wife, but I doubt whether, wi a' my love, I'll ever be worth as much to ye as twa pound. Dinna act in haste, dear; tak time to think before ye refuse this kind gentleman's offer.
Angus. Oh, sir, is not this rare modesty? Could ye match it amang your toun-bred fine ladies? I think not! Meg, it shall be as you say. I'll tak the siller, but it'll be wi' a sair and broken hairt!

The whole of *The Importance of Being Earnest* presents the same paradox. The plot and the characters are farcical (a handbag? Really!), yet as in Gilbert there is a style of language and an even greater subtlety of construction that takes it out of the realm of traditional farce or of satire. Rationally, Lady Bracknell is a monster; theatrically we, and the actresses who play her, adore her.

We are back to the problem of Falstaff. Is there something in the English temperament, along with its long tradition of nonconformity, that takes delight in the character who refuses, however outrageously, to conform to the pressures or accepted conventions of 'normal' society? The English rather more than some other nationalities have a reputation for breeding and tolerating eccentrics. Some of the best-loved, most life-enhancing characters in English comedy can be regarded as eccentrics rather than monsters, and perhaps this is how we see them – whether or not this was the playwright's intention – and warm laughter rather than condemnation is the result.

Be that as it may, with the last and greatest of the late nineteenth-century writers of comedy, Bernard Shaw, we are back firmly in the Jonsonian corrective tradition, except that for Shaw ideas and beliefs took precedence over social behaviour. If only the assumptions could be got right, he seems to have felt, the rest would follow. And so he set out to use comedy to make us re-examine our traditional attitudes:

> In order to get a hearing, it was necessary for me to attain the footing of a privileged lunatic, with the licence of a jester. . . . My method is to take the utmost trouble to find the right thing to say, and then to say it with the utmost levity. And all the time the real joke is that I am in earnest.[6]

He challenged accepted orthodoxies by standing conventional beliefs on their heads to see what happened. To audiences in a world that saw the soldier as a gallant romantic figure, he showed them in *Arms and the Man* (1894) the prosaic professional who found chocolate more useful in his holster than a revolver; to a society brought up on the notion of the male as the strong protector of the weaker female, he revealed him in *Candida* (1895) as the unknowing creature of the far stronger woman.

Candida's husband, the Rev. James Morell, vigorous and popular Christian Socialist preacher, and at the beginning of the play secure in his domestic happiness, finds his confidence undermined by the effeminate young poet, Eugene Marchbanks, who eventually declares his love for Morell's wife. At the climax of Act III, Candida challenges the pair of them to bid for her, and Marchbanks counters Morell's offer of his strength, ability and industry with a plea of his

---

[6] Quoted in A. C. Ward, *Twentieth Century Literature* (London, 1928), p. 89.

weakness and his need. Candida chooses the weaker of the two; but it is not Marchbanks, as she explains:

> *Candida.* . . . Ask James's mother and his three sisters what it cost to save James the trouble of doing anything but be strong and clever and happy. Ask *me* what it costs to be James's mother and three sisters and wife and mother to his children all in one. Ask Prossy and Maria how troublesome the house is even when we have no visitors to help us to slice the onions. Ask the trades-men who want to worry James and spoil his beautiful sermons who it is that puts them off? When there is money to give, he gives it: when there is money to refuse, I refuse it. I build a castle of comfort and indulgence and love for him, and stand sentinel always to keep little vulgar cares out. I make him master here, though he does not know it, and could not tell you a moment ago how it came to be so. And when he thought I might go away with you his only anxiety was – what should become of me! And to tempt me to stay he offered me *his* strength for *my* defence! his industry for my livelihood! his dignity for my position! his – ah, I am mixing up your beautiful cadences and spoiling them, am I not, darling? (III)

Socialist, deeply religious (though not a Christian), Shaw always tried to be a realist, often much to the surprise of his contemporaries. At the end of *Major Barbara* (1905) Barbara leaves the Salvation Army and throws in her lot with her armaments-manufacturer father, not because she approves of what he is doing – on the contrary – but because, through the material prosperity he offers, life for the major-ity of people can be improved; through idealistic poverty it can not.

Though his attempted light badinage can sometimes be excruciat-ing, at his best Shaw writes a clear, beautifully balanced and cadenced prose, shaped to some degree by the authorized version of the Bible and some of the eighteenth-century prose writers. At times he can rise to impassioned rhetoric (*Saint Joan*, 1924); Granville Barker once told his actors, rehearsing a Shaw play, to think of themselves as singing operatic arias and Shaw who was present did not demur; musically he had grown up in Dublin in a household resounding to Italian opera. Most of his lesser characters are from the traditional stock, but as such they serve as foils to the central ones, from whom his main arguments derive. They, too, have sometimes been written down as puppets, vehicles for ideas alone; certainly in his later years when he became much less concerned with conventional dramatic construction this can be true (*Man and Superman*, 1903; *Back to Methuselah*, 1921; *Too True to be Good*, 1934). But it is the heart of his method; the dance of ideas is the pattern and meaning of the comedy, so that moral purpose and the comedic structure go hand in hand.

English comedy, then, has no single aim or technique. It can aim to be a moral corrective, it can be revelatory or consolatory, it can depend on structure, it can depend on ideas. But laughter is at the heart of it. And as in all theatrical comedy the production of that laughter depends also on the art and craftsmanship of the comedians who present it. The texts may live on to be re-created, actors' performances die; but they should,not be forgotten. From Will Kemp to Miles Malleson, from David Garrick to Laurence Olivier, from Elizabeth Barry to Edith Evans, it is they who take the characters and the words and the situations, and transmute them into living delight. Let Charles Lamb, who understood the reconciliatory function of comedy better than most – and who saw in his prime Joseph Munden, one of the greatest of English comedians – have the last word.[7]

> There is one face of Farley, one face of Knight, one (but what a one it is!) of Liston; but Munden has none that you can properly pin down and call *his*. When you think he has exhausted his battery of looks, in unaccountable warfare with your gravity, suddenly he sprouts out an entirely new set of features, like Hydra. He is not one, but legion. Not so much a comedian, as a company. If his name could be multiplied like his countenance, it might fill a play-bill. He, and he alone, literally *makes faces*: applied to any other person, the phrase is a mere figure, denoting certain modifications of the human countenance. Out of some invisible wardrobe he dips for faces, as his friend Suett used for wigs, and fetches them out as easily. I should not be surprised to see him some day put out the head of a river horse; or come forth a peewitt, or lapwing, some feathered metamorphosis. . . .
>
> Can any man *wonder*, like him? can any man *see ghosts*, like him? or *fight with his own shadow* – as he does in that strangely-neglected thing, *The Cobbler of Preston* – where his alternations from the Cobbler to the Magnifico, and from the Magnifico to the Cobbler, keep the brain of the spectator in as wild a ferment, as if some Arabian Night were being enacted before him. Who like him can throw, or ever attempted to throw, a preternatural interest over the commonest daily-life objects? A table, or a joint stool, in his conception, rises into a dignity equivalent to Cassiopeia's chair. It is invested with constellatory importance. You could not speak of it with more deference, if it were mounted into the firmament. A beggar in the hands of Michelangelo, says Fuseli, rose the Patriarch of Poverty. So the gusto of Munden antiquates and en-

[7] C. Lamb, 'On the Acting of Munden', *Essays of Elia* (London, 1823).

nobles what it touches. His pots and his ladles are as grand and primal as the seething-pots and hooks seen in old prophetic vision. A tub of butter, contemplated by him, amounts to a Platonic idea. He understands a leg of mutton in its quiddity. He stands wondering, amid the common-place materials of life, like primaeval man with the sun and stars about him.

That, in the last analysis, is what great comedy is about.

7

Comedy in Northern Europe

DAVID THOMAS

CAN ANY man have such a damnable wife as I have? I honestly think she must be a Cousin to the Devil himself. People around here say that Jeppe drinks, but they don't say why Jeppe drinks; I was never beaten as much in the army in ten whole years as I am in one day by that wife of mine. *She* beats me, the bailiff drives me to work as if I was an animal and the deacon makes a cuckold of me. Haven't I good reason to drink? And don't I have a right to use whatever means nature provides to drive away my troubles? If I was just a fool, things like that wouldn't bother me, and I wouldn't drink so much; but it's quite well known that I'm an intelligent man, I'm more sensitive than others and that's why I drink. My neighbour Moens Christoffersen quite often says to me, being a good friend and all that, 'Devil take you and your fat belly, Jeppe! You just hit back and then your old woman will behave.' But I can't for three very good reasons. Number one, because I'm a coward. Number two, because my old woman has a whip hanging over the bed and my back only has to think of that for me to start crying. And number three, because, even if I say so myself, I'm a gentle person and a good Christian. I don't even try to get revenge on the deacon who gives me one horn after the other. I put my offering on his plate on the three Holy Days, but he doesn't so much as offer me a jug of ale the whole year round. Nothing wounded me more than the nasty remark he made to me last year; I was telling him how a wild bull, that had never been afraid of anyone before, took fright when he saw me. And do you know what he said? 'Well, I can see how that happened, Jeppe. The bull saw that you had bigger horns than him and he wisely decided not to challenge his superior.'

This extract from the long monologue at the opening of Ludvig

Holberg's comedy, *Jeppe from the Hill* (1722), establishes quite precisely the parameters of thought and feeling within which the remainder of the comedy will operate. Jeppe is a drunken peasant, a feckless rogue, who resorts to drink as an escape from his social and marital duties. As he himself points out, he is not only incurably work-shy but he is also, unlike others in his village, incapable of controlling his wife and running his household. Jeppe is a man who is aware of his own shortcomings, yet unable to do anything about them. Humiliated by his wife and by her lover, he takes refuge in a mixture of self-pity and ironic laughter.

The overall tone of the speech is satiric. It is funny because we are implicitly invited to contrast Jeppe with conventionally accepted ideals of manhood, and of course he fails on every score. This same implicit appeal to established norms of behaviour provides the basis for the comic incongruity running through the play. Jeppe is repeatedly made the butt of the author's satire because, in his responses to others, he infringes a code of behaviour which, it is assumed, all rational people acknowledge and share. Jeppe himself recognizes his own folly, and it is only an unusually well-developed sense of humour that keeps him from losing all self-respect.

During the course of the action, Jeppe becomes the plaything of a local aristocrat, the Baron, who finds him, in a drunken stupor, lying on top of a dungheap. The Baron transports Jeppe to his own bed, dresses him in fine linen, and then stands back to watch the result. Predictably enough, Jeppe is at first utterly confused. But he soon becomes convinced of his new identity and at once begins to indulge his voracious appetite for food and drink. His new-found authority even restores his sexual appetite, with the result that he greets the bailiff's wife by fondling her breasts and inviting her to sleep with him. All too swiftly Jeppe attempts to abuse the power he has been given. Lacking any sense of social responsibility, he threatens some of his entourage with drastic pay cuts and others with death by hanging. The point is, of course, that he is judging the wages of the Baron's staff and the roles some of his officers play, notably the bailiff, from a feudal peasant's perspective. Fortunately the draconian measures Jeppe threatens come to nothing as he falls into yet another drunken stupor.

At this juncture the Baron underlines the point the action has just made:

> He's sound asleep, and our game is over. But we were almost
> made to look like fools. He intended to use us harshly like a tyrant
> so that we would have been obliged to spoil our game or else allow
> ourselves to be mistreated by a rude yokel. From his conduct we

may learn how arrogant and proud such people become when they rise too swiftly from the mire to positions of honour and dignity.

There is admittedly an element of self-criticism in this speech: the Baron recognizes that his game with Jeppe is a trifle silly and possibly even dangerous. But the overwhelming impression conveyed by the Baron is one of class-based, or rather caste-based, arrogance in his response to the rude yokel he has fooled, a rude yokel who is in every sense of the word no more than the Baron's creature. Not only would any change of social class be unthinkable for a peasant like Jeppe; even to move from his village or work for himself, without his Lord's express permission, would be quite impossible.

At the end of the play Holberg makes it apparent that he shares the Baron's point of view, in an epilogue spoken by this character:

Of this adventure, children, the moral is quite clear:
To elevate the lowly above their proper sphere
Involves no less a peril than rashly to bring down
The great who rise to power by deeds of just renown.
Permit the base-born yokel to gain untutored sway,
At once the scepter of dominion to the scourge gives way.

There is nothing particularly surprising about finding such deeply conservative views expressed in comedy; Molière's work, for instance, is based upon similar assumptions, even if normally they are rather more subtly expressed. What is surprising, on the other hand, is that such a view of society should find expression in Northern European drama in the eighteenth century. During the course of this century, the spread of bourgeois liberalism had a growing influence on intellectuals and creative writers throughout Europe. Holberg, however, was implacably opposed, from an ideological point of view, to this development, and when he wrote his most famous comedies, some fifteen of them, within the space of a mere eighteen months in 1722 and 1723, it was back in time to the work of Molière that he looked for his inspiration.

Like Molière in the France of Louis XIV, Holberg not only endorsed the absolutist structure of the society in which he was living but took it for granted that its values were rational and just and based upon an understanding of man's eternal and unchanging nature. The neoclassical style of comedy that Molière had perfected was ideally suited to express this kind of world-view. As Henri Bergson pointed out in *Laughter* (1900), the aim of neoclassical comedy was social rather than moral; its intention was 'to humiliate and consequently to correct' any behaviour that departed from accepted social norms. This is precisely the spirit in which Holberg wrote his comedies. Following the example of Molière, he used satire and irony to castigate the folly and excess of various character types within contemporary Danish society: the feckless peasant in *Jeppe from the Hill*, the knowall amateur politician in *The Political Tinker*, the bumptious undergraduate in *Erasmus Montanus*, the slave of fashion in *Jean de France*, and so on. Throughout these plays laughter is used as a social corrective.

Holberg, like Molière, produced a series of comedies without the slightest trace of sentiment or genuine emotion. He did, it is true, frequently convey a certain sympathy and even warmth for the fools, cowards and rogues who populate his plays – and this is particularly true of Jeppe – but invariably there is an element of condescension in this. Holberg, who was a professor at the University of Copenhagen, regarded himself as an aristocrat of the spirit (later in his life he became an aristocrat in the flesh when the king made him a baron in 1747) and tended to view the victims of his satire with the kind of ironic detachment at which dons so often excel. Hidden beneath the gay exterior of Holberg's richly faceted opus, there is an intellectual coldness of heart that is typical of seventeenth-century neoclassical comedy and the essentially pagan tradition of a comic low style on which it is based. Holberg's comedies, written for the first public theatre to be opened in Denmark in 1722, were the last artistically important expression of the neoclassical tradition in eighteenth-century Europe.

Originally the neoclassical tradition in Europe had come into being as medieval feudalism gave way to Renaissance absolutism. In the drama, playwrights had abandoned the medieval mixture of styles – a mixture of styles that owed its origin to the recognition that Christ, through His own life, had brought dignity within the scope of the common man – in favour of a rigid separation of tragedy and comedy, a high and a low style, modelled on the practice of ancient Greece and Rome.[1] Renaissance kings and princes were not inclined to view themselves in anything like a comic perspective, nor were they apt to acknowledge the rights of their lowlier subjects to sublime thoughts and deeds. Hence the separation of styles in the drama. As the eighteenth-century German critic Gottsched expressed it in his *German Poetics* (1730): 'The characters appropriate to comedy are ordinary citizens or at least people of modest rank. Not that the great of this world never commit any folly. It is merely that to depict them as objects of derision would be contrary to the deference one owes them.'

The eighteenth century saw a gradual return to a militantly Christ-

[1] See E. Auerbach, *Mimesis: The Representation of Reality in Western Literature* (1946; Princeton, NJ, 1953), ch. 3.

ian view of comedy, a view of comedy that acknowledged no essential distinction between high and low styles. In the main, this development was sustained by writers from Europe's professional and merchant classes who presented in their plays liberal Christian sentiments that were fundamentally opposed to the assumptions of Renaissance absolutism.

In 1722, the same year in which Holberg wrote Europe's last great neoclassical comedies, the English writer Richard Steele wrote *The Conscious Lovers*, the first liberal bourgeois comedy in Europe. It was a play that presented the moral and social ideals of England's merchant classes in an assertive, self-confident manner. In his Preface to the play, Steele argued the case for a new style of serious comedy: 'for anything that has its Foundation in Happiness and Success, must be allow'd to be the Object of Comedy; and sure it must be an Improvement of it, to introduce a Joy too exquisite for Laughter, that can have no Spring but in Delight . . .' During the action he not only mingled laughter and his 'Joy too exquisite for Laughter' but also succeeded in expressing the unashamedly propagandist viewpoint that men of humble birth are as capable of sublime thoughts and actions as any aristocrat. In the dialogue this viewpoint is expressed, albeit with a hint of ironic exaggeration, by Mr Sealand, a rich merchant:

> Sir, as much a Cit as you take me for – I know the Town, and the World – and give me leave to say, that we Merchants are a Species of Gentry, that have grown into the World this last Century, and are as honourable, and almost as useful, as you landed Folks, that have always thought yourselves so much above us; For your trading forsooth! is extended no farther, than a Load of Hay, or a fat Ox – You are pleasant People, indeed; because you are generally bred up to be lazy, therefore, I warrant you, Industry is dishonourable.
>
> (IV. ii)

More sublimely it is fleshed out during the action in the noble demeanour of Sealand's long-lost daughter Indiana who proves herself, in her responses to others, the equal of any true-born aristocrat. It comes as no surprise when, at the end of the play, she obtains her just place in society by marrying into the aristocracy.

Steele's play is selfconsciously propagandist in intent and of course suffers from all the aesthetic weaknesses of propagandist drama. Its characters are subservient to situation and are not so much rounded individuals as representative ciphers. Nevertheless it established a pattern of mixed styles in drama that was to have considerable significance for Europe's middle-class writers throughout the remainder of the century.

The vision of social mobility between the classes, expressed at the end of *The Conscious Lovers*, was already becoming a reality in the England of 1722. Elsewhere in Europe such mobility was unheard of. In Germany, for instance, there were irreconcilable differences between the aristocracy and the bourgeoisie, and these were reflected in domestic tragedies written towards the end of the century. Most of them were propagandist melodramas with no real aesthetic merit, but at least two authors managed to transcend the limitations of the genre and produce domestic tragedies of lasting value: Lessing with his play *Emilia Galotti* (1772) and Schiller with *Kabale und Liebe* (*Love and Intrigue*, 1784). In taking class antagonism as the basis for their plays, both Lessing and Schiller drew on ideas the French writer Diderot had first suggested in the essays accompanying *Le Fils naturel* (*The Natural Son*, 1757), in which he had stressed the dramatic potential of conflict between different social groups and classes. Lessing openly acknowledged the debt he owed to Diderot's ideas.

Lessing also thought highly of Steele's play *The Conscious Lovers*, and it had considerable influence on his early attempts at comedy.[2] More particularly he endorsed, in his criticism, Steele's mixing of comic and serious effects. In his essay *Treatises on Tearful or Sentimental Comedy* of 1754 he advocated precisely the kind of middle-class comedy Steele had pioneered: 'Farcical comedy only attempts to provoke laughter, tearful comedy to engage the heart; true comedy attempts both'. In his final comedy, *Minna von Barnhelm* (1767), written against a background of the Seven Years War between Saxony and Prussia, Lessing significantly refined and developed Steele's notion of serious comedy.

In *Minna von Barnhelm* the major characters are aristocrats, but their pattern of behaviour is influenced by middle-class sensibility. The play in fact celebrates the triumph of middle-class ideals of liberal humanism over the rigid and outmoded ideals of the conservative aristocracy. There are touches of genuine comedy in the play, notably in the behaviour of the servants, Just and Franziska, but there is also a good measure of Steele's more sentimental comedy in the interaction between Minna von Barnhelm, a delightful and spirited young lady from Saxony, and her stubborn Prussian fiancé, Major von Tellheim. The most noticeable improvement over Steele's play *The Conscious Lovers* is Lessing's abandonment of overtly class-based propaganda in favour of a more subtle and oblique insinuation of middle-class ideals.

The main body of the action traces out Minna's determined efforts

[2] See Paul Kies, 'Lessing's Relation to Early English Sentimental Comedy', *Publications of the Modern Language Association of America*, XLVII (1932), pp. 807–26.

to persuade the reluctant Tellheim to marry her. Tellheim, we soon learn, still loves Minna deeply, but he refuses to agree to the marriage on grounds of honour. At the end of the war between Prussia and Saxony, he was retired from the army with something of a slur against his name: this has caused him acute financial and psychological embarrassment. Until his name is cleared and he is restored to his former social status, he refuses to have anything to do with Minna. This stubbornly aristocratic insistence on honour at the expense of personal wellbeing is viewed critically by the author and by Minna, whose responses are very close to Lessing's own. She decides to take extreme measures to make Tellheim change his mind, even to the point of fooling him into thinking that she has decided to break off their engagement. Indeed she pushes her game with their engagement rings so far that there is, for a moment, a danger of their relationship breaking up in earnest. However, the various misunderstandings are resolved at the last moment; Tellheim has learnt his lesson and the couple are united in a way that is clearly intended to bring tears to the eyes of the audience. For good measure, Minna's quickwitted maid Franziska is married off to one of Tellheim's men in the last scene of the play, reinforcing the final impression, which the author clearly wishes to leave with his audience, of a 'Joy too exquisite for Laughter'.

Even from this sketchy account of the play it should be apparent that there is an emotional seriousness of texture in the main body of the action that is very different from that of neoclassical comedy. And the role of laughter is proportionately diminished. Individual comic scenes that are more straightforwardly laughter-provoking are for the most part confined to 'low-life' episodes involving the servants. (In *The Conscious Lovers* Steele had used a similar division between a serious high action involving the main characters and a comic low action involving the servants.) There is, however, one occasion in the latter half of the play when Minna is driven by Tellheim's obduracy to use laughter as a social corrective, but only as a last resort, when Tellheim's obstinacy threatens to harden into an inhuman obsession. By exposing him to ridicule she hopes to teach him the error of his ways. Even her bluff with the engagement rings, when she pretends to hand back her ring, but in fact gives back to Tellheim his own ring that he has pawned through lack of ready cash, is part of this same comic stratagem.

Minna only resorted to her comic stratagem under duress and at the end of the play confesses that she found her role as a comic actress none too easy. Significantly what provoked her into using laughter as a social corrective was an inhumanly rigid pattern of behaviour inspired by an outmoded aristocratic code of conduct. What she hopes to achieve by her victory over Tellheim is a relationship based on trust and humanity rather than inherited codes of conduct. Where there is no rigidity, there will be no need for corrective laughter. Instead there can be human interaction founded on mutual respect and understanding. This vision of union with which the play closes is one that could not be further removed from contemporary aristocratic notions as to the purpose of marriage. In place of the eighteenth-century aristocratic concern with caste, honour and estates, Minna offers a vision of union based on equality, trust and sensitive understanding, an essentially humane vision inspired by the ideals of bourgeois liberalism.

Lessing's play was widely acclaimed by his contemporaries. By concentrating on individual patterns of response and avoiding blatant class propaganda, Lessing succeeded in pleasing everyone. But of course his approach begged a number of important issues, both financial and social, and perhaps above all the question of class antagonism which was such a distinctive feature of contemporary German life. Had Tellheim and Minna belonged to different social classes, instead of both belonging to the privileged aristocracy, Lessing would have found himself writing not a serious comedy but a domestic tragedy, which is precisely what happened in his later play, *Emilia Galotti*.

The following passage from a play written a mere eight years after *Minna von Barnhelm* indicates clearly enough the seriousness of this particular issue which Lessing had glossed over in his comedy:

Countess (*to Marie*). Come now, no false modesty. You know you're beautiful; heaven has imposed that penalty on you. You met people above your station who made promises to you. You saw no difficulty at all in rising to a higher station in life. You scorned the girls you had known in your youth, you thought it unnecessary to cultivate any finer qualities in yourself; you shrank from hard work, you treated young men from your own class with contempt and were hated in return. Poor child! How happy you might have made some honest citizen if only your unblemished features and charming manner had been imbued with a spirit of modesty and charity. How you would have been worshipped by your equals, admired and imitated by your betters. But you wanted to be the envy of your peers. Poor child, what were you thinking of and for what miserable fortune did you want to exchange all these advantages? To become the wife of a man who, on your account, would be hated and despised by his whole family. And for the sake of this ill-starred game of chance you were prepared to risk your entire happiness, your honour

and even your life. What were you thinking of? And what were
your parents thinking of? Poor misguided and mistreated child,
poor little victim of vanity. (*Presses Marie to her breast.*) I would
have given my own blood to prevent this from happening.

There is an urgency and directness here in defining the nature of the
problem that is radically different from the oblique tactfulness of
Lessing's approach. And there is none of the humane understanding
that informed the behaviour of Lessing's heroine. The Countess, it is
true, professes to feel sorry for Marie but only after subjecting her to a
verbal attack that is expressly intended to destroy Marie's belief in
herself and her sense of the place she occupies in the world. Motivated by an urgent desire to prevent this young merchant's daughter
from seducing her son, the Countess leaves nothing to chance. Her
analysis of Marie's social pretensions is not only witheringly accurate
but is also expressed with a confusing mixture of mockery and profes-
sedly warm concern, a warm concern that has in it the merest hint of a
sexual overtone. Not surprisingly, after being subjected to this
intensely confusing experience, Marie finds it difficult to believe any
longer in the validity of her own ideas and responses. Shamed and
humiliated, she is prevented from venting her feelings against the
woman who has undermined her belief in herself by the ambiguous
warmth of that same woman. For a time at least, the Countess has her
way with Marie.

In this scene from J. M. R. Lenz's play *Die Soldaten* (*The Soldiers*,
1776) there is no trace of the sentimentally tinged warmth one finds in
Lessing or Steele; instead there is a dispassionate and almost
naturalistic focus on the way two figures interact within a clearly
defined social framework. Lenz seems to have admired Lessing's
work as a critic and as a dramatist – indeed such is his admiration that
Minna von Barnhelm is mentioned warmly by the characters in his play
Der Hofmeister (*The Tutor*) – but in his own plays he raised, in a
painfully direct manner, most of the issues Lessing had instinctively
avoided. In so doing, his work provides something of a bridge between the humane rationalism of eighteenth-century bourgeois comedy, with its careful exclusion of all things unpleasant, and the growing pessimism of nineteenth-century realist comedy.

Unlike Lessing, Lenz was no optimistic rationalist. He was a man
who in his own life knew only too well the power of instinct and
emotion. Increasingly he found his emotions difficult to control and
by the end of the 1770s suffered the first of many schizophrenic
breakdowns that were eventually to make life intolerable for him. In
view of this, it is not surprising that Lenz felt little sympathy with the
liberal humane ideals of Europe's professional and merchant classes.

Significantly, where Lessing had looked to the work of middle-class writers in England and France for his inspiration, Lenz looked back to Shakespeare. In Shakespeare Lenz found a baroque extravagance and vitality similar in spirit to his own; he also found in Shakespeare an understanding of intuitive patterns of feeling of the kind he himself had experienced.

In his *Notes on the Theatre*, written early in his career in 1773, Lenz repeatedly underlined the significance of Shakespeare's work for his own development as a writer. Apart from his advocacy of Shakespeare, the essay also contained Lenz's thoughts on tragedy and comedy which he distinguished as follows: 'In my view, the main thing in a comedy should always be an event, in a tragedy a character'. In his own work as a playwright the distinction is blurred. His major plays are tragicomedies in which the primacy of character alternates, at times almost disconcertingly, with the primacy of event. Two years after his *Notes*, Lenz defended his approach on the grounds that German dramatists were in something of a special position 'because the nation for which they are writing, or for which at least they ought to be writing, is such a hotchpotch of culture and coarseness, civilization and barbarism'. In view of this he felt German dramatists had a duty to write 'comically and tragically at one and the same time. . . . In this way the comic writer creates an audience for the tragic writer'.

Of Lenz's two best-known plays, *Der Hofmeister* (*The Tutor*, 1774) is the more overtly comic in mood and texture. Even so, much of what happens in the play has tragic implications. The main body of the action revolves around the experiences of a young man, a priest's son called Läuffer, who is appointed tutor to the children of an aristocratic family. Constantly humiliated by his aristocratic patrons, Läuffer nevertheless chooses to stay with the family rather than attempt to make his way in the even more frightening world outside the house. Eventually, through sheer boredom, Läuffer seduces the young lady he is supposed to be tutoring, and, when she becomes pregnant, is forced to flee from the family literally to save his life. In other subsidiary actions there are further violent and unhappy episodes including a duel scene and a prison sequence where a young student is committed to gaol, having rashly stood as financial guarantor to a friend who absconds. Meanwhile the young woman whom Läuffer seduced attempts to commit suicide after the birth of her child, while Läuffer, who has taken refuge from her irate father in a small country school, bitterly regrets his action and actually castrates himself in order to still his violent sexual longings.

Against this sort of background, there may not seem to be much scope left for laughter. But in fact throughout the play there is a strong sense of grotesque incongruity between human aspirations and human actions which provokes laughter in even some of the darkest episodes. Läuffer, for instance, discovers that, even without his genitals, he still feels the itch of unstilled sexual appetite and at the end of the play attempts to woo a coquettish young peasant girl with an ardour that is both grotesque and comic.

The play ends, with calculated irony, in a series of sentimental tableaux: Läuffer in a bourgeois idyll with his bride-to-be; his former aristocratic mistress reconciled to her father and with a potential husband willing to marry her despite her past, and so on. But there is no cosy warmth behind these various tableaux, which are engineered with the most improbable twists of plot. Life, as Lenz saw it, was not a cosy sentimental affair; it was a serious and at times grotesquely comic business in which, more often than not, men behaved with destructive irrationality, slaves to their impulses and victims of their emotions.

Lenz's ironic style of tragicomedy was clearly inspired by Shakespeare's dark comedies, but it is nevertheless unique in the way socially conditioned attitudes and prejudices of his own day are built into the very stuff and fabric of his plays, affecting not only the plot but also the pattern of interaction between the various characters, with all that this implies in terms of language, gesture and physical posture. By comparison with the routinely sentimental middle-class dramas written by authors such as Iffland and Kotzebue in the final decades of the eighteenth century, Lenz's plays seem to belong almost to a different age. They point forward to the darker, more problematic plays of Ibsen and Chekhov at the end of the nineteenth century in which comic and tragic elements are woven together in increasingly complex and intricate patterns.

Lenz was, however, only the first of several German writers whose work anticipated future developments in European drama. At the turn of the century Heinrich von Kleist wrote a series of plays that completely bewildered his contemporaries, including Goethe, who finally rejected Kleist's pleas for help, delivered, as Kleist put it, 'on the knees of my heart'. Among these plays was a comedy called *Der zerbrochene Krug* (*The Broken Jug*, 1808) which Goethe did try producing at the Weimar court theatre but with disastrous consequences.

The action of *Der zerbrochene Krug* is full of rumbustiously comic scenes, but there is a serious undertone running through the play, as the author examines a world in which truth and deception seem inextricably mixed. A village judge called Adam tries a case involving ostensibly a broken jug but which, more importantly, involves the reputation and self-respect of a young village girl called Eve. By the end of the play it emerges that Adam was attempting to blackmail Eve into granting him sexual favours under threat of having her fiancé sent as a conscript to the East Indies. Adam the judge is himself judged and some semblance of order is restored to the world, not unlike the semblance of order re-established at the end of *Measure for Measure*, but Eve remains embittered at the fact that no one trusted her, least of all her fiancé, when appearances went against her. There is a dark and potentially tragic edge to this comedy which is played out in a world where appearances are deceptive and confusion is the norm rather than the exception.

   Some thirty years after Kleist had terminated his seemingly hopeless career as a writer by committing suicide with a woman companion, Georg Büchner, a young university lecturer in biology, wrote a handful of plays which were completely neglected by his contemporaries but which have since been acknowledged as belonging to the finest achievements of nineteenth-century German drama. Passionately concerned with man's alienation in a socially unjust and even absurd world, Büchner was above all a writer of tragedies. There is not much laughter in his work, although there are touches of poignantly dark humour in his expressionistic tragedy *Wozzeck* (1836–7); Büchner did, however, manage to write one world-weary comedy called *Leonce und Lena* (1836) in which he laughed, with an irony reminiscent of Musset, at the absurdity of life that normally so oppressed him. 'Dear God, is it true then that we must redeem ourselves with our suffering? Is it true that the world is a crucified saviour, the sun his crown of thorns and the stars the nails in his feet and the spear in his side?' This is the persistent theme of Büchner's work, explored in depth in *Dantons Tod* (*Danton's Death*, 1835) and *Wozzeck*, but here, in the context of *Leonce und Lena*, it is presented with an elegantly brittle sense of *déjà vu*. Life is a pointless game; death and suffering offer the only promise of redemption or at least self-transcendence. But in the world of comedy that particular avenue is closed to the protagonists. All that is left is endless boredom, the boredom that even God felt when He created the world. *Leonce und Lena* closes on a note of profound melancholy as young prince Leonce and his bride Lena face a life that seems to both of them totally devoid of meaning.

   Lenz, Kleist and Büchner, in their different ways, were all precocious harbingers of things to come. And significantly they were rewarded for their insight by the almost complete neglect of their contemporaries. Middle-class theatregoers in the early nineteenth century were not yet ready to tolerate the degree of probing introspection one finds in the work of these writers. On the other hand, they were willing, in the early decades of the century, to see current social attitudes and even problems discussed in an overtly entertaining and rather less sentimental fashion than before. By comparison with the previous century, the middle classes were no longer on the defensive. The drama of mixed styles that middle-class writers had pioneered was now an accepted fact. The innovation of popular nineteenth-century writers was to replace, albeit gradually, the sentimental basis of middle-class comedy – summed up in the notion of a 'Joy too exquisite for Laughter' – with an increasingly realistic and serious treatment of modern social themes. In this way middle-class comedy slowly developed into the middle-class problem play.

By the 1820s vaudevilles and comedies treating social themes, written by the prolific French author Eugène Scribe, were already beginning to find their way into the repertoire of theatres all over Europe. In Scribe's literally hundreds of plays, contemporary bourgeois responses to life were reflected in a lighthearted manner that was simultaneously satiric and flattering. Scribe shared the tastes and prejudices of the middle-class audiences who flocked to his plays and what he offered them in his 'well-made' comedies was an amusing confirmation of their materialistic values. There was some gentle satire in his own work directed against individual excesses, but, for the most part, plays like *Mariage de raison* (*A Marriage of Convenience*, 1826) and *Une Chaîne* (*A Chain*, 1841), which are typical examples of his approach, acknowledged the importance attached to money and social rank by the bourgeoisie of contemporary France and advocated, in the light of this, a hardheaded attitude to marriage and human relationships in general that would enable people to lead, if not happy lives, then at least lives of affluence and quiet contentment. Scribe was no more aware of the philistine limitations of such a view than were his audiences, which undoubtedly contributed to his unparalleled success. But it was also the sheer technical virtuosity of his work that appealed to people – the blatant theatricality of his plots, full of endless surprises and reversals, the tangled web of misunderstandings that kept his characters tied up in knots, the unexpected *coups de théâtre* that filled his audiences with astonishment – and it was this technical virtuosity that spread the influence of his work abroad.

In France, Scribe's comedies provided the starting point for social dramatists like Dumas *fils* and Augier who used his intrigue-play conventions to explore, rather more critically than he would ever have done, increasingly serious problems from bourgeois life. The vogue for social comedies and problem plays gradually spread from France throughout Europe during the nineteenth century. In Scandinavia the influence of French social theatre was particularly strong. In the late 1820s J. L. Heiberg introduced Scribe into Denmark, translating and producing many of his comedies for the Theatre Royal in Copenhagen and drawing on Scribean ideas in his own half-romantic, half-realistic vaudevilles written during the 1830s. Scribe's influence was equally important in the social comedies of Herz and Hostrup, written in Denmark during the 1840s. In Norway, the early problem plays and social comedies of Bjørnson and Ibsen owed a great deal to the combined influence of Scribe and Augier. While Augier had first suggested the kind of themes explored in plays like *A Bankruptcy* (1874) by Bjørnson and *The League of Youth* (1869) by Ibsen, it was Scribe who had established the conventions both dramatists exploited in these early plays. Bjørnson never quite succeeded in overcoming the heritage of Scribean conventions in his work, but it was one of the marks of Ibsen's greatness as a dramatist that he not only assimilated the powerful impact of French writing – his plays were always in the best sense well made – but went on to establish in his mature plays a new and indeed unique type of social tragicomedy that was totally different in spirit from anything seen before.

The Wild Duck, for instance, contains an astonishing mixture of genuinely tragic feeling and an ironic, almost black comedy, bordering on the farcical. Hedvig, a young girl, commits suicide in an adolescent gesture of despair at the incomprehensible behaviour of the adults around her. Gina, her mother, responds with instinctive tenderness and dignity after this shattering event. Hjalmar, her father, weak and self-indulgent by comparison with Gina, takes refuge from real experience in the rhetoric of sentimental melodrama; relieving himself of any guilt feelings at his part in the child's death, he shakes his fist at God in Heaven. Meanwhile Gregers, the incorrigible idealist, believing passionately in the redeeming power of suffering, asserts that Hedvig's death will ennoble her father and bring out the best in him. In contrast Doctor Relling, the intellectual cynic, sees life as a black comedy and Hjalmar as a rather poor ham actor. What is remarkable about the play is the way Ibsen brought together a number of fundamentally divergent responses to experience without in any way damaging the overall fabric of his work. In so doing, he added an entirely new dimension to the mixing of styles attempted by earlier middle-class writers. Even in Lenz's work, for instance, there was at least some alternation between scenes of comedy and tragedy; here the comic and the tragic coexist without in any way invalidating each other. It was this that made *The Wild Duck* unique in European drama when it first appeared, and Ibsen was well aware of its unique status. In a letter to his publisher, Frederik Hegel, dated 2 September 1884, he commented:

This new play in many ways occupies a place of its own among my dramas; the method is in various respects a departure from my earlier one. I do not want to say anything more about this for the present. The critics will, I hope, find the points; in any case they will find plenty to quarrel about, plenty to interpret. Furthermore, I think *The Wild Duck* might entice some of our younger dramatists onto new paths, and that is something I consider desirable.[3]

The Wild Duck remained, in some respects, a unique achievement even for Ibsen. Most of his later plays were tragedies in which comic scenes fulfilled the same kind of function as the comic scenes in Shakespeare's tragedies: they were a means of achieving a momentary release from tension and at the same time a way of underlining, in bitter counterpoint, the tragic texture of the remaining scenes, as, for instance, in the Ulrik Brendel scenes in *Rosmersholm* (1886). In one other play, however, *Hedda Gabler* (1890), Ibsen made use of tragicomic techniques not unlike those he had pioneered in *The Wild Duck*.

In this play it is the main character herself, Hedda Gabler, who experiences life simultaneously as a tragedy and a comedy and, in so doing, provokes a wide range of response from the various people with whom she interacts. Once a general's daughter, Hedda is now married to a none-too-wealthy academic, Jørgen Tesman, who is more interested in the domestic industries of Brabant in the Middle Ages than in the complex emotional make-up of his young and disdainfully beautiful wife. The incongruity of Tesman's response to Hedda is consistently comic. Her cobra-like swiftness of wit and subtlety of response are beyond him, so much so that he is not aware of her ridicule even at those moments when he is the immediate object of it.

Judge Brack, on the other hand, a close friend of Hedda's and Tesman's, is intellectually Hedda's equal. Now that Hedda is safely married, there is nothing Brack would like more than to see her become his mistress. The sparring between then is accordingly rich with sexual innuendo and subtly comic undertones. In Act II Hedda laughingly fires her pistols near the Judge as he enters their house through the garden and comments somewhat ambiguously: 'That'll teach you to come in the back way!' The full implications of her remark are followed up by Brack towards the end of the next act:

> *Hedda.* (*Gets up.*) Are you leaving through the garden?
> *Brack.* Yes. It's shorter.
> *Hedda.* Yes. And it's a back door, isn't it?
> *Brack.* Very true. I have nothing against back doors. They can be quite intriguing – at times.
> *Hedda.* When pistols are fired out of them, perhaps?

[3] *Henrik Ibsen: A Critical Anthology*, ed. J. McFarlane (Harmondsworth, 1970), p. 104.

Brack. (*In the doorway, laughs.*) Oh, people don't shoot their tame cocks.

Hedda. (*Laughs, too.*) No, I suppose not, when they've only got one.

Laughingly, both of them share the sexual innuendo. But there is tension under the laughter. Hedda is determined that this kind of sexual pleasure is the only one the Judge will ever manage to share with her. She has no intention of becoming his plaything.

Brack understands Hedda as a woman of wit, but he does not see the more reflective and serious side of Hedda's personality. The only character who appreciates Hedda's deeply felt longing for truth and beauty, for a life of emotional and sexual fulfilment without subterfuge and shame, is the writer Ejlert Løvborg. Ejlert is a man who dares to live out his deepest longings and face the consequences; because of this he fills Hedda with fascination and horror. Hedda is terrified of scandal and the destructive potential of public opinion. Her repressive and sexually confusing upbringing – her father insisted on treating her as if she were a boy – has filled her with severe inhibitions. She is ashamed of her secret thoughts and fantasies, afraid to reveal to anyone what she really thinks. Her life seems to her a half-life, except in the presence of Løvborg. Long before she was married, Løvborg used to visit her at her father's home and she would make him confess all the extravagant and outrageous things he had done since their last meeting. Through Løvborg Hedda lived, if only vicariously. For her he became a fantasy hero.

In the play itself the interaction between these two is extremely complex, and it culminates in tragedy. Løvborg has become a reformed man. Under the influence of another woman, Thea Elvsted, he has given up his drink and brothels and dedicated himself to writing. Hedda cannot bear the thought of Ejlert, her Dionysian hero, being reduced to the level of domesticated responsibility by any woman. She wantonly destroys the manuscript of the book Ejlert has written under the calming influence of Thea Elvsted and subsequently encourages his frenzied death-wish in the light of this irreparable loss. As Hedda sends Ejlert away from her to commit suicide with one of her pistols, she pleads with him to do it beautifully. What she envisages is a gesture of aristocratic contempt for the world and its petty tribulations, an act of wilfully beautiful self-destruction. But here the tragic fiction Hedda has constructed begins to break down.

Ejlert proves to be human, comically human, at the very moment when Hedda expects most from him. Drunk and confused, he ends up in a local brothel, quarrels with a redheaded singer, and accidentally shoots himself in the crotch. A more grotesque distortion of

Hedda's tragic fiction it would be difficult to envisage. The world of real experience, where intense emotions can be fully and truthfully lived out without any comic taint, for ever seems to elude her. After Ejlert's almost farcical end, all that is left her is the cosy domesticity of her husband, now ironically determined to reconstruct Ejlert's 'lost' manuscript with the help of Mrs Elvsted, and the sexual blackmail of Judge Brack who has enough evidence to link Hedda with Ejlert's death but is prepared to remain silent – at a price. Faced with these alternatives, Hedda decides to live out her tragic fiction for herself.

Hedda's suicide has in it the makings of tragedy, but perhaps there is something too selfconscious about it for it to be totally convincing. Tragedy, at its most intense, leaves no room for reflection. Hedda, even in her death, remains a creature of intellect. She is a woman who has carefully weighed up the odds and found them so stacked against her as to make life hardly worth living. She therefore opts out. And there is almost more comedy than tragedy in her going. The sudden-ness of her departure produces a grotesquely incongruous response both from Tesman and from Brack, a response that Hedda almost certainly anticipated:

> Tesman. (*Shouts at Brack.*) She's shot herself! Shot herself in the head! Just think!
> Brack. (*Half paralysed in the armchair.*) But, good God! People don't do such things!

Even at this point Hedda remains more of a comic than a tragic heroine. One cannot, after all, have the last laugh, as Hedda insists, and still provoke that mixture of fear and pity appropriate for a tragic heroine. Nevertheless, there is something deeply disturbing and tragic in the fate of this woman, intelligent and sensitive, perhaps even gifted, and yet so emotionally stunted by her upbringing, so cowed by the repressive values of her social environment, that she cannot relate spontaneously and openly to any of the people around her. Prevented from relating to others, Hedda can achieve no satisfac-tory vision of what she herself is or even might be. Instead she lives out a series of increasingly destructive fantasies that culminate in her own suicide and the death of the potentially brilliant Løvborg.

Hedda Gabler was a tragicomedy in which Ibsen, in the text and in the hidden poetry between the lines of the text, showed the spiritual and psychological alienation of modern man. The destructive pattern of process he saw in modern life was something his contemporaries were at first unwilling to recognize. *Hedda Gabler* was dismissed as a drama of abnormal psychology; Hedda herself was described as 'a horrid miscarriage of the imagination, a monster in female form to whom no parallel can be found in real life'.[4] It was perhaps the austerity of Ibsen's vision that disturbed his contemporaries. Even the laughter provoked by *Hedda Gabler* brought no sense of spiritual release. At its best it might be seen as a last defence against absurdity; at its worst an ironic gesture of despair. But the validity of Ibsen's vision was soon affirmed in the work of other contemporary writers.

Closest in spirit to Ibsen was the Russian author Anton Chekhov. His tragicomedies from the late 1890s could hardly have been written without the example of Ibsen's pioneering work. Chekhov was, however, less austere in his approach than Ibsen, more inclined to be wistfully elegiac in the face of life's absurdity. There were also other influences on his work, notably that of earlier Russian authors such as Griboyedov, Ostrovsky and Turgenev who had developed a peculiarly Russian style of character drawing in their comedies during the course of the nineteenth century.[5] But the blending of comic and tragic responses in his plays owed a great deal to Ibsen's exploration of tragicomic patterns of experience in *The Wild Duck* and *Hedda Gabler*.

Chekhov always insisted, to the bewilderment of his contemporaries, that his late plays were comedies. To a certain extent they were. There was comedy in all of them even at moments of great seriousness, perhaps above all at such moments, but a major part of their action traced out serious and tragic events. The point was that Chekhov had little faith in human dignity and even less in man's ability to cope nobly with adversity. There is, as a result, something ridiculous and yet at the same time pathetic in the way his characters respond to the inevitable suffering and tragedy that life brings, provoking in an audience a peculiar blend of laughter and poignant sympathy. The following passage from *The Seagull* (1896) illustrates this very simply:

> *Sorin.* I'd like to give Constantine a plot for a novel. It ought to be called *The Man who Wanted* – *L'homme qui a voulu*. In youth I wanted to become a writer – I didn't. I wanted to speak well – I spoke atrociously. (*Mocks himself.*) 'And all that sort, er, of thing, er, don't yer know.' I'd be doing a summing-up sometimes, and find myself jawing on and on till I broke out in a sweat. I wanted to marry – I didn't. I wanted to live in town all the time – and here I am ending my days in the country and so on.
>
> *Dorn.* You wanted to become a senior civil servant – and did.

[4] Quoted by M. Meyer, *Ibsen: A Biography* (Harmondsworth, 1974), p. 670.
[5] See M. Valency, *The Breaking String: The Plays of Anton Chekhov* (London, 1966), ch. 1.

Sorin. (Laughs.) That's one thing I wasn't keen on, it just happened.

Dorn. To talk about being fed up with life at the age of sixty-two –
that's a bit cheap, wouldn't you say?

Sorin. Don't keep on about it, can't you see I want a bit of life?

Dorn. That's just silly. All life must end, it's in the nature of things.

Sorin. You're spoilt, that's why you talk like this. You've always
had what you wanted, so life doesn't matter to you, you just
don't bother. But even you'll be afraid of dying.

Dorn. Fear of death's an animal thing, you must get over it. It only
makes sense to fear death if you believe in immortality and are
scared because you've sinned. But you aren't a Christian for a
start, and then – what sins have you committed? You've worked
for the Department of Justice for twenty-five years, that's all.

Sorin. (Laughs.) Twenty-eight.

Sorin is seriously ill; he realizes he is about to die and is afraid of
death. His immediate response is to complain, somewhat self-
indulgently, of his pointless life. He has never achieved anything of
significance, never really done any of the things he wanted to. He has
existed but never truly been alive. Now that death faces him, he
panics, and is filled by a totally incongruous urge to live, fully and
meaningfully, in a way that has always eluded him. The fact that he is
totally incapacitated, confined to a bath-chair, makes his urge all the
more incongruous. His predicament is essentially comic. And yet his fear
of death, manifested in his awareness of the absurd waste of his life,
is full of genuine pathos. One laughs at Sorin and yet one feels for him.

Sorin's life has been wasted, but he is far from being a tragic figure,
as Chekhov shows in the way Dorn responds to him. Dr Dorn, rather
like Relling in *The Wild Duck*, is a realist who knows only too well the
limitations of life and has learnt to accept them. He recognizes at once
that Sorin's complaints of his pointless life are not to be taken at face
value but are an expression of Sorin's fear of death. His response is to
try to help Sorin come to terms with his fears by making him laugh at
his predicament instead of wallowing in it. His oblique technique
succeeds. Despite all the pathetic appeals for sympathy, Sorin himself acknowledges that he is a comic figure and laughs at himself.

All of the characters in the play are to some extent comic, including
the young writer Constantine to whom Sorin refers in the above
passage. Unlike Sorin, however, Constantine is oblivious to the
comic undertones in his behaviour. Instead he views himself and his
emotional problems with committed earnestness, dramatizing his
various failures in a way that provokes almost more laughter than
sympathy. Nevertheless Constantine does suffer genuinely from his

uneasy relationship with his actress mother, Irina Arkadin, a beautiful but no longer young woman who is far too preoccupied with her career and her love life to give much thought to the complex emotional needs of her son. He also suffers deeply from his relationship with Nina, a young country girl with whom he falls in love but who deserts him in favour of the mature and successful writer Trigorin. And certainly his passionate jealousy of Trigorin, who for years has been his mother's lover and who now takes Nina from him, is perfectly justified.

What makes Constantine's behaviour comic, however, is the exaggerated seriousness with which he responds to his misfortunes. In the opening scene of the play he is plunged into suicidal despair when his mother and some of her friends dare to laugh at his clumsy attempt at playwriting. In Act II he actually threatens to shoot himself when Nina cools in her feelings towards him, symbolically laying at her feet a seagull he has shot that same morning to suggest her wanton destruction of his spirit. Even by the end of the play, when he has begun to achieve some success as an author, he is still pathetically unaware of anything beyond the narrow horizon of his own immediate world of suffering. After a final abortive attempt to win back Nina, he decides to shoot himself in earnest. Appropriately, his last comment as Nina leaves him and he tears up his manuscripts is completely incongruous: 'It'll be a pity if anyone sees her in the garden and tells Mother. It might upset her.' The thought that his mother might be more upset at his suicide than at a report of Nina's presence simply does not cross his mind.

Constantine's life is as wasted as Sorin's, although for very different reasons. And yet whatever sympathy one feels for him is tempered by the comic perspective in which so many of his responses and actions are viewed in the play. For Chekhov life is an absurd tragicomedy, Constantine a hapless victim of life's tragicomic rhythm. Ultimately his death is of no particular significance, nor will it have any profound effect on those he knew most intimately.

One need only compare the ending of *The Seagull* with, say, *Ghosts* to realize something of the difference between Chekhov's and Ibsen's vision of life. Ibsen's characters are victims of tragic process, caught in a vicious spiral from which they simply cannot escape; but they are aware of life's beauty and mystery and that only heightens the poignancy of their failure. In *Ghosts* Osvald Alving's tortured relationship with his mother drives him into madness, despite his longing for light and happiness, for a life of creative independence.[6] At the end of the play a strong sense of tragic waste is communicated to an audience.

[6] See David Thomas, 'Patterns of Interaction in Ibsen's *Ghosts*', *Ibsenårbok 1974*, ed. D. Haakonsen (Oslo, 1974), pp. 89–117.

At the end of *The Seagull*, which revolves around an equally tortured relationship between a mother and her son and culminates in Constantine's suicide, there is simply a sense of emptiness. Passions have been stirred, thoughts expressed, words written down, but nothing has fundamentally changed and all too soon the characters who are left will have forgotten Constantine and his problems. In their turn, they too are aware of the transient nature of their existence and of the fact that they also will disappear without trace. 'Yes, we'll be forgotten. Such is our fate and we can't do anything about it. And the things that strike us as so very serious and important, they'll all be forgotten one day or won't seem to matter.' The words are spoken by Vershinin, one of the characters in Chekhov's play *The Three Sisters* (1900–1), but the sentiments they express apply equally well to *The Seagull* and to Chekhov's last play *The Cherry Orchard* (1903–4).

To write tragedy means in some sense to believe, if not in God or some other metaphysical order, then at least in human dignity. It was that that made Ibsen above all a writer of modern tragedy who occasionally used comic techniques in his work to communicate an essentially tragic vision. Chekhov, as an extreme rationalist, was too sceptical a man to believe in anything except life's comic absurdity. In his view man was too frail a creature to be capable of real dignity. He clearly felt a certain sympathy with his characters in their different predicaments, but, like the well-trained doctor that he was, he never allowed his sympathy to extend to empathy. It was that, as he well knew, that made him above all a comic dramatist.

What emerges from this review of the way Northern European comedy developed during the eighteenth and nineteenth centuries is a major shift in emphasis during the period from the social to the existential. For the neoclassicist Holberg, comedy was essentially a social corrective, the aims of which were to castigate folly and, through the use of ridicule, to bring deviant behaviour into line with accepted social norms. For middle-class writers in the eighteenth century, comedy was a vehicle for expressing the social aspirations and moral sentiments of their particular class. For writers of social comedies in the nineteenth century, it was a means of examining specific social issues and problems. But for a small group of writers towards the end of the eighteenth century, and for Ibsen and Chekhov at the end of the nineteenth century, comedy became a means of expressing insight into man's existential situation. By definition that included a social perspective, but the overall sweep was wider than anything seen before in European comedy. For these dramatists, writing in an age of growing unbelief, laughter was a last defence against absurdity, for some even a last gesture of defiance as the darkness closed in around them.

8

Twentieth-century comedy

GEORGE BRANDT

Laughter . . . indicates a slight revolt on the surface of social life.
. . . It . . . is a froth with a saline base. Like froth, it sparkles. It is
gaiety itself. But the philosopher who gathers a handful to taste
may find that the substance is scanty, and the after-taste bitter.
(HENRI BERGSON, *Laughter*
(London, 1921), p. 200)

Man's freedom manifests itself in laughter, his necessity
in crying; today we have to demonstrate freedom. The tyrants of
this planet are not moved by the works of poets, they yawn at their
lamentations, they consider their heroic lays silly nursery tales,
they fall asleep over their religious poetry, there is only one
thing they fear: their mockery. So parody has crept into all
genres, into the novel, into drama, into lyrical poetry.
(F. DÜRRENMATT, *Theater-Schriften und Reden*
(Zürich, 1966), p. 128)

. . . I wrote some plays. One of them, *Huge Cloudy Symbols*,
was performed, twice on the same night, as a farce and as a
serious drama. I didn't know it then, but this was an exact
statement of the ambivalence within myself. Later in life, I
tried to combine comedy and drama, feeling that things were
both ridiculous and tragic at the same time.
(E. KAZAN in M. CIMENT, *Kazan on Kazan*
(London, 1973), p. 14)

TO ATTEMPT to squeeze twentieth-century comedy into one chapter
is, appropriately enough, absurd.

For one thing, the field is vast. Also, it does not subdivide neatly
along national lines as do earlier periods of drama. It is less meaningful than it used to be to speak of English, French, German or Ameri-

can theatre as wholly separate entities. Even the famous Iron Curtain is theatrically speaking full of holes, holes moreover that face both ways (as holes are apt to do). They wait for Godot in the East, Mrozek's Tango is danced in the West, Brecht's Arturo Ui rises resistibly everywhere. True, comedy is still a shade more national than other forms of drama since it depends on shared reflexes. Nevertheless, the broad trends in playwriting do not stop at frontiers. Indeed the field is vast.

For another thing, the twentieth century is a somewhat vague chronological abstraction. For many purposes it began in 1914. From the point of view of comedy it began in 1896. Let us be more precise: the twentieth century began on 10 December 1896 with the first of two performances that season of Alfred Jarry's *Ubu Rex* (*Ubu roi*) at the Théâtre de l'Œuvre in Paris. The scandal provoked by the play, with its opening expletive 'Merdre!' (variously translated: 'Shittr!' – 'Shittle!' – or 'Pschitt!', none of which quite catches the satisfying sonority of the original) has passed into theatre history.

Did the first-night audience, wincing at this slap in the face of card-carrying members of the bourgeoisie, i.e. themselves, see the full significance of the event? Does the acknowledged influence on Jarry of the German playwright Christian Dietrich Grabbe's *Jest, Satire, Irony and Deeper Meaning* (1822) spoil my neat scheme of the genesis of modern comedy? Rhetorical questions to which there is no answer. No matter whether the author, or the play's director, Lugné-Poe, or Firmin Gémier, the first Ubu, or the rioting audience, knew it; regardless of the play's links with earlier drama, we can now see in retrospect that the voice of the new age had spoken, some three years before the turn of the century.

To an outside observer – say, a Martian historian – the twentieth century might seem unpropitious for comedy. It has witnessed some of the greatest disasters in human history: worldwide economic crises, two world conflicts, a Thirty Years War in Vietnam, fascism, systematic genocide, the invention of fission and fusion bombs, the threat of biological and environmental warfare. More a time, the outsider might think, for tragedy. In fact, the twentieth century has produced very little tragedy. The dramatic reflection of an age is not so direct or simple. What matters more than the facts themselves is the model of the world in people's heads: our self-image moulds our perception of events. 'The pursuit of tragedy', writes George Steiner of recent times, 'is marred by a great failure of nerve.'[1] The idealized picture of man that made tragedy possible was based, perhaps more than would-be revivers of the genre would have us believe, on the

[1] Steiner, *The Death of Tragedy* (London, 1961), p. 304.

concept of rigid social divisions. Renaissance theorists were quite explicit about this. Writing in 1561, Julius Caesar Scaliger made the following class-based distinction:

> Tragedy, like comedy, is patterned after real life, but it differs from comedy in the rank of its characters, in the nature of the action, and in the outcome. . . . Comedy employs characters from rustic, or low city life. . . . The beginning of a comedy presents a confused state of affairs, and this confusion is happily cleared up at the end. The language is that of everyday life. Tragedy, on the other hand, employs kings and princes, whose affairs are those of the city, the fortress, and the camp. A tragedy opens more tranquilly than a comedy, but the outcome is horrifying. The language is grave, polished, removed from the colloquial.[2]

This strict genre distinction reflects not just social stratification as such but a consciousness of, a *belief* in, this stratification. Kings and nobles were held to be creatures different in kind from the common herd. The ordinary citizen, at least as a stage figure, was inevitably mean and ridiculous. In English seventeenth-century usage the word 'cit' implied contempt.

Now what has been changing in our century is not merely the old class structure as such; what has gone is, even more significantly, the belief that status expresses an inherent quality. Divinity no longer hedges kings; aristocrats are just people with a handle to their names. Even the difference between the rich and the rest of us is merely this: the rich have more money. This blurring of *felt* distinctions among men has led to a blurring of the genre distinctions in drama. Comedy has proved less vulnerable in this than tragedy. Not walking on high stilts, it is less easily shaken by the winds of change. Even so, in its classical high form it needs, or at any rate best flourishes in, certain social conditions. As George Meredith put it in his well-known essay in 1877: 'A society of cultivated men and women is required, wherein ideas are current and perceptions quick, that [the comic poet] may be supplied with matter and an audience. The semi-barbarism of merely giddy communities, and feverish emotional periods, repels him . . .'[3] This idealistic image of society may be vague; it does, however, sketch a picture sufficiently different from today's world for us not to be greatly surprised to find that classical, i.e. class-based, comedy is not what it used to be.

Let us not overstate our case. Obviously comedies of a traditional type continue to be written and performed. In England, for instance,

---

[2] In B. H. Clark (ed.), *European Theories of the Drama* (New York, 1947), p. 61.
[3] Meredith, *An Essay on Comedy and the Uses of the Comic Spirit* (London, 1918), p. 8.

writers like Noël Coward and Ben Travers have been able to ply their
craft with commercial and critical success, without breaking the
mould of comedy of manners and farce respectively, several generations after the *Ubu* affair. It has been said of the most prolific English
writer of comedies in the sixties and seventies, Alan Ayckbourn, that
he has '. . . most consistently avoided any suggestion of deeper
meaning in his plays. Try as we may we cannot find any trace of social
or political indoctrination masquerading as harmless diversion, let
alone of cosmic anguish.'[4] Indeed, Ayckbourn himself has made this
very point in the Introduction to his first widely acclaimed comedy:

> In general, the people who liked this play when it was first seen
> remarked that it was 'well constructed'; those that didn't called it
> old-fashioned. If the latter is true, then I suppose it's because, as
> the song goes, I am too.[5]

And in the United States Neil Simon is alleged to have made more
money than any writer in the history of the theatre with his far from
revolutionary comedies, from *Barefoot in the Park* (1963) onwards.

To bring an essential point into focus, however, I propose to limit
my survey of twentieth-century comedy to its specifically twentieth-
century elements. There is a *new comic response* palpably different from
that of the past. The new response arises precisely out of the blurring
of genre boundaries I have mentioned. This shift works in two ways.
Internally, the distinctions between the various branches of comedy
have weakened; high comedy mingles with farce, satire frequently
intrudes. Externally, the realms of comedy and tragedy now share
certain border territories or coalesce. Playwrights are, of course, well
aware of this. Hence their frequent attempts to invent generic names
other than that of straightforward 'comedy'. Thus Apollinaire called
his polemical piece *The Breasts of Tiresias* (a farcical clarion call for more
lovemaking in order to increase the population of France, which was
written in the wake of *Ubu Rex* in 1903 but not staged until 1917) a
'surrealist drama'. Though the label anticipated the founding of the
surrealist movement by several years, it was intended to emphasize
that this was a comedy of a new type. In the Prologue, the Director,
emerging from the prompt box in evening attire and carrying a
swagger-stick, made these programmatic points (among others):

> Here you will find actions
> Which add to the central drama and augment it
> Changes of tone from pathos to burlesque

[4] J. R. Taylor, *The Second Wave: British Drama for the Seventies* (London, 1971),
   p. 156.
[5] Ayckbourn, *Relatively Speaking* (London, 1968).

And the reasonable use of the improbable
And actors who may be collective or not
Not necessarily taken from mankind
But from the universe.[6]

Later, the movement under André Breton's leadership was to take over the surrealist label with somewhat different connotations. But surrealist drama *proprement dit* – the provocative work of Breton, Tzara and others – certainly had its comic aspect. While this was largely a French affair, in Italy the Theatre of the Grotesque had a brief vogue after the First World War. The outstanding example, Luigi Chiarelli's *The Mask and the Face* (written in 1913, first produced in 1916), is subtitled 'A Grotesque Comedy in Three Acts'. Its grotesquerie consists less in any formal innovations (structurally it is in fact quite traditional) than in its (for the time) bold challenge to upperclass Italian notions of honour.

Count Paolo Grazia lacks the courage to kill his unfaithful wife Savina. He sends her away in secret but pretends to have done 'the right thing' by drowning her in Lake Como. He is sent to prison for this imaginary crime. When he is released he becomes something of a hero to his circle. But Savina returns unexpectedly. An unrecognizable body had actually been fished out of the lake, and all was on the point of sorting itself out. But Paolo and Savina decide that they love one another after all. In order to keep intact his reputation as an implacable defender of his honour, Paolo is forced to steal away out of his own house with his wife and leave his social circle for ever. What is grotesque is not so much Paolo and Savina themselves as a society that forces them to act in so unnatural a manner.

As early as 1908, Luigi Pirandello had defined the difference between the comic and what he called the humorous in his essay on *Humourism*. According to him, 'humourism' was a fusion of laughter and grief, a trespassing of the comic into the region of feeling. As the century wore on there was to be more and more of this trespassing. The expressions 'sick humour' and 'black comedy' have become the small change of critical journalism. (Paradoxically, Peter Shaffer's one-act play *Black Comedy* (1965) is free of any such stylistic ambiguity. This farcical comedy uses the convention derived from Chinese theatre of presenting in full view scenes supposed to be happening in the dark: the blackness of the title refers to a reversed lighting scheme, not a mixture of moods.)

Other dramatists have invented other generic names for their works or have tortured old names into new meanings. The Spanish

[6] *Modern French Plays: An Anthology from Jarry to Ionesco*, ed. M. Benedikt and G. Wellwarth (London, 1964), p. 66.

author Ramón del Valle-Inclán termed the satirical pieces he wrote in the twenties, such as *The Horns of Don Friolera* (1921), *esperpentos* (i.e. 'scarecrows' or 'grotesques'). The Polish proto-absurdist Witkiewicz stuck some odd labels on his plays. Of the two visions of collapsing civilization he wrote in 1921, one, *Gyubal Wazahar or Along the Cliffs of the Absurd*, was called 'A Non-Euclidean Drama in Four Acts' and the other, *The Water Hen*, was 'A Spherical Tragedy in Three Acts'. Some of Eugène Ionesco's play-descriptions stress the fact that conventional categories do not apply. Calling *The Bald Prima Donna* (1950) an 'anti-play' was an aggressive declaration of hostility to traditional theatre; calling the grotesque *Jacques or Obedience* (written 1950, first performed 1955) a 'naturalistic comedy' was no less intentionally provocative.

If Beckett names the English version of *Waiting for Godot* (1954) a 'tragicomedy', he may appear to have placed himself within a long mixed-genre tradition. This fails (perhaps deliberately) to reveal the novelty of what he had done. The word 'tragicomedy' has been used down the ages with varying shades of meaning. To Plautus it was an action drawn from contrasting spheres of life, including the divine. In the Prologue to *Amphitryon*, he made the god Mercury, disguised as the slave Sosia, say:

> Are you frowning because I said that this would be a tragedy? . . . I will bring about a mixture: let it be tragicomedy. For I do not think it proper to make it wholly comedy, since there are kings and gods. What then? Since there is also a slave, it will be . . . a tragicomedy.

In Renaissance usage, the term tended to describe a potentially tragic action that ended happily. 'A tragi-comedy', wrote John Fletcher in his preface 'To the Reader' of his pastoral play *The Faithful Shepherdess* (1608–9?), 'is not so called in respect of mirth and killing, but in respect it wants deaths, which is enough to make it no tragedy, yet brings some near it, which is enough to make it no comedy . . .' Though he emphasized the nature of the *action*, he followed Plautus concerning the persons in tragicomedy in stating that 'a god is as lawful in this as in a tragedy, and mean people as in a comedy'.

Now *Waiting for Godot* is not a tragicomedy in either sense. There is no mixture of persons drawn from different spheres, nor is there a fatal outcome narrowly averted. The waiting of Estragon and Vladimir is comic or tragic according to viewpoint or, more properly, to viewing distance. The nearsighted view of their attempts to kill time with chitchat, the odd nibble and clownish business with hats and boots is (for lack of a better word) comic. The panoramic view of their endless wait, twice and perhaps eternally frustrated, verges (in a sense) on the tragic. Neither word quite covers the mixed feelings evoked. The tragic note is brusquely undercut at the end when Estragon takes off the string that holds up his trousers in order to hang himself – and his trousers fall down. So tragicomedy in *Waiting for Godot* is not a mosaic of happy and unhappy events. The event itself, or perhaps the lack of it, is pitched in a no man's land which the older categories are powerless to fix.

When Dürrenmatt calls *The Visit* (more properly *The Old Lady's Visit*, 1956) a 'tragical comedy', he too means this in a specifically modern sense. The elderly Claire Zachanassian, the richest woman in the world, returns to the small town of Güllen from which she had been driven in disgrace as a young girl. She offers the citizens of Güllen fabulous endowments if they will do away with one Alfred Ill, her former lover who had betrayed her. Step by step the citizens are corrupted by greed; in the end, turning into a lynch mob, they kill their profitable victim. But the tone of the play is not as black as this summary may suggest. Dürrenmatt presents his ironic view of human motivation with plenty of theatrical trickery: scene changes take place in full view, four citizens act the part of a forest, the Old Lady has her seventh, eighth and ninth husbands in her suite as well as the judge who had once sentenced her but who is now her butler. Like *Waiting for Godot*, the play straddles the comic and tragic at once. '*The Visit*' is' – according to the author – 'an ill-natured play, but just for that reason it must not be produced in an ill-natured but in the most humane way, sorrowfully rather than angrily, indeed humorously too, for nothing is more damaging to this comedy which ends tragically than total seriousness.'[7]

Borrowing a term from Shakespearian criticism, J. L. Styan has called this new type of play the 'dark comedy'. Although, in the book by that title, he casts his net rather wider in time than I am doing here, it may be useful to quote his definition of this very contemporary genre. 'Dark comedy is a drama which impels the spectator forward by stimulus to mind and heart, then distracts him, muddles him, so that time and time again he must review his own activity in watching the play.'[8]

A variant of this dark comedy that established itself in the fifties in a good many countries is the Theatre of the Absurd. Deriving in part from surrealism, this genre has been clearly pinpointed since the publication of Martin Esslin's authoritative book on the subject. Absurdism largely accepts that the world is beyond 'mere' rational comprehension. It is nevertheless the case, according to Esslin, that 'since . . . the incomprehensibility of the motives, and the often

---

[7] Dürrenmatt, *Der Besuch der alten Dame* (Zürich, 1956), p. 103.
[8] Styan, *The Dark Comedy* (Cambridge, 1968), p. 262.

unexplained and mÿsterious nature of the characters' actions . . . effectively prevent identification, such theatre is a comic theatre in spite of the fact that its subject-matter is sombre, violent and bitter.'[9]

True, the Theatre of the Absurd may be comic, but it carries a powerful charge of anguish. If drama is a mirror of life and the images in this mirror are undecipherable, it follows that the life whose reflection is so baffling must itself be baffling. This bafflement is felt to be painful; our world of traps, pitfalls and delusions is basically unfriendly – a world of menace.

The label 'comedy of menace' (a journalistic pun on 'comedy of manners') has been hung on the work of Harold Pinter. His earlier plays are perhaps too rooted in a recognizable environment to be fairly classified as absurdist, as is sometimes done. But, like Beckett or Ionesco, Pinter often makes a bleak utterance sound like a joke. Thus, in the one-act play *The Dumb Waiter* (premièred in Germany in 1959), the action of which has been likened to a Hitchcock story with the last reel missing, two smalltime gunmen, Ben and Gus, are waiting to perform a contract killing in the basement of a former restaurant. The situation is black enough; but theatrically the struggle for dominance between the two killers, which turns out to be a life-and-death struggle, comes over as funny. Their trivial chitchat is in violent contrast to their lethal mission; they quarrel furiously over whether one should say 'light the gas' or 'light the kettle'.

I have suggested before that, when class divisions no longer express the essence of a person, old genre distinctions have largely lost their *raison d'être*. But there is more than the blurring of class lines to modern comic drama. Modern man sees himself (at least in so far as he is a theatregoer) as involved in a complex urban society. Now the scale of urban life has altered strikingly, a change of quantity becoming one of quality. There are not merely more individuals around than ever before; the role of the individual in society has, or appears to have, shrunk drastically. Friedrich Dürrenmatt has recognized this changed sense of life not only in his playwriting but theoretically as well:

> Tragedy presupposes guilt, suffering, balance, insight, responsibility. In the muddle of our century, in this last dance of the white race, no one is guilty and no one is responsible any longer. Nobody could help it and nobody wanted it to happen. Everybody really is dispensable. . . . That is our bad luck, not our guilt: guilt only exists now as a personal achievement, as a religious act. All we are entitled to is comedy. . . .[10]

[9] Esslin, *The Theatre of the Absurd* (London, 1964), p. 300.
[10] Dürrenmatt, *Theater-Schriften und Reden*, p. 122.

But if tragedy has always rested on the bedrock of established values, so traditionally has comedy. The new sensibility has not only changed the quality of our laughter, it has also changed its target. The social framework itself, rather than the deviant individual, has become matter for mockery.

In the past, when spectators were rocking with laughter, they were safe. The butt was up there on the stage and could be mocked without any self-questioning. Now when the auditorium is rocking it may be an earthquake right under our feet. As likely as not we are ourselves the butts – not in our personal capacity as misanthropes or imaginary invalids but as members of a society that is palpably sick. Laughter used to confirm social norms and in that sense was conservative. Now it often becomes a means of insight into social contradictions and in that sense disturbs the norm.

Ours is the first epoch in which the word 'disturbing' has been used as a term of critical approbation. It is just this disturbing quality that gave the first night of *Ubu Rex* its claim to have brought in a new vision of man. Yeats's shuddering reaction – 'After us the Savage God' – is well known.[11] Was he right – or was Mallarmé right when he called the homicidal clown Ubu 'a prodigious personage' and claimed that he would enter 'into the repertoire of high taste' henceforth?[12]

History has played its own joke with this archetypal modern comedy. The original notion of its grotesque antihero had not been Jarry's at all. Nor was Jarry's idea of building a play around Ubu at first intended for the live theatre. The fact is that Pa Ubu was modelled on a physics teacher at the Rennes lycée, an unfortunate gentleman by the name of Monsieur Hébert. The butt of his pupils' hatred, he collected a generous number of nicknames: Père Heb, P. H., Eb, Ébé, Ébon, Ébance, Ébouille. In 1885 two lycée students, Henri and Charles Morin, wrote a satire entitled *The Poles* in which the detested teacher, under the name of 'le père Ébé', had a series of unfortunate adventures as the King of Poland. When Alfred Jarry joined the school in 1888, he converted this ready-made story into a puppet play which still bore the title *The Poles*. But the figure of the monstrous pedant took hold of Jarry's mind and continued to preoccupy him. When he went to Paris in 1891 he wrote the two plays (for live actors, not puppets this time), *Ubu Cuckolded* and *Ubu Rex*. In 1896 he managed to persuade Lugné-Poe, for whom he was working as secretary, to put on *Ubu Rex*. Why exactly was the play felt to be such a new departure in comedy?

The opening word only epitomized an aggressiveness that knocked older notions of comedy sideways. There is an element of literary

---

[11] Yeats, *Autobiographies* (London, 1955), p. 349.
[12] J. Robichez, *Le Symbolisme au théâtre* (Paris, 1957), pp. 359–60.

parody in *Ubu* – not so much a dig at Sophocles as the title suggests, more of a mock Macbeth. Ubu is the classical usurper of tragedy, but seen from a gutter perspective. Stripped of its prestige and glamour, the historical chronicle dwindles to the level of the crime page. The villain-hero – Macbeth, Nero, Tamburlaine – is caught with his trousers down; his sordidness shatters the myth of 'greatness'. A century and a half earlier Fielding had done something comparable in his novel *Mr Jonathan Wild the Great*. But Ubu is not merely a comment on the myth-making of the past. He looks forward to the new age when tyranny was to take on petty bourgeois guise, unrestrained not only by morality but also by any notion of decorum. Jarry saw Ubu as a universal type. Addressing the first-night audience he said: '. . . the action which is about to start takes place in Poland, that is to say Nowhere'. In part this referred to Poland being at the time a geographical expression rather than a political reality; but it also meant that the theme was a general one. Ubu may or may not be what Cyril Connolly dubbed him, the 'Santa Claus of the Atomic Age': who ever heard of a Santa Claus with sharp claws or a Santa Claus with a shittlesword? But Jarry's protagonist seems to prefigure, in madly caricatured form, some of the 'great men' of the twentieth century.

What does Ubu do? Captain of the dragoons to King Wenceslas of Poland, he is pushed by Ma Ubu, a monster Lady Macbeth, into seizing the throne for himself. He prepares his plot with Captain Bordure and the Palotins, a clutch of mindless thugs. The king is murdered while reviewing his troops, as are his sons Boleslas and Ladislas. However Buggerlas, the youngest prince, escapes together with Queen Rosamund who then dies in a bathetic scene in a cavern in the mountains. Having become king, Ubu at first ingratiates himself with the populace by throwing them handfuls of gold. He in turn fills his own coffers by exterminating and expropriating the nobles, the judges and the financiers. Then of course he attacks the peasants and robs them as well. Captain Bordure falls out with Ubu and flees to the Tsar's court. When war breaks out between Russia and Poland as the Tsar wishes to restore Buggerlas to the throne, Bordure fights on the Russian side. While Ubu is away at war, Ma Ubu steals the royal treasure from Warsaw Cathedral; but she is put to flight when Buggerlas leads a revolt. In a parody of Shakespearian battle scenes, the Poles under Ubu are beaten by the Russians; Ubu flees, accompanied by the Palotins. They take shelter in a cave in Lithuania where they are attacked by a bear; while his companions are killing it, Ubu sits on a rocky ledge and recites the Lord's Prayer. He falls asleep, and his comrades sneak away. Enter Ma Ubu; she sees her husband and pretends to be a ghost in order to scare him into forgiving her for her misdeeds. Dawn breaks, he recognizes her and beats her up.

Then Buggerlas arrives with his followers and routs them both. The final scene shows Pa and Ma Ubu together with their gang again, aboard a ship sailing off to France. Instead of poetic justice the audience gets feeble puns, broad slapstick and a disgustingly happy ending.

There is no denying that Pa Ubu has a certain shabby attractiveness, the criminal charm of Mr Punch. 'Mr Ubu is a base creature,' wrote Jarry in the first-night programme, 'which is why he is like all of us (seen from below). . . . He is rather naughty, and nobody speaks up against him as long as he doesn't touch the Tsar who is what we all respect. . . .'[13]

Some of the moral repulsiveness of Ubu was mitigated by his puppetlike character. He had after all started life as a marionette. Shortly before his death Jarry again prepared a shortened version of the stage play, *Ubu Rex*, for the puppet theatre. While this linked Ubu with a long clown tradition, it also linked him with the retreat from realistic psychology which was to be such a feature of twentieth-century drama. Indeed Jarry, who took a keen interest in the staging of the original production, asked Lugné-Poe to bring out his characters' puppet qualities. In a letter dated 8 January 1896, months before the performance, he made the following suggestions to the director: Ubu should act in a mask and speak in a special voice; the equestrian scenes should be done by hanging a cardboard horse's head around an actor's neck; and a single actor, rather than hordes of extras, should represent crowds and armies.

So *Ubu Rex* attacked convention on all fronts. There was the attack on decorum of speech and conduct as practised in the bourgeois drawing room; the attack on morality; the attack on verisimilitude of action and consistency of character; and the attack on the very notion of theatre, at any rate in its rationalist form. Once the 'as if' of the theatrical occasion is called into question, the absurdity of performing a make-believe action in front of passive adults squeezed into rows of seats becomes apparent.

The noisiest propagandist for aggressive new forms of theatre – as well as aggressive new forms in *all* the arts – was the futurist Filippo Tommaso Marinetti who made culture a matter of riots and demonstrations between 1909 and the period immediately after the First World War. The manifestos he launched in French and Italian, alone or together with friends, were stridently innovatory but ideologically confused. How else could this 'revolutionary' so quickly become a panegyrist of Mussolini and an advocate of fascist 'culture'? The fact remains that futurism theoretically anticipated a great many

---

[13] Jarry, *Tout Ubu* (Paris, 1962), p. 32.

developments in the theatre that were to take place in the half-century following its brief career – Dada, surrealism, expressionism, the Theatre of the Absurd, not to mention the fantastic cinema, ploughing many of the furrows first traced by Marinetti. The Jarry element in Marinetti's thought and style of utterance is unmistakable: it was no accident that Lugné-Poe produced his Ubuesque play *King Bombance*. There was a theatrical aspect to all of Marinetti's public gestures; but the ones most relevant to our concerns here were his manifestos *The Variety Theatre* (1913) and *The Futurist Synthetic Theatre* (1915), the latter written in collaboration with Emilio Settimelli and Bruno Carra. *The Futurist Synthetic Theatre* calls for a fast-moving, alogical, amoral, unrealistic, naïve and deliberately chaotic drama; but it touches on comedy only obliquely.

The earlier manifesto is more to the point. It exalts the variety theatre because of its opposition to all that is traditional and well made – 'passéist', as Marinetti liked to call it – and it has a distinct bearing on comedy. The virtues he saw in the variety theatre were its freedom from tradition; its readiness to 'distract and amuse the public with comic effects, erotic stimulation, or imaginative astonishment'; its 'ironic decomposition of all worn-out prototypes of the Beautiful, the Grand, the Solemn, the Religious, the Ferocious, the Seductive, and the Terrifying'; its dynamism of form and colour; its audience involvement, which included encouraging the spectators to smoke (here Marinetti anticipated by a decade Brecht's idea of a 'smoker's theatre'); its contempt for idealized love in that it 'mechanizes senti-ment, disparages and healthily tramples down the compulsion towards carnal possession, lowers lust to the natural function of coitus, deprives it of every mystery'; its anti-academic primitivism; its destruction of all received notions of perspective, proportion, time and space; and its placing of action above psychology.

The manifesto advocated the 'futurist marvellous' which would have the following characteristics:

> . . . powerful caricatures . . . abysses of the ridiculous . . . delicious, impalpable ironies . . . cascades of uncontrollable hilarity . . . profound analogies between humanity, the animal, vegetable, and mechanical worlds . . . flashes of revealing cynicism . . . plots full of the wit, repartee and conundrums that aerate the in-telligence . . . the whole gamut of stupidity, imbecility, doltish-ness and absurdity, insensibly pushing the intelligence to the very border of madness . . . instructive satirical pantomimes . . . caricatures of suffering and nostalgia, strongly impressed on the sensibility through gestures exasperating in their spasmodic, hesitant, weary slowness; grave words made ridiculous by

funny gestures, bizarre disguises, mutilated words, ugly faces, pratfalls.[14]

This breathless catalogue lists practically all the devices that were to typify twentieth-century comedy.

One of the prophetic insights of the *Variety Theatre* manifesto was its praise of the cinema. In the group manifesto *The Futurist Cinema* (1916) Marinetti went further in this direction. Here he called for boldly comic devices in the cinema, such as dramas of objects ('animated, humanized, baffled, dressed up, impassioned, civilized, dancing') and absurd fantasies ('a big nose that silences a thousand congressional fingers by ringing an ear, while two policemen's moustaches arrest a tooth' or 'a thirsty man who pulls out a tiny drinking straw that lengthens umbilically as far as a lake and dries it up *instantly*').[15]

Even apart from its obvious connection with animated cartoon films, the relevance of all this to early American cinema is considerable. Equally important is the influence the twentieth-century entertainment media of film and radio have had on stage comedy. (Television, an inherently more theatrical medium, has had a far less innovatory effect.) Less class-bound than traditional theatre, film reflects contemporary lifestyles more immediately. Its comedy is the comedy of today. The American silent cinema in particular proliferated comic types of a vigour and universality that the theatre had not been able to create since the days of the *commedia dell'arte*. Charlie of the bowler hat, cane, baggy trousers and desperate gentility enjoyed a wider if more shortlived following than Harlequin had had over a period of centuries. Much of his appeal lay in a recognition of the urban alienation of our times. Chaplin's tramp was not merely the universal vagabond (he was that too, of course) but more specifically the little man of today knocked down by the juggernaut of industrial 'progress'. He is knocked down, leaps to his feet, is knocked down again, and so on ad infinitum, or at any rate till the final walk down the endless road into the sunset. He is an image of survival *malgré tout*. If this 'message' was merely implicit in his Keystone, Essanay, Mutual and First National pictures, it became overt in later full-length features such as *The Gold Rush*, *City Lights* and *Modern Times*. The Charlie image has had a clear influence on drama – from Ghelderode's political-innocent-in-a-time-of-trouble Pantagleize to Ionesco's recurrent Everyman figure of Bérenger.

The universality of the silent American film may have been brief. But even when sound brought the limitations of language, the cinema

[14] Marinetti, *Selected Writings*, ed. R. W. Flint (London, 1972), p. 117.
[15] Ibid. pp. 133–4.

continued to enrich comedy. The Marx Brothers, it is true, originally hailed from the stage; but the immortal trio of Groucho, Chico and Harpo (let us forget the bland Zeppo) owed their worldwide resonance to the screen. To trace them to the *commedia dell'arte* has become a critical commonplace – historically pointless but indicative of the nature of their art: fixed types operating in a framework of thin plots which are nothing more than pretexts for their brilliant *lazzi*. Though traditional in this sense, the Marx Brothers were nevertheless clowns of the age of change. According to John Grierson, it was 'the job of a Marx Brother to destroy all . . . evidence of social equilibrium'.[16] What better comment on modern fiscal policy than that of Groucho's Firefly, dictator of the Ruritanian state of Freedonia in *Duck Soup* (1933)? When told by the Minister of Finance, 'Your Excellency, here is the Treasury Department's report. I hope you'll find it clear,' he replies, 'Clear? Huh! Why, a four-year-old child could understand this report . . . Run out and find me a four-year-old child. I can't make head or tail of it.'[17] When war is declared between Freedonia and Sylvania, the equally ridiculous country next door, the Freedonian legislature bursts into a minstrel-type song-and-dance routine with lots of hi-de-ho and arms flung skywards. Of course the Brothers were Marxian, not Marxist, and this is primarily fun on a showbiz level. But it does puncture the insanities of nationalism; war hysteria is unmasked as just another form of showbiz.

No wonder the Marx Brothers have left their mark on diverse stage authors. Brecht modelled the overcrowded wedding scene in *The Caucasian Chalk Circle* (1944–5) on the sardine-like crushing of people into the ship's cabin in *A Night at the Opera* (1935). And Brecht's tireless detractor Ionesco claimed that the three greatest influences on his own work had been Groucho, Chico and Harpo.[18]

The impact of radio on stage comedy is rather harder to assess. It has probably been less than that of film: radio is after all a more parochial and evanescent medium. It is common in Great Britain to accord legendary status to *The Goon Show*, and there is no doubt that between 1951 and 1960 the British airwaves were strangely troubled. But how strong outside the English-speaking world was the influence of Milligan's, Secombe's and Sellers' surreal types and their adventures in such fondly remembered episodes as *The Dreaded Batter Pudding Hurler*, *The Phantom Head-Shaver* or *The House of Teeth*? The reaction of Lithuanian, Basque and Albanian playwrights has not been recorded. In Britain at any rate the Goons swept away the distinction between mainstream and avant-garde comedy. They

---

[16] *Grierson on Documentary*, ed. F. Hardy (London, 1946), p. 36.
[17] Marx Brothers, *Monkey Business and Duck Soup* (London, 1972), p. 120.
[18] Ionesco, in *Time*, 12 December 1960; quoted in Esslin, op. cit. p. 240.

dramatized the anarchy of our times, sometimes prophetically – as in this brief summary of *Foiled by President Fred*:

> Before he lapses into unconsciousness Ned overhears the mysterious Count Jim booking reservations for South America, and he realizes that once more he has become enmeshed in the plot to kidnap President Fred and relieve him of his historic portion of the International Christmas Pudding. . . .[19]

The Goons' sound effects ('great sack of pennies dropped onto floor' . . . 'gorilla fighting another gorilla' . . . 'organ starts up, then falls to pieces') and Bluebottle's catch-cry of 'You rotten swine! You deaded me!' were the aural equivalent of the Keystone Cops running at a demented eight frames per second (or less). Goonery, no less than Buster Keaton's feats on trains, ships and balloons, Harold Lloyd's cliff-hanging and football gags, or Mack Sennett's armoury of tricks with cars and custard pies, set the theatre high standards of speed in comedy. The theatre ignores this competition at its peril: action speaks faster than words.

In contemporary drama's retreat from psychology, the recorded media are best able to show mankind in a mechanical way – robots predictable but for the fact that the machinery seems out of control. But the comic theatre often takes a similar line. The robot image reflects the actual mechanization of life. Twentieth-century man lives in vast malfunctioning conurbations; he eats processed food and swallows processed ideas; he is socially engineered; his leisure is packaged; he works in huge factories run by faceless combines, turning out tiny components of products which are trivial, unsaleable or deadly; and all his life he is pushbuttoned – at school, at work, in the army or caught up in the machinery of the state. Now this reduction of man to a robot (the very word 'robot' originated in drama, though not in a comedy – in Karel Capek's *R.U.R.*, 1920) can be seen in a tragic light. That is how expressionist drama saw it in the second and third decades of our century. The note of horror was clearly struck by Ernst Toller who, still a political prisoner at Niederschönenfeld, wrote in the Preface to his *Masses and Man*:

> I see inmates in a prison-yard sawing wood in a monotonous rhythm. People, I think with emotion. That one may be a factory-worker, that one a peasant, that one a lawyer's clerk. . . . I see the room in which the worker used to live, I see . . . the special gestures with which he might toss away a match, embrace a woman, walk through the factory gate in the evening. . . . Then . . . suddenly . . . these are no longer the human beings X and Y and Z

[19] S. Milligan, *The Goon Show Scripts* (London, 1972), p. 120.

but horrific puppets, fatally driven by a dimly perceived compulsion.[20]

But if Bergson was right in claiming that the root cause of laughter was 'something mechanical encrusted upon the living', these horrific puppets can also be seen in a comic light. 'Any arrangement of acts', said Bergson, 'is comic which gives us, in a single combination, the illusion of life and the distinct impression of a mechanical arrangement.'[21] Behaviourism, which treats man as controllable and alterable, is, in a sense, comic. It is this behaviourist joke that lies at the bottom of Bertolt Brecht's *Man is Man* (a better translation would be *Man Equals Man*). The play, written in 1924–5 and first produced at Darmstadt in 1926, is subtitled 'The Transformation of the Docker Galy Gay in the Army Barracks of Kilkoa in the Year Nineteen Hundred and Twenty-Five'; it is explicitly called a comedy.

The setting of this fantastic action is in a pantomime India (then still part of the British Empire) which in its way is no more real than Jarry's Poland. The physically powerful, mentally pliable Irish docker Galy Gay goes out to buy a fish for his wife. (An Irish docker in India? An Irish docker called Galy Gay?) He runs into three British soldiers who, having lost one of their comrades, one Jeraiah Jip (!), in an attempted temple robbery, urgently need a replacement. Galy Gay is systematically reconditioned to fill the gap in the ranks of the army. First he is enticed to the beer saloon run by the Widow Begbick (Brecht's first charcoal sketch for the later Mother Courage) to join the soldiers in a smoke. That's easy: he likes cigars. Then he is persuaded to impersonate the missing soldier at roll-call: he likes to make himself agreeable. Then he is tempted with a business deal – buying an elephant. (The building-up of the artifical elephant out of bits and pieces is just like a Marx Brothers gag.) Having made the purchase, Galy Gay is ready for the full conditioning routine – conditioning by terror. He is accused of having offered the elephant (which is army property) for sale, and condemned to death. In his fear he even denies his own identity. The soldiers go through the motions of a mock execution, and he faints. When he comes to he is ready to assume the new identity of Jeraiah Jip; he even gives a funeral oration over the dead docker, i.e. himself, and goes off with the others on a colonial campaign against the Tibetans. On the train Widow Begbick pretends to have slept with him: sex is another conditioning factor. So is his liking for army rations. The attack on a mountain fortress begins, and the new 'Jeraiah Jip' distinguishes himself: it is he who blasts it to

[20] Toller, *Masse-Mensch* (Potsdam, 1922), p. 5.
[21] Henri Bergson, *Laughter* (London, 1921), p. 69.

pieces. The easygoing docker has been turned into a 'human fighting machine'.

This change is paralleled by two other transformations. The real Jeraiah, captured by the priest of the temple, is first made to impersonate a heathen god in exchange for grub; later, when he rejoins the regiment, he is given Galy Gay's army pass and thus 'becomes' the man who has taken his own identity. And Sergeant Fairchild, whose reign of terror over his troops motivated the switch in the first place, is so much at the mercy of his sex drive that it destroys his disciplinarian image. He has to choose between passion and efficiency. As a good behaviourist, he castrates himself.

The outlook underlying these transformations is expressed by one of the soldiers as follows:

> I'm telling you, Widow Begbick, looked at from a broader point of view, what's going on here is an historical event. . . . Technology takes a hand. Clamped in a vice and on the conveyor belt the great man and the little man are the same as regards stature. The individual! Even the ancient Assyrians represented the individual as a tree that unfolds. Unfolds, see? So then it's just going to be collapsed again, Widow Begbick. What's Copernicus say? What's turning? The earth's turning. The earth, meaning man. According to Copernicus. So man isn't in the centre any longer.[22]

It is this technological view of human personality, sinisterly comical in its implications, that Widow Begbick puts in a direct address to the audience before the conditioning of Galy Gay:

> Mr Bertolt Brecht claims, one man's the same
> As any other, and it's easy to make that claim.
> But then Mr Bertolt Brecht will actually prove that you can
> Do anything whatever to any man.
> Here tonight a man will be reassembled like a car in a way
> That none of his bits and pieces go astray . . .
> And whatever rebuilding they may undertake
> In assessing him they haven't made a mistake.
> If we don't watch out, it's possible he might
> Even be turned into a butcher overnight.[23]

The human engineering of Galy Gay is shown not in psychological but in mechanistic terms. Each of the stages in the transformation is treated as a music-hall number, with the soldier Uriah Shelley serving as a compère.

How are we to read the view of man Brecht is putting forward here?

[22] Brecht, *Erste Stücke*, Vol. II (Berlin, 1953), p. 235.
[23] Ibid. pp. 229–30.

From a communist angle, Ernst Schumacher regards it as a straight attack on capitalism:

> Young Brecht had Galy Gay transformed from a civilian worker into a uniformed mercenary of imperialism. The dehumanization, the wiping out of individuality, the reduction to a mere number and the utilization of the individual as 'human material' by capitalism is strongest in the army. Nowhere does capitalism produce more horrendously barbaric results than in the colonial army.[24]

Arguing from a liberal position, Esslin on the other hand sees the 'restructuring' of Galy Gay as being achieved by

> . . . methods which foreshadow the brain-washing techniques of totalitarian society with an accuracy as uncannily prophetic as that with which *Die Massnahme* foreshadowed the Stalinist purge trials. . . . In the light of recent researches on the techniques of brain-washing, Brecht's intuitive anticipation of the essence and the methods of this process as early as 1924–6 is staggering. And . . . what he intended as an attack on the brutality of the existing social order turned in fact into a forecast of the reality of his own brand of totalitarianism.[25]

The temptation to enlist a man of Brecht's stature on behalf of one's own ideological position is very strong. There is of course something to be said for both readings of the play; both, in my view, sell it short by making the application too specific. The slotting of individuals into predetermined social roles is found in most social systems. The critic Michael Billington has written perceptively, apropos of a revival of *Man is Man* by the Royal Shakespeare Company:

> Brecht is best approached not in a mood of dogged cultural piety but with a lively awareness of his pungent humour, delight in theatre and profound moral ambivalence. . . . The play states something true about human beings yet is open to many interpretations: and that seems to me a fundamental test of a work of art.[26]

If *Man is Man* slips through too coarse an ideological net, Ionesco's *The Chairs*, first produced at the Théâtre Lancry in Paris in 1952, mocks ideology as such. Called a 'tragic farce', it also scoffs at genre distinctions: it is at one and the same time very funny (more in performance than on the printed page) and arctically desolate.

An Old Man and an Old Woman – they are jocularly described as

[24] Schumacher, *Die dramatischen Versuche Bertolt Brechts 1918–1933* (Berlin, 1955), p. 113.
[25] Esslin, *Brecht: A Choice of Evils* (London, 1973), p. 221.
[26] Billington, in *The Guardian*, 25 September 1975.

respectively ninety-five and ninety-four years old – live in a tower wholly surrounded by water. (So, by the way, do the Captain and his wife in Strindberg's *Dance of Death*. Islands occur repeatedly in Ingmar Bergman's films as images of desolation. John Donne's 'No man is an island entire of itself' no longer rings quite true to post-religious man in the twentieth century.) The room is empty; the old couple are expecting visitors. In the course of their rambling conversation it emerges that Paris was destroyed 4000 years ago; maybe this is aeons after a nuclear holocaust; civilization appears to be dead. Tonight's visitors will be coming for a special purpose – to hear the Old Man's 'message'. This, the fruit of a lifetime of thought and experience, is going to be delivered by a professional orator, the Old Man not being much of a speaker. To be sure, after a while visitors do begin to turn up: first a few – a lady, a colonel, a photographer; then more and more; the room fills up completely; at last the emperor himself arrives.

All the visitors have one thing in common: they are invisible. Their presence is represented in theatrical terms by the old couple setting out more and more chairs till the entire stage area is totally cluttered. All is ready for the great moment. The Orator comes, ready to deliver the message. This is the culminating point of the old couple's career. There is nothing further for them to look forward to. So they happily commit suicide by jumping out of the window into the water below.

And the message? It never comes. The Orator turns out to be a deaf mute. The few sounds he manages to utter are a meaningless gabble. He writes a few letters on the blackboard: more gibberish. The Orator leaves. The stage is empty but for the chairs. 'The very last scene,' Ionesco wrote to the first producer of the play,

> after the disappearance of the old couple and the Orator's departure, must be very long; the sound of murmuring, of wind and water, should be heard for a very long time, as though coming from nothing, coming from the void. Thus the audience will not be tempted into giving the easiest explanation of the play, the wrong one.[27]

But what is the right explanation? One hesitates to pin down a play so well protected by false leads, non sequiturs and barbed-wire fences against facile rationalism. But, obviously, it satirizes any attempt to give life a meaning, metaphysical, religious or ideological. Life simply is: the search for a 'message' is merely a self-delusion.

This need not in principle be wholly pessimistic. It could be read as a suggestion, nothing more, that all we ever have is the immediate

---

[27] Ionesco, *Notes and Counter-Notes* (London, 1964), pp. 196–7.

present, that nostalgic retrospect and hopes for the future are distractions from the business of living in the here and now. In the words of a Japanese Zen poem:

> We eat, excrete, sleep and get up;
> This is our world.
> All we have to do after that –
> Is to die.[28]

The play *need* not be pessimistic; but in fact it *is* pessimistic. It makes its effect not so much by plot as by metaphor. The central metaphor is composed of the chairs that take over the stage. It is almost irrelevant to ask whether the guests are mere hallucinations or actually 'present' in some sense. All we have are the chairs; and they 'speak' of the couple's solitude, their frustrated desire for companionship; they mock their illusions; they cause them to be pointlessly busy. As Ionesco put it:

> . . . when the old couple speak they must not be allowed to forget 'the presence of this absence', which should be their constant point of reference, which they must constantly cultivate and sustain . . . absence can only be created in opposition to things present.[29]

But in *The Chairs*, more is absent than the visitors or the final message. The world of reason is dismissed; causality ceases to operate; communication breaks down; meaning drains out of words. Nonsense proliferates no less than do the chairs in this world 4000 years after the fall of Paris.

But, theatrically at any rate, it must be admitted that Ionesco's pessimism is fun. The bleakness of the outlook is kept in balance by a mad comic invention. When the Old Man says to his wife, 'Semiramis, drink your tea', this is followed by the stage direction 'Naturally, there is no tea.' When she asks him to amuse her by doing imitations, he replies, 'All right, then. This is February,' and he scratches his head like Stan Laurel.

The lack of psychology with which the old couple are portrayed invites the actors to do a lot of clowning. They undergo unaccount-

---

[28] Ikkyu, quoted in A. W. Watts, *The Way of Zen* (London, 1957), p. 182.
[29] Ionesco, op. cit. p. 196. When the play was performed in the author's presence at Cardiff in 1974 as part of a Welsh Ionesco Festival, the French company presenting it, the Atelier de Boulogne-Billancourt, chose to omit the chairs: the director felt that the visitors were invisible anyway, so there was no need for the chairs either. No wonder Ionesco wrathfully denounced this production in his honour. The crucial absence, i.e. that of the visitors coming to hear the 'message', was fatally undermined by the absence of any stage furniture.

ably rapid and grotesque changes. For a while the Old Man turns into a whining infant; later on the Old Woman sheds the burden of her years in an alarming manner: according to the stage directions, she 'should become more coquettish . . . throwing her head back, hands on hips, uttering erotic cries, thrusting her pelvis forward, standing with legs apart, she laughs like an old whore'.[30]

What the clowning represents is, perhaps more than anything, imaginative energy. And it is this energy that makes the pessimism bearable. Ionesco once said in a speech:

> When the theatre could be the place of the greatest freedom, of the wildest imaginings, it has become that of the greatest constraint. . . . We are afraid of too much humour, (and humour is freedom). . . . I personally would like to bring a tortoise onto the stage, turn it into a racehorse, then into a hat, a song, a dragon and a fountain of water.[31]

In our highly selective lightning tour around twentieth-century comedy we have noted certain recurrent features. Our comedy may well be bold; it is often poetic; but it rarely exhibits the unqualified gaiety of more confident ages. Its vision of man as clown or puppet tends to reduce the role of the word as against the physical side of stage action. Farce and tragedy reach out towards one another in a world that no longer makes sense in the old terms. Comedy views present-day society with a quizzical eye.

But there is no reason to suppose that pessimism must prevail for ever. Comedy may have turned dark and chilly; but time and again there have been attempts, beyond mere efforts to be cheaply 'popular', to restore its healing function. Among others, John Arden has called for a 'vital theatre'. In the 'Author's Preface' to *The Workhouse Donkey*, a play with the challenging subtitle 'A Vulgar Melo-Drama', Arden demanded:

> . . . the theatre must be catholic. But it never will be catholic if we do not grant pride of place to the old essential attributes of Dionysus:
> noise
> disorder
> drunkenness
> lasciviousness
> nudity
> generosity

[30] Ionesco, *Plays*, Vol. I (London, 1958), p. 58.
[31] Ionesco, *Notes and Counter-Notes*, p. 46.

corruption
fertility
    and
ease.
The Comic Theatre was formed expressly to celebrate them: and whenever they have been forgotten our art has betrayed itself and our generally accessible and agreeable god has hidden his face.[32]

There is nothing further to add to this. Except perhaps: AMEN.

[32] Arden, *The Workhouse Donkey* (London, 1964), p. 9.

Suggestions for further reading

THESE have been limited to works written in English, or available in English translation.

Introduction: general studies of comedy; theories of comedy; theories of laughter

BENTLEY, E. *The Life of the Drama*. London, 1965.

BERGSON, H. *Laughter* (1899). Trans. C. Brereton and F. Rothwell. London, 1911.

COOK, A. S. *The Dark Voyage and the Golden Mean*. Cambridge, Mass., 1949.

COOPER, L. *An Aristotelian Theory of Comedy*. London, 1922.

DUCHARTRE, P. L. *The Italian Comedy* (1925). Trans. R. T. Weaver. New York, 1966.

FREUD, S. *Jokes and their Relation to the Unconscious* (1905). Trans. J. Strachey. London, 1976.

FRYE, N. *Anatomy of Criticism*. Princeton, NJ, 1957.

HERRICK, M. T. *Tragicomedy*. Urbana, Ill., 1955.

—— *Comic Theory in the Sixteenth Century*. Urbana, Ill., 1964.

HODGART, M. *Satire*. London, 1969.

HOY, C. *The Hyacinth Room*. London, 1964.

HUIZINGA, J. *Homo Ludens: A Study of the Play Element in Culture*. London, 1949.

KERR, W. *Tragedy and Comedy*. London, 1968.

KOESTLER, A. *Insight and Outlook*. London, 1949.

LAUTER, P. (ed.) *Theories of Comedy*. New York, 1964.

MERCHANT, M. *Comedy*. London, 1972.

MEREDITH, G. *An Essay on Comedy and the Uses of the Comic Spirit* (1877). London, 1919.

MONRO, D. H. *Argument of Laughter*. Melbourne, 1951.

NIKLAUS, T. *Harlequin Phoenix*. London, 1956.

OLSEN, E. *The Theory of Comedy*. Bloomington, Ind., 1968.

POTTS, L. J. *Comedy*. London, 1949.

SEDGEWICK, G. G. *Of Irony, especially in Drama*. Toronto, 1948.

STATES, B. O. *Irony and Drama: A Poetics*. Ithaca, NY, 1971.

The comedy of Greece and Rome

ARNOTT, P. D. *The Ancient Greek and Roman Theater*. New York, 1971.

ARNOTT, W. G. *Menander, Plautus, Terence*. Oxford, 1975.

BEARE, W. *The Roman Stage* (1950). Rev. ed. London, 1964.

BIEBER, M. *The History of the Greek and Roman Theater*. Enlarged ed. Princeton, NJ, and London, 1961.

CORNFORD, F. M. *The Origin of Attic Comedy*. Ed. T. H. Gaster. New York, 1961.

DEARDEN, C. W. *The Stage of Aristophanes*. London, 1976.

DOVER, K. J. *Aristophanic Comedy*. London, 1972.

DUCKWORTH, G. E. *The Nature of Roman Comedy*. Princeton, NJ, 1952.

MURRAY, G. *Aristophanes: A Study*. Oxford, 1933.

NORWOOD, G. *Greek Comedy*. London, 1931.

—— *The Art of Terence*. Oxford, 1923.

SANDBACH, F. H. *The Comic Theatre of Greece and Rome*. London, 1977.

SEGAL, E. *Roman Laughter: The Comedy of Plautus*. Cambridge, Mass., 1968.

WEBSTER, T. B. L. *An Introduction to Menander*. Manchester and New York, 1974.

WHITMAN, C. H. *Aristophanes and the Comic Hero*. Cambridge, Mass., 1964.

Medieval comic drama and the beginnings of English comedy

AXTON, R. *European Drama of the Early Middle Ages*. London, 1974.

BRADBROOK, M. *The Growth and Structure of Elizabethan Comedy*. London, 1955.

COGHILL, N. 'The Basis of Shakespearean Comedy'. In G. Rostrevor Hamilton (ed.), *Essays and Studies*. London, 1950.

FRANK, G. *Mediaeval French Drama*. Oxford, 1954.

JANICKA, I. *The Comic Elements in the English Morality Plays against the Cultural Background, particularly Art*. Poznan, 1962.

MAXWELL, I. *French Farce and John Heywood*. Melbourne, 1946.

NICOLL, A. *Masks, Mimes and Miracles*. London, 1931.

RODWAY, A. *English Comedy: Its Role and Nature from Chaucer to the Present Day*. London, 1975.

WICKHAM, G. W. G. *The Mediaeval Theatre*. London, 1974.

Comedy in Italy

HERRICK, M. T. *Italian Comedy in the Renaissance*. Urbana, Ill., 1960.

KENNARD, J. S. *Goldoni and the Venice of his Time*. New York, 1920.

—— *The Italian Theatre* (1932). 2 vols. New York, 1964.

LEA, K. M. *Italian Popular Comedy: A Study in the Commedia dell'arte*

1560–1620, with special reference to the English stage. 2 vols. Oxford, 1934; New York, 1962.

RADCLIFF-UMSTEAD, D. *The Birth of Modern Comedy in Renaissance Italy.* Chicago, Ill., 1969.

SALERNO, H. F. (trans. and ed.) *Flaminio Scala's Il Teatro delle favole rappresentative: Scenarios of the Commedia dell'arte.* New York and London, 1967.

SYMONDS, J. A. (trans.) *Memoirs of Count Carlo Gozzi . . . with Essays on Italian Impromptu Comedy, Gozzi's Life and the Dramatic Fables, and Pietro Longhi, by the Translator.* London, 1890.

Comedy in Spain and the Spanish comedia

BENTLEY, E. (ed.) *The Classic Theatre.* Vol. III: *Six Spanish Plays.* New York, 1959. (Includes Tirso de Molina, *The Trickster of Seville.*)

BOOTY, J. (trans.) *Lope de Vega, Five Plays.* New York, 1961. (Includes *Justice Without Revenge* and *The Dog in the Manger*).

JONES, R. O. (ed.) *A Literary History of Spain.* 8 vols. London and New York, 1971–2.

SHERGOLD, N. D. *A History of the Spanish Stage from Medieval Times until the end of the Seventeenth Century.* Oxford, 1967.

WILSON, M. *The Spanish Drama of the Golden Age.* Oxford, 1969.

Comedy in France

BRERETON, G. *French Comic Drama from the Sixteenth to the Eighteenth Century.* London, 1977.

GOSSMAN, L. *Men and Masks: A Study of Molière.* Baltimore, 1963.

GUICHARNAUD, J. (ed.) *Molière: A Collection of Critical Essays.* Twentieth-Century Views. Englewood Cliffs, NJ, 1964.

HUBERT, J. D. *Molière and the Comedy of Intellect.* Berkeley and Los Angeles, Calif., 1962.

JEFFERY, B. *French Renaissance Comedy 1552–1630.* Oxford, 1969.

JOURDAIN, E. F. *Dramatic Theory and Practice in France 1690–1808.* London, 1921.

LANCASTER, H. C. *French Dramatic Literature in the Seventeenth Century.* 9 vols. Baltimore, 1929–42.

MCKEE, K. *The Theatre of Marivaux.* London, 1958.

MOORE, W. G. *Molière: A New Criticism.* Oxford, 1949.

RATERMANIS, J. B., and IRWIN, W. R. *The Comic Style of Beaumarchais.* Seattle, 1961.

TILLEY, A. *Three French Dramatists.* Cambridge, 1933.

Comedy in England from 1600

BENTLEY, E. *Bernard Shaw.* 2nd ed. London, 1967.

CHARLTON, H. B. *Shakespearian Comedy.* 2nd ed. London, 1938.

GORDON, G. *Shakespearian Comedy and Other Studies*. London, 1944.

HAZLITT, W. *Lectures on the English Comic Writers*. London, 1819.

—— *Dramatic Essays*. Ed. W. Archer and R. W. Lowe. 1895.

KNIGHTS, L. C. *Drama and Society in the Age of Jonson*. London, 1937.

LOFTIS, J. (ed.) *Restoration Drama*. New York, 1966.

MUIR, K. (ed.) *Shakespeare: The Comedies*. Englewood Cliffs, N.J., 1965.

PRICE, C. *Theatre in the Age of Garrick*. Oxford, 1973.

ROWELL, G. *The Victorian Theatre*. London, 1956.

WARD, A. C. (ed.) *Specimens of English Dramatic Criticism*. Oxford, 1945.

WILSON, J. D. *The Fortunes of Falstaff*. Cambridge, 1943.

Comedy in Northern Europe

BENN, M. *The Drama of Revolt: A Critical Study of Georg Büchner*. Cambridge, 1976.

BRUFORD, W. H. *Theatre, Drama and Audience in Goethe's Germany*. London, 1950.

MARKER, F., and MARKER, L.-L. *The Scandinavian Theatre: A Short History*. Oxford, 1975.

VALENCY, M. *The Flower and the Castle: An Introduction to Modern Drama*. New York, 1963.

—— *The Breaking String: The Plays of Anton Chekhov*. New York, 1966.

Twentieth-century comedy

BRECHT, B. *Brecht on Theatre* (1957). Trans. J. Willett. London, 1964.

ESSLIN, M. *The Theatre of the Absurd* (1962). Rev. ed. London, 1972.

—— *The Peopled Wound: The Plays of Harold Pinter*. London, 1970.

GROSSVOGEL, D. *The Blasphemers: The Theater of Brecht, Ionesco, Beckett, Genet*. Ithaca, NY, 1965.

GUTHKE, K. S. *Tragicomedy: An Investigation into the Nature of the Genre*. New York, 1966.

IONESCO, E. *Notes and Counter-Notes* (1962). Trans. D. Watson. London, 1964.

MATTHEWS, J. H. *Theatre in Dada and Surrealism*. Syracuse, NY, 1974.

SHATTUCK, R. *The Banquet Years: The Arts in France 1885–1918*. London, 1959.

STYAN, J. L. *The Dark Comedy*. Cambridge, 1968.

WEBB, E. *The Plays of Samuel Beckett*. London, 1972.

WILLETT, J. *The Theatre of Bertolt Brecht: A Story from Eight Aspects*. Rev. ed. London, 1967.

Index